THE INTERNATIONAL
WINE AND FOOD SOCIETY'S GUIDE TO

BAKERY

CAKES AND SIMPLE
CONFECTIONERY

THE INTERNATIONAL
WINE AND FOOD SOCIETY'S GUIDE TO

BAKERY

CAKES AND SIMPLE
CONFECTIONERY

by

MARIA FLORIS

with color photographs by
KENNETH SWAIN
and drawings by
LESLIE THOMPSON

The International
Wine and Food Society

Bonanza Books
NEW YORK

A Publication of
The International Wine and Food Society Limited

President : André L. Simon

Bonanza Books,
a division of Crown Publishers Inc.,
419 Park Avenue South, New York, N.Y. 10016

Library of Congress Catalog Number 67-21385

This book was designed and produced by
Rainbird Reference Books Limited
Marble Arch House
44 Edgware Road, London W2

Phototypeset in Monophoto Imprint by
Oliver Burridge Filmsetting Limited, Crawley, Sussex
Printed and bound in Yugoslavia

House Editors : J. E. M. Hoare and Rosemary Joekes

Designer : Anthony Truscott

Index : Dorothy Frame

First published, 1968
Second printing, 1970

CONTENTS

Throughout this book English measurements are given first:
the American equivalents for both solids and liquids follow in
brackets.

COLOR PLATES

ILLUSTRATIONS

ACKNOWLEDGEMENTS

I would like to thank some of those who so kindly helped me; first, my editors, John Hoare, who encouraged and bullied me alternately, and Mrs Rosemary Joekes. I am grateful to Miss Elizabeth Werner, who typed the manuscript and whose knowledge of cookery was a great help to me. I must mention my sons; George, who typed many drafts and helped in my researches, and Christopher, who did likewise and kept up my spirits besides. I would like to express my thanks to my manager, Mr Ivor Dyer, for his help in testing recipes and for the loan of books. Many of my staff also gave me their time and help in testing recipes. I am grateful to them all.

Publisher's Note to the Second Edition

Madame Floris unfortunately died shortly after this book was first published. In consequence she has not been able to make the revisions for the second edition that she might have wished. In the circumstances it has been thought best to incorporate only a few minor corrections, but in the main to leave the text untouched as the last work of one of the greatest pastry cooks of our time.

INTRODUCTION

After writing my first book, and this surprised me that it was a success, I began writing again, but my husband, my partner, my friend, died and I lost heart and nerve. I know time and work are most wonderful healers and the next best thing perhaps is vanity. I had to look right; I had to keep up my home, my household, just as I had done before. When, later, the Editor to the Wine and Food Society wrote that he and Monsieur André Simon would interest themselves in my writing a book again, I was rather interested, more excited and a little bit frightened. My new Editor issued a challenge to me just very casually, that I write a book – only 70,000 words – about bread, buns, rolls, any yeast pastry or cake, cakes, petits fours, *mignons*, gâteaux – anything to do with flour confectionery, and of course, if I would, some easily-made sweets. But the book should be written in such a way that even the greatest simpleton like him could understand. How easy it is to say a few sentences like these. Nobody on earth would believe how very difficult it is to explain sometimes, for me at least, the simplest things, and I am sure I am not quite clever enough to write a book which simpletons could understand. Take a very simple thing, such as *Strudel* – I don't think anything is so easy, but you have to know how to make it. It is very easy to explain, very difficult to do, but I promise you I shall try to do my best and a little more.

Now my Editor wants me to tell you about bread – all kinds of bread, to explain, for instance, what I mean when I say 'use a sour dough'. A sour dough is an ordinary piece of dough which you may keep 3 or 4 days. Everything depends on the temperature. In a warm room it goes sour more quickly, and in a cold room it goes sour less quickly. How much sour dough should you put in with so much flour? Yes, you can weigh the flour, you can weigh the sour dough; this is all true, but how does it come out just right? I experiment twenty times before I can tell you this exactly.

He wants me to tell you all about cakes. How many kinds of cakes – Madeira, Christmas cake, birthday cake, seed cake, oh, so many kinds of cakes. All right, I will give you all the recipes but don't blame me if it does not come out exactly as you wish. Fingertip feeling must play its part. For instance, I know a little story about a wonderful blacksmith who for years and years removed cataracts. Not only did the people from his own village come to him, but from miles and miles around. He would just finish shoeing a horse and not even bother to wash his hands, but would sit the patient down and in 5 minutes remove the cataract and be paid just a shilling or two and the person would go happily home. He did this for years, but once a University professor in Budapest I knew heard about this and decided he would go and see this man. He went and watched him and said to him, 'Now I have seen you, I would like you to come and see how we do it in my hospital'. The blacksmith was very proud and happy and promised next time when he went to Budapest he would visit him. When he did, the professor made him take off his coat and waistcoat and put on a white sterilised coat; and made him wash his hands very thoroughly even though he had nothing to do with the operation. He went into the operating theatre, but only to watch. The professor, his assistant and two nurses prepared the patient and the operation was performed. He was deeply impressed, but very shocked, and went home and never, never again in his life touched eyes – he was just terrified. Now, that is how I feel. I can do all these professional things without thinking and without fear of the outcome, and the outcome must be good. I am a good cook, but I wonder will I ever be able to write down all these things for you. Never mind, I will try and I hope I will succeed.

Now I have to start writing the book. I am foremost a pastrycook, but a lover of bread and of cooking in general. The first subject should be bread. I do this with love because my most loved food is bread; nothing interests me more than bread or rolls. I feel bread is a very important food in our lives. We sit down three times a day to eat and each time we have bread, rolls or buns. Bread is important in many other ways too; it is the food of all the hard-working people and hard-working people are the most important in this world. So bread has to be good, very good.

Because bread is the basic food, therefore, it ought to be made very carefully. You never can, or never should, have short-cuts if you prepare any food. But bread more than anything has to be made very well. There is now a new school which amazes but does not delight me: to mix the flour and other ingredients very lightly and bake it even more lightly. I just don't like it, and don't approve of it. I tell my bakers to

Hungarian oven

knead the bread but with all the ingredients so long and so well until it comes up to the brim, then bake it very carefully, and definitely very well. I like a good crust which for my liking has to be crisp. But I am afraid it is very difficult to prepare a really good bread at home unless you live in the country and have a proper bread oven which could very easily be built at little expense; it is worthwhile. A household oven will never bake as well.

BREAD

We eat bread at least three times a day and I wonder whether anybody ever thinks how bread comes into being. Most of us only know so much as to go or send to the local baker's shop and buy bread and rolls.

A few years ago even that was not necessary, because the local baker would bring to the door the famous 'baker's dozen', – rolls or anything else. But now life is more difficult, so we have to fetch our bread or rolls from the baker's shop.

But now, I like to tell you about bread and as my job is to make cakes, bread and rolls for you, I know a little more than you. You, all of you, take bread for granted, I want now to explain what bread is made of.

We seldom think what an enormous amount of work, together with much knowledge, research and ingenuity, was needed to turn tiny cereal germs into the ultimate refinement of flour. I don't know how it was achieved in the dark ages when hand grinding was in use before mills developed. As a mill could not use untreated corn, the grains were cleaned and separated from the little white wheat seeds, then washed very carefully; after the washing they had to be dried. So development came gradually until we arrive at the very modern methods of scientific and mechanised milling with push-button systems. I personally don't like this but I have to move with the times, because time will not stand still for my benefit. Bread, which is made of flour – wheat or rye – gives, of course, a lot of work and thought. Poor bakers are not appreciated enough for the very hard work they still do to provide us with good bread. I read in one of the papers that a baker in this country was fined heavily for selling short-weight bread in his shop or shops. Next day in my research reading I happened to note that gluten and flour, and so naturally bread too, lose weight. Before I bore you with technical expressions I want to find out how much the average housewife knows about bread.

I have, in my shop, four intelligent girls – one or two of them above average. I asked them, 'Do you know, what is gluten?' One, the most knowledgeable, said: 'I've never heard this word'. The other asked, 'Who?' (meaning 'who is gluten?'). The other two simply admitted of having never heard about it. I don't think that it would be right, if I were to say much more than tell you that gluten is a part of the flour and gluten's behaviour in baking and confectionery is a very important factor. Gluten expands, gluten stretches, gluten has a breaking point, gluten can play havoc with cakes and with bread.

Why is it that a cake may sink in the middle, why does the fruit in it sink to the bottom? These are all very difficult questions and all of them are handled very scientifically. Can I explain all this to you? I can just give a few helpful hints and show you a glimpse of how the making of bread has evolved over the centuries.

The Stone Age housewife baked a kind of bread – but from what? I read a story that wheat was sown by ants and that the people learned from them how to grow it. It is true that it was believed that wheat came from Heaven. The first recorded bread was made by the Egyptians, the Jews and the Chinese. Millet and buckwheat are among the earliest known cereals. The grain was crushed between stones and then pounded by hand. I have been told by an Indian friend of my son that in some parts of India the peasants make a form of bread to this day in ways not unlike those used in biblical and even pre-biblical times. In one method a flour and water dough is prepared – the flour is, of course, whole flour and will contain salt if they are wealthy. This dough is then moulded into discs between $\frac{1}{4}$ in. and $\frac{1}{2}$ in. thick and covered over with fat, normally sheep fat. While this is being prepared a small pit has been dug in the sand and a fire is lit in this pit. When the fire has died down to the embers, the pit is cleared of the ashes, the dough discs are put into the pit and covered with hot sand and left there for an hour or more. When the baked bread is removed from the pit it is brushed over with sheep fat to prevent the sand from penetrating the dough. An alternative way in which this dough is baked is again by preparing a fire in a pit and then placing stones, as nearly spherical as can be found, in the fire. When these stones have become hot, they are removed. The dough is wrapped round the stones and left out for the heat of the stones to bake the bread.

While I would not like to say how authentic this story is, it is interesting; and it is especially so to note that this last method is noteworthy as a prototype of a new type of oven in which the bread is cooked from the inside out. It is interesting that this revolutionary new method is only 3,000 years old!

Unleavened bread influenced the lives of the Israelites, Jews and Christians alike. We know much about early unleavened bread from the Old Testament and in particular from the Book of Exodus. This describes the sad fate of the Israelites when Moses led them out of Egypt and they had no time to think or prepare for their long and perilous journey. In their terrible haste they forgot to take with them the vital ingredients for making bread. In those times the method of making dough rise with sour dough was not known. This is simply to keep a small piece of dough for three or four days. It will then ferment and help the bread to rise. So the Israelites had to make their bread without any yeast. Orthodox Jews preserve the memory of the privations of their historic past by fasting eight days before the Passover. This fast was called *pesach*. During this time only unleavened bread is eaten. As far as I am aware, there is no proper recipe for this, but one way to make it at home is this. Mix some sieved white wheat flour into a very soft dough with salted water. Roll out about $\frac{1}{4}$ in. thick and cut into 6 in. squares. Put these on baking sheets, prick very thoroughly and bake in a very low oven. They are dried out rather than baked. The Egyptians baked the first leavened bread, and also were the first to use ovens.

The first leavened bread came about by accident as have so many famous recipes and discoveries. A young Egyptian, perhaps in love, left some bread dough out in the warm sun so that it fermented. This produced the first sour dough. The story is that the young Egyptian's accidental discovery led to beer and yeast being discovered. Breadbaking was learnt from the Egyptians by the Romans; from them the Greeks learned it and then they became the world's greatest bakers in their time. The discovery of sour dough and yeast was revolutionary. Not so long ago Spanish ladies, famous for their beauty, used sour dough with great success as a beauty treatment for their faces. I find sour dough or any cream or mud useful – if you believe in it.

I find the history of bakers most interesting and at the same time, I feel the treatment of bakers has been unjust. The regulations imposed on them were absolutely cruel. The 'baker's dozen' originated in the Middle Ages when the bakers who didn't abide by their oaths, or bake enough bread for each day – or gave short-weight bread were beheaded in England; in Germany they were 'ducked' in public. Even now I find it unjust that every price is going up – travel, cigarettes, beer; nearly everything – no mourners about it. Bakers' wages, very rightly, have to go up as well; good luck to them, they deserve this rise, as baking really is very hard work. But if the price of bread goes up a penny a loaf, there are big headlines in all the papers and politicians make speeches about it in Parliament. The price of bread should go up in England, as it is cheaper than anywhere else. If the price went up, the bread would also be better, much better in quality.

In 1948 Parliament passed an act which prohibited bakers from working more than 26 weeks in any one year on night work. This was a great blow to the smaller bakers who previously had always baked bread on night shift. Three choices faced them. They could either bake half their bread on the day shift, and the rest at night, or they could bake in advance and deep freeze the bread. Or the dough could be made by day, placed in a *retarde* (a kind of cold chamber) and then proved and baked by night. The first way was not satisfactory for the bread was sometimes 18 hours old before it reached the customer, and bread, such as Vienna bread and French bread, is only good when it is fresh out of the oven.

Bread can be placed in a deep freeze and kept for several days, but I am sure that any cooked article loses a lot of its natural flavour when it is frozen. Also the crust of frozen bread becomes very brittle and is liable to break away and fall off, thus spoiling the whole appearance of the bread.

If space is available, retardation is by far superior to freezing, for in this way bakers can ensure that their customers have oven-fresh bread at all times. To do this the loaves are first moulded and placed in tins and on baking sheets; then instead of leaving them in a warm prover as is customary, they are placed in a cold cabinet with a temperature of 45–50°F. (6–10°C.). This reduces the fermentation to a minimum and bread can be kept sweet, i.e. without turning sour, up to a period of 12–16 hours. The bread can then be taken from the cold cabinet and the proving finished in a warmer temperature; it is then baked at the required time. After all, what is better than oven-fresh bread?

Much of the bread in England is made in automatic plant bakeries and requires very little baking skill or attention. Of course, there are various opinions about this 'automation' bread and many people do not like it, and it is often referred to as 'cotton wool' bread. However, it is nicely sliced and wrapped in wax paper and the public (whether they like it or not) buy it, for it is convenient and keeps well. In warm humid weather this bread will easily develop a mould; this is prevented by the addition of a little acid. This kind of bread is not baked in the usual way and often has a clammy feel to its texture.

Oven-bottom bread is baked on the floor of the oven and steam is injected into it. This steam gelatinises the gluten on the surface of the bread and when it has finished baking gives a biscuit crust to the bread. This bread is by far the most appetising of all and is very popular with those who are real connoisseurs.

I think that the bread baked today does not contain enough salt: this makes the taste dull and insipid. I firmly believe that all bread should contain 1 oz. salt to every 3 lb. flour, which is practically 3 lb. salt to every bag of flour (140 lb.).

Yeast and salt are not very good friends and I may go so far as to say that they

Granary French bread; wheatsheaf loaf; white caraway bread; granary loaf;
'Loaves and Fishes' Harvest Festival bread; black Polish rye bread

don't like one another at all. Therefore, in breadmaking they must be added as far away in time as possible from each other. Generally, the salt is added at the first stage with the fat, sugar and water and when the dough is half mixed the yeast (dissolved in a little more water) should then be added. Sometimes in a way that is known as the 'salt delayed action', the salt is added (dissolved in a little water) 1 hour after the first mixing.

Salt does two things in bread. First it gives it flavour and brings out the natural flavour of the wheat and also retards the fermentation slightly. Therefore, the more salt you use the more yeast you must use. Many years ago a very eminent heart specialist often sent his patients to me for salt-free bread and I wondered why. Later he told me that salt hardens the arteries and any person liable to suffer this way should go on a salt-free diet for 3 weeks each year.

Although bread is so very much taken for granted its manufacture is most interesting. Every kind of flour contains a small percentage of natural sugar; the yeast and this sugar start the fermentation in which a gas (carbon dioxide) is formed. While this is going on the other enzymes convert the starch in the flour into maltose and give the yeast more sugar to act upon. With the liberation of this gas the dough becomes full of gas and this is why it rises in the bowl. To ensure that no pockets of gas are left in any one spot the dough is 'knocked back' that is, as much of the gas in the dough is forced out as is possible and then fermentation starts again. The dough is ready for 'moulding' when it has risen for the second time. The dough is divided into pieces of the required weight and then 'moulded' into the required shape.

Breadmaking has not altered much since the old days. Naturally the enormous 'plant' bread factories use different methods, but we are not concerned with them. We try to make bread as it was made by our mothers and their mothers. Breadmaking was – I would love to know whether it will ever be again – sacred and romantic. When we knew that it was the day of the week for breadbaking, it was a very special day, a gay and happy day. We children all rushed home from school, because all of us got one tiny loaf, each received a little, oddly-shaped loaf. It was better than any pastry or cake and we never tired of looking forward to this great treat.

Most housewives find that baking bread at home is very difficult but if they would only follow a few simple rules they would find it very easy and what tastes better than home-made bread? What better than the joyful and proud moment when you watch your family and friends demolish your bread! Home-made bread is 'healthy and honest'.

Breadmaking is simple but as with everything else it has to be precise. Short-cuts in the end make double work or give a bad result. I think there is no truer proverb than 'what is worth doing is worth doing well'.

Austrian rye bread;
White cob loaf; double plait loaf; cob wholemeal loaf

I will tell you the general rules or methods for breadmaking and then give you very many breadbaking recipes. But you should always try to experiment. My mother used to tell us that whatever we did, as long as we made the dough properly, it would bake itself all right. I say that everything takes just so much time. If you overcome the difficulty of starting, whether it be cooking, baking or breadmaking, you will master it after a while, and then you will experiment and goodness only knows what masterpieces will come of your trying. You just go on trying.

There are two important operations or methods of preparing bread dough for baking:

The Long Method. The yeast with liquid, milk or water, sugar, flour and a few other ingredients is left overnight before being mixed with the rest of the dough. Kneading and rising follow.

The Straight Dough Method. All the ingredients are mixed in the order above before the kneading and rising period which follows immediately afterwards.

Mix vigorously and confidently in preparing the dough. To help the distribution of the ingredients and yeast cells a prolonging of the flour blending helps, and dissolving the yeast in the liquid before adding to the flour is also beneficial. Work the dough energetically by hand or with a wooden spoon. I prefer the hand, it is exercising and relaxing, pleasant and satisfying, in a primitive way. The slushing sound; the forward clumping; the hand against the board, all relieve frustrations and inhibitions. Maybe the modern woman will naturally prefer to use an electric mixer. That I do not mind as long as she mixes the dough very thoroughly until it is smooth and silky like satin. It is, some believe, better to knead it lightly and then let it rest. I don't believe in short-cuts in anything and definitely not in cooking or baking. The kneading stretches the gluten into a minute elastic network and thoroughly blends the ingredients. Then use a slightly-floured board. If the dough becomes very sticky, don't panic but sprinkle the working surface with a little flour. The dough will become a little heavier and will rise more slowly and it will make a coarser-textured bread. If it is very coarse a little oil on the hand will help. Knead until the dough becomes smooth and elastic, and you can see small bubbles under the dough. Let it rest for 10 or 15 minutes, then roll the dough into a ball, cover it with a clean cloth and leave to rise in a spot free from draughts, not too cool and not too warm, about 80–90°F. (25–30°C.), a kind of damp-proof box is ideal. We did not make much fuss at home, were not in the least bit scientific, but the result was beautiful

A selection of loaves (reading from top to bottom)
French bread; English bread; cottage loaf; granary loaf

bread. The Hungarian peasant woman who used to make the best bread put the
bread dough, rolled into a ball and covered, to rise in her bed. You can do almost
anything also. Put the dough in a bowl over a pan of hot water, or on the water
heater, or the radiator. You can even put your bread ball on the television set while
you watch your favourite programme. It will add flavour to the bread and maybe
your programme will be improved! Lucky people who live in a sunny climate can
put the dough in the hot sun and let it prove there. To know when the dough has
risen enough, press two fingers or knuckles deeply into the dough and if the dents
remain and the bubbles shyly present themselves and pop, then you can start
shaping or moulding the bread. Cut the dough into equal portions and roll them
into balls. Well-worked dough will obey and will shape to your will. It is best to use
your hand but you can use a rolling pin. Flatten the dough and press out all the

bubbles. Shape the dough into a loaf, sealing and tucking under the inner edges. Place in a greased tin with the seam side at the bottom. For a softer crust, brush the top of the loaf with shortening or butter after baking. For a glossy, crispy crust, brush the top of the loaf with a mixture of egg white and water before baking. Baking stops the rising process. A well-baked loaf should look golden yellow or light brown on the top and bottom. I like my bread crusty and I like a thick crust. A good bread test; if you press a slice of bread together it should regain its original shape immediately. A good loaf has to have holes, but not big ones and not too small.

The loaf should tumble from the tin and should be cooled on a wire rack. Now comes the hardest job of all. Keep the bread from the family until it is cool! Our cook at home could never do this! If you have to cut hot bread, use a saw-edged knife; it helps if the knife is a little warm. Cool loaves completely before putting them into a bread bin or tin, plastic bag or foil. All of these keep bread moist and fresh. Bread will keep in a refrigerator if wrapped in moisture-proof plastic or foil. The smell or aroma of fresh bread should be good, very good, nothing is better than a good bread smell. For me nothing gives more appetite than the smell of fresh bread. Brown bread again depends on taste; it is definitely tastier; it keeps fresh longer and moist, but most people prefer snow-white bread; it is still a status symbol. When I went to America immediately after the Second World War the hotel where I stayed was sorry for me coming from poverty-stricken England and showed me, proudly, snow-white bread which tasted like cotton wool!

Bread with potato in it again not only keeps much better fresh but tastes better; but very few people in this country will touch such bread.

Sometimes customers bring back to my shop a loaf of bread that they bought a few days before, saying that they have just bought it and it is mouldy. They forget that they may have a bread tin containing spores from mould in it already because there are mould spores in countless millions in the atmosphere. The only solution is to sterilise a bread tin; it is not enough merely to wash it. This applies also to keeping Christmas pudding. If you make Christmas pudding at home and the basin is not filled with pudding mixture the water will penetrate the cover and mould soon forms.

But to return to breadmaking. First, you should have a large wooden bowl. I think that is the best. I find it so because we had a huge oblong wooden bowl at home. Put in some warm and sieved flour, make a well in the middle; dissolve the yeast in warm water; put this in the middle of the flour; mix a little, sprinkle it with a little flour on the top and cover it with a linen cloth and let it rise for about 2 hours. When this so-called 'little' dough is risen add the remainder of the flour and if necessary warm water and salt. All of us have different tastes; I find bread made with yeast and sour dough tastier than without sour dough. I love caraway seed in my bread; very many, especially English people can't stand caraway seed. There are different schools of thought for making bread; some of the health enthusiasts don't believe in kneading, just mix the flour and water and let it rise; mould and bake. I like it very well kneaded till it is silky and produces bubbles; I love the taste of a little maize flour and I like to sprinkle cornflour on the top of the already moulded bread. I like it washed over first with a little milk and sprinkled with cornflour afterwards, but you can do it just as well with water or sprinkle it with wheat or rice flour. It is always better to use warm water. If you like you can grease the tin with lard, oil, or butter; I love butter but not for this purpose. To bake bread in steam produces a very good bread, but to do this at home is complicated, but just before you put your bread in the oven you can sprinkle the whole oven with a little water; this will give a little steam.

But no more red herrings. Here is my first recipe and method, it is very simple and should be easy to follow.

Breadmaking techniques: kneading bread; knocking back; shaping or 'scaling' bread dough

BREAD DOUGH (1)

3 lb. (12 cups) flour
2 oz. ($\frac{1}{4}$ cup) fat
1 oz. (2 tablespoonfuls)
   sugar
1 oz. (1$\frac{1}{4}$ tablespoonfuls)
   salt
1$\frac{1}{2}$ oz. (2 cakes) yeast
1$\frac{1}{2}$ pints (2 pints) warm
   water

Mix well together the flour, fat, sugar and salt. When well mixed add the yeast dissolved in the water and mix until a firm dough is formed. Place the dough in a pan, cover with a cloth and leave in a warm place for 1 hour to prove. After 1 hour take the dough from the pan and give it a good kneading on the table, making sure that all the gas has been expelled. Now place the dough back in the pan, cover with the cloth and leave in a warm place for a further half an hour.

When the half hour has elapsed, divide the dough into 1-lb. pieces, mould into shapes to fit well-greased tins. Allow to prove until they reach nearly to the top of the tin and then bake at a temperature of 450°F. (233°C.). If the crust appears a little dull after baking, gently brush the top with a little melted fat, which will give the bread a most attractive appearance.

BREAD DOUGH (2)

3 lb. (12 cups) flour
1 tablespoonful (1$\frac{1}{4}$
   tablespoonfuls) salt
1 oz. (1$\frac{1}{2}$ cakes) yeast
1 teaspoonful (1$\frac{1}{4}$ tea-
   spoonfuls) sugar
1$\frac{1}{2}$ pints (2 pints) warm
   water
a little corn oil or
   butter

Put 2 lb. of the flour in a large bowl – a wooden one if possible – add the salt (a little less or a little more, depending on how you like your bread – I like it tasty). Blend the yeast and sugar into a smooth paste with a spoon. If you mix it long enough then it becomes emulsified, like cream. Then add the warm water and stir, adding a little flour until it becomes a thick batter. Sprinkle the top of this with flour. Make a small hole in the flour in the big bowl and put this batter in it. Cover the bowl with a cloth, then leave it in a warm place for about 30 minutes until the yeast works, and the dough rises. Then mix it with the rest of the flour and knead the dough till it becomes silky and elastic. Your hand should come out clean from the dough. The kneading time is about 15 minutes. Grease the top of the dough with a very little corn oil or butter and cover it with a damp cloth and let the dough prove for well over 1 hour. It has to rise well. After this, turn the dough onto a well-floured board, make three pieces of it, knead each again for a few minutes and shape according to your baking tin. Grease the tins with a little corn oil, put dough in each, cover them again with a warm cloth and leave them in a warm place to prove again for 20 minutes. Bake in a hot oven – 450°F. (233°C.) – baking time 45–50 minutes.

BREAD DOUGH (3)

2½ lb. (10 cups) plain flour

1 oz. (2 tablespoonfuls) cooking fat

1 oz. (1¼ tablespoonfuls) salt

4 oz. (6 cakes) yeast

1 pint (1¼ pints) water

Sieve the flour into a bowl and carefully rub in the cooking fat. Next sprinkle in the salt (using more or less depending on taste). Dissolve the yeast in the water, which should be lukewarm. The amount of water may vary but be sure to mix in just enough to make a firm dough. Proceed as before with the proving and kneading.

BISHOPS BREAD

2 eggs

3½ oz. (⅞ cup) flour

3½ oz. (7 tablespoonfuls) butter

3½ oz. (scant ½ cup) sugar

grated lemon rind

2 oz. (⅔ cup) raisins

2 oz. (2 squares) chocolate, grated

2 oz. (½ cup) almonds or walnuts, grated

2 oz. (½ cup) glacé cherries, grated

Separate the yolks of the egg from the whites. Chop the chocolate and almonds. Cream the butter with half the sugar, add the yolks of eggs and mix well. Whisk the whites of eggs stiffly then whisk in the rest of the sugar. Fold the whites of eggs into the yolks alternately with the flour. Add lemon rind, raisins, almonds, glacé cherries and chocolate gradually. Place mixture in a buttered and floured oblong tin and bake in an oven 350°F. (177°C.) for about 45 minutes. Cool on a wire rack and when cold slice.

COBS

Use one of the above bread doughs, scale off at the required size and mould into balls. Rest the dough for 1 hour. Allow to prove and at the halfway stage 'dock' the loaves. Finish the proving and when the dough has doubled in size bake at 420–440°F. (216–228°C.) on a greased sheet for 30–35 minutes. This method should give a nice thick crust.

COTTAGE LOAF

Use an ordinary bread dough as shown above. The shape, which is well known, is made by forming two different-sized balls of dough. One should weigh 1 lb. 8 oz. for the base and a smaller piece 10 oz. for the top. First mould into balls and flatten slightly to help adhesion of the two halves. Place the smaller piece on top of the larger one and use the thumb and forefinger to pierce through the centre of the top piece to the lower piece. Prove in a warm place until double the size. Bake in a very hot oven, approx. 460°F. (238°C.) for 35–40 minutes.

ENGLISH BREAD

English bread was mostly used on the Continent as a very special bread. They used it for canapés, for special hors d'oeuvre or toast for tea. You can make English bread in any shape, or you can make it in a tin; if you have the right kind of oven you can make a bottom-baked oven bread out of it.

5 lb. (20 cups) flour
2 oz. (3 cakes) yeast
2 oz. (2½ tablespoon-
fuls salt
water

Use enough warm water to make a dough. Leave it in a warm place to rise for about 2 hours; but this depends on the temperature of the room. When it has risen enough, then start to knead till it is smooth and bubbling, then cover it and leave it again to rise for another 1½–2 hours. Meanwhile heat your oven to 440°F. (228°C.) put the dough when well risen on a floured board and cut into eight pieces and shape them in any way you like. Then put the loaves in the oven and bake them till golden brown and firm. Test this by knocking; which will give a hollow sound when the bread is ready. When you take out from the oven brush with butter; this gives a fine golden colour to the loaves.

FRENCH BREAD

We hear much about how wonderful French food is. Of course, I appreciate French cooking as much as anybody else, but my greatest joy in France is the bread. In my bakery we make thirty-seven kinds of bread, but there is not one I like so much as real French bread. I think that it never tastes so good as in Paris in the Café de la Paix, sitting outside in the street, having a glass of wine, with a long, very long sandwich made with wonderful French butter and ham.

I could eat twice as much, if I had not been ashamed before the waiter.

French bread is made from a very special flour, which is not obtainable in Britain.

A kind friend of mine took the trouble to obtain for me a recipe from his local baker and sent it to me with a friend who himself brought a few pounds of the flour as well. Even from this French flour my copy of the French bread did not taste the same as the one I ate in the Café de la Paix. Maybe it is the water, as we used to say in Budapest when we got tea from England and tea made from it was still not so good as a cup of tea in England.

I make French bread here with English or Canadian flour, but I mix in a little brown flour. But for me it is still not the same. I give the recipe:

$\frac{3}{4}$ **lb. (3 cups) flour**
$\frac{1}{4}$ **lb. (1 cup) brown flour**
a pinch of salt
a pinch of sugar
$\frac{1}{2}$ **oz. ($\frac{3}{4}$ cake) yeast**
1 oz. (2 tablespoonfuls) butter
$\frac{1}{2}$ **pint (1$\frac{1}{4}$ cups) water**

Mix the yeast and sugar together and add to the water, add the flour slowly, then the butter and salt and mix these all very well. Then start to knead till it is smooth and silky, cover it with a teacloth and let it rest for a good 90–95 minutes in a warm room. The volume should double with the rising. When it is well risen, knock it back and leave it until it rises again. That should take 35–45 minutes, it really depends how warm the room is. We, in my bakery, prove our bread in a heated prover. When your bread has risen enough turn it on a flour board and roll it out about a $\frac{1}{4}$ in. thickness, then roll it together very tightly. It should make a nice 12 or 14 in. long, shaped loaf which you should shape carefully with your hands and press down at both ends.

Grease a baking tin, I think the best oil to use is corn oil, put the bread on it, shape it again with your hands, then slit it with a sharp knife four or six times, about $\frac{1}{4}$ in. deep. Brush the top of the loaf with cold water, let it rest again about half an hour and bake in a moderate oven until it is nice golden brown and very crisp.

This will take about 50 minutes; the heat should be about 400°F. (205°C.).

FRENCH LOAVES
Scale off at various weights according to size required. Mould into cylinder shapes and point the ends. With a sharp knife cut several shallow cuts in the top of the loaves. Place on a flat, greased baking sheet. Prove until double the original size. Bake at 440–450°F. (228–233°C.) for 25–30 minutes.

FLORIS BREAD

1 lb. (4 cups) plain flour
½ oz. (2 teaspoonfuls) salt
½ oz. (¾ tablespoonful) oil
½ lb. (1 cup) finely-mashed potatoes
2 oz. (3 cakes) yeast
½ pint (1¼ cups) water

Mix the flour with the salt, oil and finely-mashed potatoes. Add the yeast dissolved in ½ pint water at 98°F. (37°C.). Mix to a firm dough and allow to rest for 1 hour. Knock back and mould into Coburg shape (*see* p. 32) and bake on a flat, greased tray in an oven at 450°F. (233°C.) with steam for about 30–35 minutes.

GRANARY BREAD

2 lb. (8 cups) granary flour
1 oz. (2 tablespoonfuls) oil or fat
1 oz. (1¼ tablespoonfuls) salt
1 oz. (1 tablespoonful) malt
1 oz. (1½ cakes) yeast
½ pint (1¼ cups) water

Place the flour, oil, salt and malt in a bowl. Dissolve the yeast in the warm water and use this to form a firm dough. Allow this to relax for 1 hour and then knock back. Mould into oblong, cylinder or ball shape and place in prepared baking tins that have been greased. Bake the bread at 400°F. (205°C.) for 30–35 minutes. It is essential to use a relatively cool oven for otherwise the malt will burn and the loaf will be over-coloured and undercooked. For variety, raisins or chopped dates may be added to the dough.

HONEY BRAN

2 lb. (8 cups) wholemeal flour
1 oz. (1 tablespoonful) malt
1 lb. (11 cups) bran
6 oz. (¾ cup) honey
1 oz. (1¼ tablespoonfuls) salt
2½ oz. (3¾ cakes) yeast
1 pint (1¼ pints) lukewarm water

Place 1 lb. wholemeal flour with 1 oz. malt in a bowl and mix in 1 pint water with ½ oz. yeast dissolved in it. Leave this for 24 hours in a warm place. When the ferment is slightly sour add 1 lb. wholemeal flour, 1 lb. bran, 6 oz. honey and 1 oz. salt and mix all this together with 2 oz. yeast dissolved in 1 pint lukewarm water. As soon as it is thoroughly mixed, divide into 1 lb. pieces and place in greased tins. Prove until double the original size and bake in a moderate oven at 440°F. (256°C.) for about 35–40 minutes. This is a very unusual type of bread with a distinctive flavour of its own and contains all the roughage needed in a modern diet.

OAT BREAD

**8 fl. oz. (1 cup) scalded
  milk**
8 fl. oz. (1 cup) water
**11 oz. (1⅓ cups) golden
  syrup**
**1 teaspoonful (1¼ tea-
  spoonfuls) salt**
1 oz. (1½ cakes) yeast
1½ lb. (6 cups) flour
**8 oz. (3 cups) rolled
  oats**
melted butter

Cool the milk to about 80°F. (27°C.) and heat the water to the same temperature, then pour them both into a basin and add to this the syrup and salt. Add crumbled yeast and stir until the yeast is dissolved. Add 1 lb. (4 cups) sifted flour, beat until smooth then stand in a warm place for about 2½ hours until double its size. Stir in rolled oats and the rest of the flour. Knead the dough until it is smooth and elastic. Put the dough into a greased bowl and turn it until it is coated slightly all over with the grease. Leave it to double its size for 1¾ hours. Knock back and let it prove again for 1 hour. Cut into 2 pieces and knead the dough into 2 loaves of the same size. Put them in well-greased loaf tins. Brush the surfaces with melted butter and leave for 40 minutes. Bake in a moderately hot oven 375°F. (191°C.) for 20 minutes then lower the temperature to 350°F. (177°C.) and bake for another 40 minutes. When the loaves are ready, they should look lovely and brown.

MILK BREAD (1)

**2¼ lb. (9 cups) plain
  flour**
**1 oz. (2 tablespoonfuls)
  fat or oil**
**½ oz. (2 teaspoonfuls)
  salt**
**1 pint (1¼ pints) luke-
  warm milk**
2 oz. (3 cakes) yeast

Mix the flour, fat and salt with the lukewarm milk in which the yeast has been dissolved. Mix to a firm dough and prove for about 30 minutes and then mould into oval shapes. Place on a greased baking sheet and cover with greased oval tins. Some people like to make a series of inverted Vs down the centre before covering. Re-prove for a short while and then bake at 420°F. (216°C.) for 35–45 minutes.

MILK BREAD (2)

I have eaten this good milk bread in the Palace Hotel at St Moritz. All the food in the hotel was very good. I got this recipe from the manager of the confectionery depart-ment of the hotel kitchen under whose management everything had to be perfect. Now I give you her recipe:

2 lb. (8 cups) flour
5 oz. (⅔ cup) butter
1 oz. (1½ cakes) yeast
12 fl. oz. (1½ cups) milk
** (if necessary you can**
** use a little more)**
1 oz. (1¼ tablespoon-
** fuls) salt**
1 oz. diamalt powder
** (optional)**
1 oz. (2 tablespoonfuls)
** sugar**
2 eggs

Put the flour in a bowl and keep it in a warm place. Make a well in the middle and put in the yeast, which first ought to be diluted with a little warm milk. Add the salt, the sugar and as much milk as will make a firm but not hard ball. Add eggs and the *diamalt* powder; this is a German product which gives any bread, roll or bun a very specially good flavour. If this is unobtainable, it may be left out without harm. Mix the ingredients together; add the butter which should have been warmed and add slowly bit by bit. Work the dough till it is smooth and silky and let it rest for 1½ hours. Put it into two 1 lb. baking tins. Let it rise again for 30 minutes, wash it over with a little milk or yolk of egg. Bake at 350–375°F. (177–191°C.) for 30–40 minutes.

NEWBARNS FRUIT LOAF

½ lb. (1 cup) butter
½ lb. (1 cup) caster sugar
1 lb. (4 cups) flour
2 teaspoonfuls (2½ tea-
** spoonfuls) baking**
** powder**
2 eggs
½ lb. (1½ cups) currants
½ lb. (1⅓ cups) sultanas
2 oz. (½ cup) blanched
** almonds**
milk to blend

Cream the fat with the sugar. Add sieved flour and baking powder with the eggs, which have been previously beaten, to the fat and sugar. Lightly stir in the fruit. Chop the almonds and add with the milk. Mix lightly till blended and pour into a large greased loaf tin. Bake in a moderate oven, 350°F. (177°C.) for 2½–3 hours, till dry when tested in the centre with a skewer.

PLAIN CURRANT BREAD

2 lb. (8 cups) flour
1 oz. (1½ cakes) yeast
sugar to taste
1 pint (1¼ pints) tepid
** water**
2 teaspoonfuls (2½ tea-
** spoonfuls) salt**
¾ lb. (2 cups) currants

Put sifted flour into a warm basin. Cream the yeast with the sugar, add ½ pint (1¼ cups) water and pour into the centre of the flour. Mix together to make a thick batter then sprinkle in the salt. Cover and stand in a warm place for 15 minutes. Stir in the remainder of the water and flour. Knead the currants into this dough. Prove again for 30 minutes until well risen then shape into 2 loaves. Place each in a greased loaf tin, filling it half full. Cover and stand in a warm place for about 20 minutes or until the dough has risen to the rim. Brush the tops lightly with milk. Bake in a hot oven 450°F. (233°C.) for 15 minutes, then lower to 375°F. (191°C.) for another ½ hour till the loaves sound hollow when tapped. Cool on a wire tray.

PLAITED LOAF

1 lb. (4 cups) flour
4 yolks of eggs
5 oz. (full ½ cup) sugar
4 oz. (½ cup) butter
¼ pint (1¼ cups) milk
1 oz. (1½ cakes) yeast
1 oz. (¼ cup) grated almonds
a little salt

Mix the yeast with a little warm milk and a very little sugar. Let it rise for 15 minutes. Then put your flour in a warm bowl, put in the yeast which by now has risen; add the yolks of eggs and the other ingredients and knead well till it is smooth and very silky; it should have some bubbles in it, by this time. Let it rise again. The dough should rise to double its original size. When it has risen pour onto a floured cake board, cut it in 3 pieces and roll the pieces into balls. Then roll each ball into long rolls 12–14 in. long and then make a long plait out of it. Make the ends nice and neat; then take another egg yolk and mix it with a little sweetened milk; brush the loaf once, let it dry and brush it again and then bake it in a moderate oven 375°F. (191°C.) for 30–35 minutes. Let it cool and then eat fresh with a good coffee. I am sure you will enjoy it. The plaits can be made with 3, 5 or 6 strands.

RYE BREAD (Austria)

1½ lb. (6 cups) white flour
2½ lb. (21 cups) fine rye flour
1½ pints (2 pints) water
2 oz. (¼ cup) sugar
3 oz. (¼ cup) salt
2 oz. (6 tablespoonfuls) finely-ground caraway seeds
1 oz. (1½ cakes) yeast

Place ½ lb. white flour and ½ lb. fine rye flour into a bowl with the warm water and the sugar and allow to stand in a warm place for 24 hours. When sour add 1 lb. white flour, 2 lb. fine rye flour, the salt, finely-ground caraway seed, 1 oz. yeast; add enough warm water to make into a smooth firm dough. This type of bread is moulded into round pieces and proved in small cane baskets which have been well greased. Before baking they are turned out of the baskets onto baking sheets. This bread must be baked slowly and well.

RYE BREAD

1 lb. (6 cups) medium rye meal
1 pint (1¼ pints) lukewarm water
1 oz. (1½ cakes) yeast
1 oz. (2 tablespoonfuls) sugar
1 lb. (4 cups) white rye flour
½ lb. (2 cups) plain white flour
1 oz. (1¼ tablespoonfuls) salt (optional)
caraway seed (optional)

Place the rye meal in a bowl and add the lukewarm water in which ½ oz. yeast has been dissolved and the sugar. Place in a warm place for 24 hours, until the dough ferments. After fermentation add the white rye and plain white flours. Also add the salt and caraway seeds, if used. Add to this ½ pint (1¼ cups) of water in which ½ oz. yeast has been dissolved and mix all to a firm dough. Allow to stand for 20 minutes and then knock back. Divide into 1 lb. pieces and mould into Coburg shape by forming into cylinders roughly as long as they are broad and with tapered ends. Allow to prove until double the size and bake at 460°F. (238°C.) for 40 minutes. Steam should be used with this, as with all crusty breads and can be obtained by placing a saucepan of water in the bottom of the oven.

RYE BREAD (Denmark)

1½ lb. (9 cups) coarse rye flour
½ lb. (2 cups) white flour
1 oz. (1½ cakes) yeast
2 oz. (¼ cup) sugar
1 oz. (1¼ tablespoonfuls) salt
2 pints (2½ pints) water

Place 1 lb. coarse rye flour with ½ oz. yeast, the sugar and water into a bowl and leave in a warm place until sour. To this add ½ lb. white flour, ½ lb. coarse rye flour and the salt and knead to a firm dough. Mould into 1 lb. pieces and place in a baking tin. As this is a sour dough ferment, the final proving will take rather longer than ordinary bread. It must be baked slowly and well.

RYE BREAD (Poland)

4 lb. (16 cups) rye flour
3¼ pints (4 pints) warm water
1 oz. (2 tablespoonfuls) sugar
1 lb. (4 cups) white flour
1 oz. salt
½ oz. (¾ cake) yeast
3 oz. (8 tablespoonfuls) caraway seeds

Place half the rye flour mixed with 2½ pints of water and the sugar in a small bowl and leave it in a warm place for 48 hours, till it ferments and turns slightly sour.

Now place the other half of the rye flour, the white flour, caraway seeds and salt in a bowl, add the sour ferment and ¾ pint of water to which the yeast has been added. Mix a fairly firm dough. Allow it to rise for about 1 hour, then shape into 1 lb. pieces. Mould into long loaves and prove for 30–45 minutes. Before baking, make cuts across the loaf and wash lightly with warm water. Bake at 440°F. (228°C.) for 50 minutes.

SODA BREAD

1 lb. (4 cups) flour
salt
1 level teaspoonful
(1¼ teaspoonfuls)
cream of tartar and
of bicarbonate of soda
1 pint (1¼ pints) buttermilk
for preference
(If fresh milk is to be
used increase cream
of tartar by 2 tea-
spoonfuls)

Sift the flour, cream of tartar, salt, bicarbonate into a basin; make a well in the centre and stir in enough milk to make a light, spongy dough. Knead very lightly and place on a floured baking sheet. Cut across about ½ in. deep and bake in the top of a hot oven at 450°F. (233°C.) for 20 minutes, until brown and well risen. When cooked wrap in a clean damp teatowel and stand on a cooling rack.

To make brown bread use wholemeal flour. For fruit bread use fruit and candied peel and 1 oz. of sugar. Make in the same way.

VERY SWEET BREAD

Whenever life is not as you like it, if you are bitter about anything or anybody, don't despair. I give you a recipe of a very sweet bread which will make you feel better. You just make the following recipe.

6 eggs
1 lb. (2 cups) caster
sugar
curaçao
2 lb. (8 cups) flour
1 lb. 4 oz. (2½ cups)
butter

Beat the eggs and the sugar; add the liqueur and one-third of the flour to make a dough. Put the remaining flour in another bowl and put the dough in it. Warm the butter a little and slowly rub into the flour; use your hands and mix it thoroughly. When it is smooth make a roundish flat loaf; brush the top with beaten egg and bake for 30 minutes in a moderate oven at about 370°F. (189°C.).

VIENNA BREAD

2½ lb. (10 cups) flour
1 oz. (1¼ tablespoonfuls)
salt
a little fat
malt extract
1 pint (1¼ pints) milk
2 oz. (3 cakes) yeast

Add the salt to the flour, then the fat and malt extract, and bind them all with the milk in which the yeast has been dissolved. When well mixed to a firm dough let it prove for 30 minutes and then knock back. Leave for 10 minutes. Scale at 8 oz. and mould into the required shape. Prove in a warm place until double the original size. Score the top with short diagonal cuts across the top. Place on greased sheets and bake at 450°F. (233°C.) for 25–30 minutes. Steam should be used for the first 5 minutes, so place a saucepan of hot water in the oven during the warming up and remove 5 minutes after the bread is put in.

VIENNA ROLLS
Use dough as above. Scale at 1 oz. and shape into cylinders. Proving, scoring and baking are as for Vienna bread.

WHITE BREAD
I give you here the recipe of another white bread which you may like.

1 lb. (4 cups) white flour
½ oz. (¾ cake) yeast
1 teaspoonful (1¼ teaspoonfuls) sugar
1 teaspoonful (1¼ teaspoonfuls) salt
1 oz. (2 tablespoonfuls) butter
½ pint (1¼ cups) milk
1 egg

Rub the butter into the flour, add the salt, sugar yeast and warm milk and egg. Mix well and then start to knead and continue until the dough is smooth and silky, and your hands are clean of the dough. Let it rise till it doubles in volume, then knock it back and let it rise for another ½ hour. Put the dough on a floured board and shape it longish, but shorter and much wider than the French loaf. Let it rest again and put it in a greased and floured baking tin, wash over with a little warm milk and again slit it three times on top. Then bake in a 400°F. (205°C.) oven for 15–16 minutes, then reduce heat a little and let it bake for another 40–45 minutes. When ready, it should be golden in colour and crisp.

WHOLEMEAL BREAD
1 lb. (4 cups) plain flour
2 lb. (8 cups) wholemeal flour
½ oz. (1 tablespoonful) oil or fat
salt
2 oz. (3 cakes) yeast
1½ pints (3¾ cups) warm water

Mix the flour, fat and salt to a firm dough with ½ pint warm water in which the yeast has been dissolved. Allow to stand for 1 hour and then knock back. Mould into round shapes and place in greased tins. Allow to prove until double the size and bake at 460°F. (238°C.) for about 35 minutes.

Rolls (reading from top to bottom); knots; granary rolls; brioches; Vienna rolls; Kaiser rolls; fancy rolls

POTATO BREAD (1)

I experimented with making bread with potato during the war, when there was a cry everywhere: 'Save flour, eat more potatoes'. The experiment resulted in very good bread, so I thought, 'Save flour and eat very good bread!' Here is the result of my experiment:

1 lb. boiled potatoes
3 lb. (12 cups) flour
1 oz. (1¼ tablespoonful) salt
4 oz. (6 cakes) yeast
water as required
1 oz. (2 tablespoonfuls) caraway seed (optional)

Make a 'little' dough with warm water, the yeast and a little flour. Leave it to rise. Mix the boiled potatoes, salt, 1 or 2 spoonfuls of warm water and the remaining flour and leave it in a warm place, if possible over night. In the morning mix these 2 doughs together. Remember that the potatoes will take up a lot of water and you may have to add more, but do not make the dough too soft. Work the dough until it is smooth, and your hands are clean and no longer sticky with the dough. If you like caraway seed you can add as much as you like. I like it very much and would add about 1 oz. Cover with a clean cloth and let it rest for about 1 hour. Mould the dough into balls, any size and as many as you like. Then place on floured cloths and put into little baskets and allow to rest for another hour at least. Bake for about 1½ hours in a medium oven – 350°F. (177°C.) – for a medium-sized loaf. Less time is required for smaller loaves.

POTATO BREAD (2)

2½ lb. (10 cups) strong Canadian flour
2¼ lb. boiled potatoes
1 oz. (1¼ tablespoonfuls) salt
¾ oz. (1½ tablespoonfuls) milk powder
½ oz. (1 tablespoonful) sugar
4 oz. (6 cakes) yeast
lukewarm water as required

Knead this dough until it becomes smooth and silky; let it rest until it doubles in volume, bake for 45 minutes in a moderate oven.

Wedding cake

DIABETIC BREAD

I have always been very concerned about diabetics and their diet. Being a professional concerned with food, naturally it was very close to me. I cannot answer the natural question – why diabetes and not one of the hundreds of other illnesses? Of course, all the illness and trouble of the world concerns me, as it does everybody else. I suppose I am particularly interested because I had an uncle, whom I liked more than the others, who died comparatively young. He was a character and a very interesting one! He was straightforward and, I could say, uncomfortably honest. As a child he was sent to a boarding school, having parents who lived in the country where no day school existed. The first holiday, his parents sent a coach to collect him, and when the time came for him to arrive, the whole family went out and waited by the gate for his arrival. When my uncle noticed the gathering, the big family reception, he started to shout from far away, 'I failed in my exam!' He just could not face the nice reception with the knowledge that he had disappointed his people, especially his mother, whom he adored. He had quite a lot of difficulty in his schooldays, but in the end he became an excellent engineer. He married in due course, and his wife was just as uncomfortably honest as he was. Unluckily for him, they had no children. This was a bitter disappointment for him; he adored children, but it was no help; he had to find other children to love. He lived a very quiet, hard-working life; if you like you can call it happy; no worry, but no joy either. Suddenly, somehow, he noticed that he was over-tired and always thirsty and his wife urged him to see a doctor, who diagnosed diabetes. My uncle asked what the remedy was. I suppose at this time insulin did not exist. The doctor prescribed a very strict diet. He gave my uncle a sheet on which were all the things he could eat; all very strict measurements. My uncle looked at it very seriously, folded the paper nicely and asked what would happen if he did not keep to the diet. The doctor answered his straight question with a straight answer: 'You will die in a very short time.' My uncle replied that was O.K. by him and never kept to the diet and in due course he died. Since then diabetes and diabetic people have been my concern.

Several times in Hungary people asked me if I would make diabetic pastries, petits fours and chocolates. I flatly refused. I dared not; I could not play with people's lives. I could not take such a responsibility. My workrooms, my business have never been big enough to have proper dieticians or proper laboratories, with chemists who could assure me that what we would make would be harmless.

NIGERIAN BREAD

During one of my holidays recently I read in the American magazine *Time* an article about Nigerian millionaires. One of them was a baker. I thought that perhaps he could help me and as a colleague I wrote to him and asked if he could send me some local or any African specialities; any bread, pastries, cakes or such like. I got back a friendly and cordial letter. He would like very much to help me but all that he knows and makes originated from this country or the United States. However, he wrote, we have one national cake. If I remember well it was a soya flour affair; I never got this recipe either. Then I got a letter from his son saying that his father, the baker from Nigeria, was ill and in a London hospital and he would like to visit me. He came and had lunch with me; he told me all about his business. Two of his 6 children are already in the business and his wife is very active, too. It seems to be that they have a very large enterprise with very many kinds of interests, 5 shops, restaurants, coffee bars, everything. He found our production wonderful; I sent him over to our chocolate factory and bakery. He was delighted with everything and in our long discussion he mentioned that in Nigeria they have a lot of difficulty with raw materials; they have to import everything. I asked him whether they grew potatoes and he said yes, plenty of potatoes, so I told him I would give him a recipe and I make for you white bread with 40 or even 50 per cent of potato. He got terribly excited and he said 'Oh, now I can take something home from here to please my wife', and I answered that I hoped it would be a success and would make him further millions. This is just my luck – I ask somebody for help and it turns out that I have to do something for them instead. But I suppose it is so because I like it this way. I now very much hope that I will get in exchange for my good deed another one, that is, the soya bread or cake.

ARAB BREAD

I search everywhere for the origin of bread, all kinds of bread, everywhere I go or have any connections from whom I could get information. Perhaps I don't tackle my job properly, or I am just unlucky in finding the right people to enlighten me about the subject. From one friend who means very well I got a recipe – if you can call it that – the title of the recipe is 'Arab Bread'. Before the recipe it says: 'Arabic, Mediterranean countries, particularly Syria, Lebanon, Iraq, use this very simple way of breadmaking.' Use flour, water, salt and sour dough. How much salt? That is always individual. How much water? Depends on the flour you make the bread from. That is simple as that.

But I have to tell you that our bread, in my country, a very much of a bread-loving population, the bread was made from a recipe like this. The imaginative housewife or baker would elaborate on the recipe. And I can assure you that these 4 ingredients – flour, water, salt and sour dough – can make a very enjoyable bread. The most important, of course, is the flour.

This form of bread baked in the Arab countries of the Middle East, particularly Syria, Lebanon and Iraq and was very popular, although in the towns less is now being baked with the introduction of modern bakeries. These bakeries produce 'Western'-type bread. The usual recipe for Arab Bread is:

8 lb. (32 cups) flour
½ oz. (2 teaspoonfuls) salt
2 pints (2½ pints) water
a little 'old' dough

This is all mixed together, together with a piece of old dough, i.e. a piece from the previous day's dough or some flour and water mixed together and left for a few days to catch wild yeasts and commence fermentation. In recent years some bakeries have been using dried yeast.

This dough is left an hour, weighed off in approximately 1 lb. pieces and then placed into an oven with top heat and left for about 8–10 minutes, normally the time required to bake the top row. The lower rows will take proportionately longer. Pieces are placed in the oven on a long, thin piece of board, similar to our peels. The bread, when put in the oven, expands rapidly like a football and then collapses while being brought out.

DAMPER LOAF (Australia)

8 oz. (2 cups) flour
salt to taste
(sifted twice with the flour)
1 small cup milk to which a little melted butter has been added

Mix with a knife, cutting through mixture instead of stirring. Half-fill a loaf tin. Bake in a moderate oven approximately 30 minutes. Then roll in a cloth until cold. (If a sweet damper is required add 2 tablespoonfuls of sugar to mixture.) They would not use self-raising flour 'out-back'; and this bread would be baked in a 'bush oven', a round iron pot with a lid which is buried in the ground surrounded by hot coals.

LANGOS

I am a terrible worrier. I have worried my life away ever since I was a little school girl. At first about the friendship of my school mates, the likes and dislikes of my school teachers. Then I was worried whether they loved me. I worried over little things; I worried over important things; I worried over things that would never happen. The silliest thing with me is that I know the basic wisdom of life and that worrying could not help me or change matters; and meanwhile I am always outwardly cheerful and most of the time nobody notices my worrying. Another wisdom I know, but do not practice, is that the simplest things in life are the most enjoyable. I do always the most complicated and difficult and expensive things. Yesterday I learned again how enjoyable and very simple the cheapest food can be; how much pleasure you can give to people with something that needs very little to do and costs hardly anything. Take *langos* as an example. The great passion of our childhood was *langos* – we always had this when bread was made. We looked forward to it, not only my own family but I could say this about nearly everybody in my country.

Langos is made from bread dough, usually white bread dough. It is made with flour, yeast, lukewarm water, as for ordinary bread. The cook would put away from a batch of bread about 1 lb. of dough and we had *langos* mostly for breakfast. The bread dough, I say about 1 lb., is rolled out with a rolling pin $\frac{1}{4}$ in. thick and cut into rounds like a pancake. Prick with a fork and bake for 15–18 minutes in a big bread oven or the ordinary kitchen oven. We used to eat them warm with butter. I would tell stories of my childhood to my elder son in his all too frequent illnesses. My stories, I noticed, helped him to recover more than medicine. Suddenly in middle age he asked me could I make him *langos*. Naturally I made it for him and I couldn't have given a greater treat for tea, but not only for him but several of my friends, than hot *langos* with butter.

My husband always accused me of 'knighting' my dishes. He meant that I refined them. Sometimes he did not approve of my variation of our *langos*. I make small bars, roll out finger-thin and then fry in hot oil with great, great success.

BREADFRUIT

In my search to find you something new, something old, something historical in our bread line I came across an interesting tree which has very unusual-shaped fruit. It looks like an overgrown acorn. The botanical name of breadfruit is *Artocarpus incisus*, or *Artocarpus communis*, as it is known in the U.S.A. It is supposed to be a beautiful tree, according to my book of reference. It is a native of the tropical regions of Asia and of the South Sea islands. It is cultivated in the islands of the Asiatic archipelago and the Pacific near to the equatorial region. These breadfruit trees were the main reason for Captain Bligh's long, terrifying journey; he wanted to bring this very useful tree with the wonder fruit to the West Indies in 1789, the time of the French revolution. The tree is about 50–65 feet tall. It has a milky sap, thick and viscous, which made into a kind of glue used for various purposes. The timber is also very useful for building huts for the natives. The leaves are enormously big and are used as roofing. They are also used as a very valuable wrapping for food. The fruit, which is my greatest concern, is large and spherical. The colour is green, really greenish-yellow and it is the most basic food for very many islanders. When it is ripe it has a short life, as it rots quickly. Before it is fully ripe, the right time for gathering, the flesh is firm and white and very floury and starchy and has nearly the same nutritive value as wheat bread. Cut in slices it is baked or toasted on hot coals; the fruit can be also baked whole in the oven until the outside skin becomes dark brown. In this way it is a very valuable and nourishing food. It tastes like fresh bread with a slight flavour of artichoke. Two or three of these trees produce enough fruit to feed one man for a whole year. The seeds of this fruit are also edible roasted in cinders or boiled like chestnuts; the taste is also a little like chestnuts.

ROLLS

Every day I eat 1 or 2 rolls for breakfast, and in my bakery we make thousands and thousands every day. Eating and seeing them and endlessly criticising them has never brought back the painful nostalgia that writing about them now does. Rolls, lovely, crisp, happy, cheerful-looking rolls. The baker's shop – clean, pleasant and with a delightful smell which you cannot find anywhere except in a baker's shop. The girls also, fresh, healthy, good-humoured, the rolls many kinds, in big baskets, always in baskets. Which I like the best it is difficult to tell. You choose the rolls according to your mood and your mood turns good when you enter a baker's shop. Friendly faces always ready for a few jokes and gossip. In Hungary, the people have always been full of jokes. The darkest Nazi era, and the terrible repressions of Stalin and Kruschev could not kill their sense of humour.

In Hungary you choose your rolls according to the food you eat them with. For coffee – plain and very crisp rolls with no butter. For tea you eat the soft or crisp rolls with butter, and that is how fresh butter came to be called tea-butter in Hungary. For elevenses you choose the so-called water or Kaiser rolls. Cut the rolls, spread very lightly with butter, and sandwich with 1 or 2 thin slices of salami. There was such a variety of salami, that you could put in a different type each time. We did not call it all salami because there were so many varieties, but some was called *wurst*. It is difficult to explain how it looked. Even more difficult to tell how it tasted, but you have to believe me it tasted heavenly. Perhaps you will call them sausage, because in England, you call everything like this sausage – and it is sacrilege. What we called sausage you sometimes call liver sausage or garlic sausage, but who am I to break your old traditions? I have to go back to my rolls – I am always inclined to wander. The large water rolls, which get their name from the recipe, are slightly sour, but very tasty.

The Kaiser roll was the most popular, and deservedly so. It got its name because the Austro-Hungarian Kaiser liked it so much. As far as I know, he was not a gourmet, in fact, he was rather frugal with little or no good taste, but the Kaiser roll was delightful, made with butter and a little milk. The next best was the plainer, crisp little Vienna roll. I could go on talking about rolls endlessly, but I have to leave you alone for a while. I must, though, tell you about *brioches* and *croissants*, which are really the best in the world.

The origin of *croissants* dates back to the seventeenth century in the year 1686, when the Turks were besieging Budapest. They had dug tunnels under the city, but a surprise attack was foiled by some bakers working at night who heard the noises made by the Turks and raised the alarm. The bakers were subsequently rewarded by the granting of the privilege of making a special pastry. This was to be crescent shaped – the crescent being the emblem borne on the Turkish flag and so symbolizing the defeat of the Ottomans.

There were three very popular *croissants* – one was very slim, very crisp, quite large with crystallized salt or caraway seeds sprinkled on the top which you could pick off and eat separately. Once you started it, was very difficult to stop. These *croissants* were mostly eaten with elevenses, with the Vienna sausages which here you call Frankfurters. Crisp plain *croissants* are eaten without butter.

BRIOCHES

Once upon a time, when life was easy and leisurely – at least for some people – *brioches* were a luxury, not so much because they were expensive, but because they have elegance and standing; they ought to be eaten in a salon, put only on a thin China plate, and eaten with drinking chocolate in delicate, thin, china cups. Nobody who did not belong to the upper classes would think of buying or ordering *brioches* in Hungary. *Brioche* is a favourite roll in France, Austria and Hungary. It is an elegant roll and it is comparatively expensive. If you make it at home, of course, it is cheaper than if you buy it, and, I suppose, better. It is served mostly with a good, rich cup of chocolate. *Brioches* are more suitable than French *croissants* for drinking with chocolate because they are lighter; a French *croissant*, as we know it, is made with a lot of butter and, therefore, it is a little bit heavier. I love drinking chocolate, but I can never have it for breakfast. In the afternoon however, I know nothing better. It is a pity that it went out of fashion; afternoon tea on the continent is at 5 o'clock. It is much more usual for young people to prefer savouries and sandwiches for tea.

BRIOCHE (1)

2 oz. (3 cakes) yeast
salt
1 tablespoonful (1¼
**   tablespoonfuls) each**
**   sugar and cream**
3 eggs
8 oz. (1 cup) soft butter
12 oz. (3 cups) flour
1 yolk of egg

Work all the ingredients very well together and store overnight in the refrigerator. Divide into 1 large ball and 1 much smaller ball. Grease a *brioche* mould with butter and flour it. Put in the large ball and make a small hole in the middle and place the smaller ball on top. Leave it for 15 minutes to rise in a warm place.

Mix a yolk of egg with just a pinch of sugar and wash it over and bake it in a moderate oven for 20–25 minutes.

BRIOCHE (2)

1 lb. (4 cups) flour
5 oz. (full ½ cup)
**   mashed potatoes**
1 oz. (1½ cakes) yeast
2 eggs
a pinch of salt
2 oz. (¼ cup) caster
**   sugar**
2 oz. (¼ cup) melted
**   butter**
2 fl. oz. (¼ cup) warm
**   milk**
1 yolk of egg

Mix all the ingredients together very well. Knit it till smooth and silky and let it rest for half an hour. Do the same as before when moulding and place in a buttered and floured *brioche* mould. Let it rise for another half an hour. Wash it over with yolk of egg. A pinch of salt helps give a nicer colour. Bake in a moderate oven for 20–25 minutes.

BRIOCHE (3)

1 lb. (4 cups) flour
8 oz. (1 cup) butter
½ oz. (¾ cake) yeast
a pinch of salt
½ oz. (1 tablespoonful)
**   sugar**
8 eggs
milk
1 yolk of egg

Take about 1 oz. of the flour and mix it with the yeast and a little warm milk and put this dough in a warm place to prove. Sift the rest of the flour and place in a bowl. Make a well and place three-quarters of the eggs, the sugar and the salt and make all into a fairly stiff dough. Then work in the remainder of the eggs and then mix in the butter. Add to it the little dough and keep in a cold place covered with a clean cloth. You can keep it for 8 or 9 hours, but it is best to leave it overnight. In the morning add a little warm milk, as much as is needed, and knit it until smooth and silky. Leave it to rise again. When risen place in small buttered *brioche* moulds, which can be bought at any kitchen equipment shop. The mould should be about $2\frac{1}{2}$ in. deep. Cut from your dough small pieces and make them into round balls. Take much smaller pieces and make them into smaller balls. Then make a hole in each of the larger balls and place the smaller on top. They should look like little cottage loaves. Leave them to rest for about an hour and then wash over with yolk of egg. If you put a very little sugar in the yolk of egg it will make the cooked *brioche* a little browner. Bake in an oven at 380°F. (194°C.) for about 30 minutes.

FRENCH CROISSANTS

Brioches and French *croissants* are among the most elegant and perhaps the most sophisticated of foods to eat with tea, coffee or chocolate. I, in my business make more *croissants* than anything else. We make thousands and thousands daily. If well made of the right ingredients they are really very attractive to look at and just as good to eat. There are very many ways to make *croissants*. In Paris they are made quite differently than in the French provinces; the Swiss make a different one and we here make our own variety. But I give you a recipe now which is originally from America and which one of my Swiss pastry cooks produced here.

CROISSANTS (1)

8 fl. oz. (1 cup) milk
1 tablespoonful ($1\frac{1}{4}$ tablespoonfuls) lard
1 tablespoonful ($1\frac{1}{4}$ tablespoonfuls) sugar
$\frac{3}{4}$ teaspoonful (1 teaspoonful) salt
$\frac{2}{3}$ oz. (1 cake) yeast
2 fl. oz. ($\frac{1}{4}$ cup) lukewarm water
10 oz. ($2\frac{1}{2}$ cups) flour
4 oz. ($\frac{1}{2}$ cup) butter cream

Mix the lard, sugar and salt with the warm water; add the yeast and add enough flour to make a little dough. Mix well together and let it prove till double in bulk. Then put it in the refrigerator for half an hour and then put the dough on a floured pastry board. Cream your butter so creamy that you should be able to spread on a slightly rolled out dough. Then fold in 3 layers from the end toward the centre. Turn a quarter way round and pat a little, then roll out as before, then spread some of the butter; repeat this process twice. Then leave for 2 hours or even longer to rest. Take half the dough and roll out into a rectangle 15 × 10 in. Measure it carefully and cut out in squares and then cut each square in half diagonally to make 2 triangles.

Making *croissants*

Roll up each triangle beginning at the long side and then curve or shape into crescent form. Put the *croissants* on a baking sheet and leave again to rest in a cold place for about half an hour. Brush with slightly sweetened yolk of egg or a little sweetened cream. Bake for about 30 minutes; starting in a hot oven at 400°F. (205°C.) and reduce to 350°F. (177°C.) when golden-brown, that is after approximately the first 10 minutes.

CROISSANTS (2)
1 lb. (4 cups) flour
1 oz. (1½ cakes) yeast
1 oz. (2 tablespoonfuls) butter
salt
sugar
8 fl. oz. (1 cup) milk
caraway seeds
1 yolk of egg

Mix the sugar and a quarter of the lukewarm milk in a little bowl. Mix the yeast into this. Add the butter and the flour to it. When the yeast has risen add enough lukewarm milk to make a soft dough. Let the mixture rise, then – when it is double the original volume – put it on a floured pastry board. Divide the dough into 4 or 6 pieces, make them into little balls, cover them with a tablecloth and let them rise for another 15 minutes. If you want to make rolls, cut out in rounds –

the size being dependent on your preference, or roll the balls out very thin and cut out triangles and roll them up into crescents. Before baking mix the yolk of egg with a little milk and brush the rolls or crescents with the mixture. If you care for caraway seed, sprinkle on top – or you can sprinkle fine crystal salt on the *croissant*. Bake them in a medium oven for 15–20 minutes. This quantity should make 6–8 average-sized *croissants* or rolls.

BAPS

1 lb. (4 cups) flour
¾ teaspoonful (1 teaspoonful) salt
2 oz. (¼ cup) lard
1 oz. (1½ cakes) yeast
1 teaspoonful (1¼ teaspoonfuls) sugar
¼ pint (⅓ pint) milk
¼ pint (⅓ pint) water

Put the sieved flour and salt into a warm bowl. Rub in the fat. Mix yeast and sugar together until liquid. Heat milk and water until tepid about 98°F. (37°C.) and add to the yeast, then strain this into the flour and mix to a soft dough. Cover and stand in a warm place until bulk is doubled. Knead lightly and divide into small, squarish pieces. Dust with flour. Place on a greased tin sprinkled with flour and allow to prove until double in size, about a quarter of an hour. Bake in a hot oven, 425°F. (219°C.) for about a quarter of an hour. Serve hot.

BRIDGE ROLLS

Vienna dough
white of egg
yolk of egg
a little sugar

Take little pieces of the Vienna dough (*see* p. 33) and make them into little balls. How big the ball should be depends on how big you want the bridge rolls. If for tea time then they should be between 2 and 3 in. long, if for cocktails half this in size. Roll the balls out into fingers, pointed at both ends, and a little thicker in the middle. Put them on a greased baking tin in rows, not too close to each other so that they do not stick together. Brush them over with white of egg, if you like them brown and add the yolk of egg with a very little sugar. Then put them in the oven at 400°F. (205°C.) but reduce it after 5–6 minutes to 350°F. (177°C.). If you like them very glossy, brush them over again with more yolk of egg mixed with a little milk. Then return to the oven for a few minutes to dry.

FINGER ROLLS
There are very many ways of making these rolls. I think this one is a very good method which would make an appetizing roll filled with him or hot dogs.

FINGER ROLLS (1)
1 lb. (4 cups) flour
5 oz. ($\frac{2}{3}$ cup) butter
1 oz. (1$\frac{1}{2}$ cakes) yeast
1$\frac{1}{3}$ cups (full 1$\frac{1}{2}$ cups) milk
fresh cream
salt according to taste
1$\frac{1}{2}$ oz. (3 tablespoonfuls sugar

Using one-third of the flour, the yeast and the milk, make a small quantity of dough. Put the rest of the flour into a bowl, make a well in the middle, add your 'little' dough and leave to rise for half an hour. Add the butter, sugar, cream and salt. Knead it very firmly till smooth and very silky. Sprinkle the top with a little flour and cover with a cloth. Then leave in a warm place to prove. When it has risen to double its original size, put the dough on a floured board and divide into small pieces. You can make them smaller or bigger as required. Roll them out into long shapes and bake in a hot oven at about 450°F. (233°C.); if you like you can brush with yolk of egg.

FINGER ROLLS (2)
1 lb. (4 cups) flour
4 oz. ($\frac{1}{2}$ cup) fat
$\frac{3}{4}$ oz. (1 tablespoonful) salt
1$\frac{1}{2}$ oz. (3 tablespoonfuls) sugar
2 oz. (3 cakes) yeast
$\frac{1}{2}$ pint (1$\frac{1}{4}$ cups) luke-warm milk

Mix the flour, fat, salt and sugar well together. Dissolve the yeast in the lukewarm milk, add this to the other ingredients and mix to a firm dough. Allow to stand for 1 hour. Knock back, scale at 1$\frac{1}{2}$ oz. and mould into finger shapes. Place on a greased baking sheet, allow to prove until double the size and bake in a hot oven at about 480°F. (256°C.) for 15–20 minutes.

HAMBURGER ROLLS
The dough is the same as for finger rolls. Scale at 2 oz. and mould into balls. Roll nearly flat and cook in the oven at 480°F. (256°C.) for 15–20 minutes.

PASSOVER ROLLS
I am always being asked if we have some special pastries or cakes that can be eaten during the Passover, so I have here some Passover rolls. They taste and look like choux paste and I suppose you can fill them with any butter cream.

¾ pint (2 cups) matzos meal

4 eggs, well beaten

8 fl. oz. (1 cup) boiling water

4 fl. oz. (½ cup) oil

1 tablespoonful (1¼ tablespoonfuls) sugar

1 teaspoonful (1¼ teaspoonfuls) salt

To the boiling water, which you should keep over a low heat, add the sugar and then slowly add the matzos meal. Beat repeatedly until the mixture is firm. Roll it into a ball. Remove from the heat, beat in the eggs slowly and then beat vigorously until the batter is nice and thick. It must be smooth. Shape into very small balls, because the dough rises and put them into a greased baking sheet. With a knife or fork slash a design on top of each. Bake them for about 1 hour in a moderate oven.

JEWISH EGG CHOLAS or PLAITED ROLLS

1 lb. (4 cups) plain flour

2 oz. (¼ cup) butter

¼ oz. (1 teaspoonful) salt

1 oz. (2 tablespoonfuls) sugar

1 egg

½ pint (1¼ cups) milk

1 oz. (1½ cakes) yeast

Dissolve the yeast in the milk. Rub the butter into the flour with the salt and sugar. Add the egg and yeast mixture and make into a fairly soft dough. Allow to ferment for 1 hour and then the dough is ready to use. This dough is very good made into small plaited rolls; you can make bridge rolls (see p. 48) out of it or you can make a large plaited loaf out of it. Wash over with warm milk and sprinkle it generously with poppyseed which is very popular because it is very tasty.

WATER SEMMEL (Austria)

2½ lb. (10 cups) strong Canadian flour

½ oz. (1 tablespoonful) butter

½ oz. (1 tablespoonful) sugar

1 oz. (1¼ tablespoonfuls) salt

1 oz. (1½ cakes) yeast

1 pint 3 fl. oz. (1½ pints) water

Mix flour with the butter, sugar and salt, add ½ pint warm water. Dissolve yeast in ⅔ pint water and mix until a smooth firm dough is formed. Allow this dough to rest in a warm place for 3 hours and then remould it. Finally divide into 2 oz. pieces, mould round, and allow to prove for 30 minutes. Bake in an oven of 460°F. (238°C.) which is full of steam.

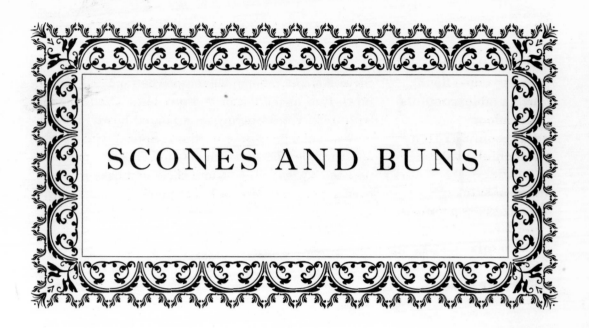

SCONES

Scones are still very popular for tea, toasted, split and buttered, or heated in the oven or under the grill. In Hungary, we had something very similar which we called butter *pogacsa*. We used to have them for breakfast, freshly made the same morning by the long-suffering cook who had to get up at 4 o'clock in the morning to have them ready for breakfast. You cannot imagine how very good these breakfasts used to be. Here you have baps and soft rolls instead. I would like your scones better, however, if they were made with less baking powder and more butter. But perhaps it is just a matter of acquired taste, and one day I may prefer scones as you make them.

BROWN FARMHOUSE SCONES

2 oz. (½ cup) **flour**
salt
2 oz. (¼ cup) **sugar**
2 oz. (¼ cup) **butter**
6 oz. (1½ cups) **whole-meal flour**
3 teaspoonfuls (3¾ tea-spoonfuls) **baking powder**
¼ pint (½ cup) **milk**

Sieve flour, salt and sugar into a bowl, rub in the butter. Stir in wholemeal flour and baking powder and mix very well. Add enough milk to make a soft dough. Knead lightly into a flat round. Place on a greased baking sheet, mark into 6 triangles with the back of a floured knife and bake in a hot oven, 450°F. (233°C.) for 15 minutes. When nearly cooked break the triangles apart. They are delicious if when still hot you split them and put butter inside.

BUTTERSCOTCH SCONES

7 oz. ($1\frac{3}{4}$ cups) flour

1 oz. (2 tablespoonfuls) cornflour

1 teaspoonful ($1\frac{1}{4}$ teaspoonfuls) baking powder

pinch of salt

1 oz. (2 tablespoonfuls) butter

milk to mix

butter

soft brown sugar

Sieve flour, cornflour, baking powder and salt into a bowl. Rub in the butter and mix to an elastic dough with milk. Knead lightly on a floured board and roll into an oblong shape $\frac{1}{4}$ in. thick. Spread with butter and sprinkle liberally with soft brown sugar and roll up like a swiss roll. Cut into slices and bake in a hot oven 475°F. (246°C.) for 8–10 minutes.

CINNAMON FARLS

$\frac{1}{2}$ lb. (2 cups) self-raising flour

pinch of ground cinnamon

salt

$1\frac{1}{2}$ oz. (3 tablespoonfuls) bacon fat

a little sugar

2 fl. oz. ($\frac{1}{4}$ cup) milk

2 fl. oz. ($\frac{1}{4}$ cup) water

Sieve flour, cinnamon and salt into a bowl. Rub in fat. Add sugar and mix to a soft dough with the milk and water. Shape lightly into a round on a slightly floured board. Roll to $\frac{1}{2}$ in. thickness then cut into triangles. Place a little apart on a greased baking sheet then bake in a moderately hot oven, 425°F. (219°C.) for about 9 minutes or until dry and a light colour.

CREAM SCONES

Prepare the dough as for sultana scones (*see* p. 54), but omit the fruit. Roll the dough and cut into rounds or triangles with a cutter. Place them on a prepared baking sheet and leave for 20 minutes. Cook them on the middle shelf of the oven at 425°F. (219°C.) until they are coloured underneath. Turn them over and colour the other side. The time for each side is approximately 6–8 minutes. After baking, cool them, split them and fill with jam and whipped cream.

CREAM SCONES (U.S.A.)

These scones rise very well and taste as good as they look.

8 oz. (2 cups) flour
4 teaspoonfuls (5 tea-
  spoonfuls) baking
  powder
2 teaspoonfuls (2½ tea-
  spoonfuls) sugar
salt
2 oz. (4 tablespoonfuls)
  butter
2 eggs
4 fl. oz. (½ cup) cream

Mix all the ingredients, work in the butter. If you have an electric mixer do it in this, if not use your hands. You can use a fork for mixing, or your fingers. Add the eggs, which you should first beat well, and then the cream. Put on a floured pastry board, work a little more and then roll out ¼ in. thick and cut out rounds 1½–2 in. in diameter. Let them rest for a while and wash over with white of egg or yolk of egg, whichever you like. Sprinkle the top with caster sugar and then bake for 15 minutes at 450°F. (233°C.). Serve hot, with butter and jam.

DROP SCONES (1)

½ lb. (2 cups) self-
  raising flour
¼ oz. (1½ teaspoonfuls)
  baking powder
2 oz. (¼ cup) caster
  sugar
2 eggs
½ pint (1¼ cups) milk
oil for frying

Sift the flour, pinch of salt, baking powder and caster sugar into a bowl. Make a well in the middle. Add 2 eggs and ¼ pint (⅓ pint) milk. Beat to a light batter, gradually adding another ¼ pint (⅓ pint) milk. Allow the batter to settle for 20 minutes after beating. Meanwhile heat a little oil in a thick-bottomed frying pan or on a griddle. Wait until a faint blue vapour rises and then drop on a tablespoonful of the batter for each scone. Cook them until bubbles come to the surface and burst, and then turn over and repeat. This will ensure a well-browned scone and they should be served hot with butter, syrup or maple syrup.

DROP SCONES (2)

½ lb. (2 cups) flour
salt
1 oz. (2 tablespoonfuls)
  caster sugar
pinch of bicarbonate of
  soda
pinch of cream of
  tartar
1 egg, beaten
about 6 fl. oz. (¾ cup)
  buttermilk

Heat a griddle or heavy frying pan. Mix all the dry ingredients together: add beaten egg and half the milk. Stir till thick; then thin with the rest of the milk till it has the consistency of thick cream. Pour into a jug. Rub griddle with a piece of suet. Pour on the batter into rounds 3 in. in diameter. Cook until bubbles form on the top and they are light brown underneath. Turn and cook the other side. They can be served either hot or cold with butter, honey or jam. Children like them hot with butter and brown sugar.

DROP BANNOCKS

1 egg
½ pint (⅔ pint) milk
**pinch of bicarbonate of
  soda**
salt
oatmeal as required

Beat egg and stir in milk, also soda, salt and enough oatmeal to make a 'dropable' batter. Pour into a jug. Rub the griddle with a piece of suet. Pour the batter into small rounds as for drop scones. Cook over a moderate heat till bubbles form on top, then turn and cook on the other side.

JAM SCONE ROUNDS

Prepare the dough as for sultana scones (*see* below), but omit the fruit. Divide into four and shape each into a round ball. Flatten each one a little and place on a greased sheet. Wash the edges with egg and spread a little jam (preferably raspberry) in the centre of each ball. Cover two rounds with the other two and press well down to ensure adhesion. To help keep the shape, flan rings can be used. Egg wash and mark each round into eight equal portions. Rest the scones for 20 minutes and then bake at 400°F. (205°C.) for 15–20 minutes.

POTATO SCONES

**½ lb. mashed cold
  potatoes**
2 oz. (½ cup) flour
butter
salt

Mash the potatoes. Melt a little butter. Mix them all together adding the salt and work in as much flour as the paste will absorb. Roll out very thinly and place on a hot greased griddle or hotplate. Prick well all over. Cook for 3 minutes on each side: cool in a towel.

SULTANA SCONES

**1 lb. (4 cups) self-
  raising flour**
**¼ oz. (¾ teaspoonful)
  salt**
**½ oz. (1 tablespoonful)
  baking powder**
4 oz. (½ cup) margarine
**4 oz. (½ cup) caster
  sugar**
4 oz. (⅔ cup) sultanas
8 fl. oz. (1 cup) milk
**Yellow colouring and
  vanilla essence**

Sift the flour, salt and baking powder together on a flat table top or slab. Rub the margarine into this to obtain a sandy texture. Add the caster sugar and sultanas and make a well in the centre. Pour in the milk, yellow colouring and vanilla essence (the latter two, optional). Mix to a light batter with a little of the flour and then mix in the rest quickly to a softish dough. This can either be rolled flat and cut with a round cutter, or rolled into a thick roll and cut with a knife into rounds. Place on a greased baking sheet, egg wash (*see* p. 59) and sprinkle with granulated sugar. Let the scones rest for 20 minutes and then cook for 15–20 minutes at 460°F. (238°C.).

SODA SCONES

1 lb. (4 cups) flour
salt
2 teaspoonfuls (2½ tea-
spoonfuls) cream of
tartar
1 teaspoonful (1¼ tea-
spoonfuls) bicar-
bonate of soda
½ pint (1¼ cups) butter-
milk

Heat a griddle slowly. Add salt to the flour and mix together with all the other dry ingredients. Add to this the buttermilk and mix to a light elastic dough. Roll out thinly on a floured board. Divide into 4 pieces. Bake on a fairly hot griddle, allowing 3–4 minutes per side. Cool in a towel. If using sweet milk, add 2 teaspoonfuls cream of tartar.

SOUR CREAM SCONES

8 oz. (2 cups) self-
raising flour
2 oz. (¼ cup) butter
salt
sour cream as required
a little beaten egg

Sieve flour and salt, rub the butter into the flour. Add enough sour cream to make a soft dough. Use a knife to mix it and toss the mixture at the same time. Roll out on a floured board to the thickness of ½ in. Cut into rounds, place on a greased tray and bake for 10–15 minutes in a hot oven 410°F. (210°C.).

TREACLE GIRDLE (GRIDDLE) SCONES

½ lb. (2 cups) flour
¾ teaspoonful (1 tea-
spoonful) bicarbonate
of soda
1 teaspoonful (1¼ tea-
spoonfuls) cream of
tartar
salt
caster sugar
mixed spice
½ oz. (1 tablespoonful)
butter
1 tablespoonful (1¼
tablespoonfuls) black
treacle
buttermilk as required

Sieve the flour with the soda, cream of tartar, salt, sugar and spices. Melt the butter with the treacle, stir into the flour with enough buttermilk to make a soft dough. Put on a floured board and divide into 2 pieces. Knead each into a round about ½ in. thick and divide into quarters. Cook on hot floured griddle over moderate heat till dry and lightly browned underneath, about 5–6 minutes, then turn and cook on the other side. Serve with butter.

BUNS

BASIC BUN DOUGH

**2 lb. (8 cups) plain
  flour**
3 oz. ($\frac{1}{3}$ cup) sugar
pinch of salt
**6 oz. ($\frac{3}{4}$ cup) fat or
  margarine**
2 eggs
2 oz. (3 cakes) yeast
**1 pint (1$\frac{1}{4}$ pints) water
  at blood heat**

Sieve the flour with sugar and salt into a bowl. Rub the fat into this and then add the eggs. Meanwhile dissolve the yeast in the water at blood heat and add this to the other ingredients, working in the water to obtain a fairly soft dough. This is a basic bun dough and is the base for doughnuts, cream and currant buns, hot cross buns and all other similar foods.

A selection of buns: 1. jam doughnut; 2. Danish pastry; 3. Chelsea bun; 4. Bath bun; 5. knotted bun; 6. Swiss bun

BATH BUNS

1 lb. bun dough
4 oz. ($\frac{3}{4}$ cup) sultanas
2 oz. ($\frac{1}{2}$ cup) peel
2 oz. ($\frac{1}{2}$ cup) sugar nibs
grated rind of 1 lemon
1 egg

Work into the bun dough the sultanas, peel, sugar and lemon peel. Roll into a thick cylinder and break off into 16 equal pieces. Place them on a slightly greased baking sheet, flatten slightly with the hand and wash them with egg. Sprinkle with nibbed sugar and prove till double their size. Bake at 450°F. (233°C.) for 10 minutes and then brush them with bun wash (*see* p. 59) after baking.

APRICOT GLAZE

1 lb. apricot jam
½ lb. (1 cup) sugar
¼ pint (⅓ pint) water

Boil together the jam, sugar and water and keep on the boil for a few minutes until reduced slightly in volume. Turn out onto a marble slab or a table top and let the mixture cool, when it will set as a jelly. Pass through a sieve and use as required.

CHELSEA BUNS

Roll out 1 lb. bun dough into a rectangle 10 in. × 16 in. and brush this with melted butter. Sprinkle the buttered dough with some small fruit, some mixed peel, some brown or nib sugar, the grated rind of a lemon and a little mixed spice. Wash the four edges with egg, roll into a fairly tight cylinder and divide into 16 pieces and while still together brush with melted butter. Place them, face down, on a lightly greased 1 in. deep, four-sided tray, fairly close together. Egg-wash the tops and prove in a warm place until double the size. All the buns should be touching each other. Bake at 425-450°F. (219-233°C.) for approximately 15 minutes, remove from the oven when cooked, and while still hot, brush with bun wash (*see* p. 59) and dust with caster sugar.

DANISH BUNS

Roll out 1 lb. basic bun dough into a rectangle 9 in. × 16 in. and mark it into three strips lengthways. Spread the centre strip with raspberry jam and wash one of the remaining strips with egg. Fold the unwashed strip onto the one with jam and then fold over the egg-washed strip to seal the others. Then turn the bun over. Divide into 16 equal pieces and place on a lightly greased baking sheet and wash with egg wash. Prove in a warm place until double the size and bake at 450°F. (233°C.) for approximately 10 minutes and complete after baking by washing with bun wash.

HOT CROSS BUNS

I wonder, who could help me to find out the origin, and history of the traditional Hot Cross bun? I think that it is the most popular bun in this country. While we sell ordinary buns by the hundreds, before Good Friday – on Wednesday and Thursday – we make and sell thousands and thousands of Hot Cross buns. I don't think that there is a family in this country that does not have Hot Cross buns on Good Friday.

I am not a lover of spice, so I am not a lover of the Hot Cross bun, but I quite like and appreciate the business part of it. I suppose, very many English ladies make their own Hot Cross buns. May I add to your collection of recipes another one? This is the way we make them.

1 lb. (4 cups) flour
1 oz. (1½ cakes) yeast
3 oz. (⅓ cup) sugar
½ pint (1¼ cups) milk
salt
cinnamon
nutmeg
4 oz. (1 cup) currants
1 oz. (¼ cup) chopped peel
3 oz. (6 tablespoonfuls) butter
2 eggs
mixed spice
milk, sugar and 1 egg to glaze

Put the flour in a large china bowl; put the yeast in the middle with the sugar, milk, salt, cinnamon, nutmeg, spice, butter, and start to mix. When it is smooth add the 2 eggs one at a time. Work it together until it is fine and silky, then add the currants and the chopped peel and knead it until your hand is clean and the dough is shiny like a piece of silk. Let it rise for about an hour in a warm place, then knock it back and let it rest for half an hour. Then put it on a floured board and shape into small round buns, each about 1 oz. in weight. Put them nicely in rows on a buttered baking tin and mark each of them with a cross.

Mix 1 yolk of egg with a little sugar and milk, brush each bun well and mark the bun with the cross again, this time a little deeper. Then bake it in a warm oven, 400–450°F. (205–233°C.) for about 15 minutes.

FRENCH BUNS

Divide and mould as for Swiss buns (*see* p. 59), but in this case, point the ends. Put them on a greased sheet and egg-wash and cut an incision with a sharp knife or scissors down the length of the back. Sprinkle with nibbed or granulated sugar and bake as for Swiss buns but do not brush with bun wash.

JAM BUNS

Divide 1 lb. basic bun dough into sixteen and mould into balls. Place them on a lightly greased baking sheet and allow them to half-prove. At this stage make a fairly deep hollow in the centre of each bun, egg wash them and then fill the hollows with raspberry jam. After this, prove, bake and wash them as with the currant buns.

PLAITED or KNOTTED BUNS

Work a few currants, about ½ cup into a basic bun dough and divide as usual into sixteen. Mould each into a large ball and then with a rolling pin flatten until the dough is about 6–7 in. across. With a sharp knife, cut through the surface of the dough into 8 equal portions and then brush with egg wash and prove in a warm place until double their size. Bake at 450°F. (233°C.) for about 10 minutes. To finish the bun rounds after baking, brush with egg wash and if desired, a little water icing.

Water Icing is made by mixing together water and icing sugar till it is adjusted to give a reasonably thick liquid that can be brushed onto the buns.

Egg Wash is made by beating together 1 egg and 2 fl. oz. ($\frac{1}{4}$ cup) water. For a richer wash, use the yolk and 1 fl. oz. water.

CURRANT BUNS

basic bun dough

4 oz. (1 cup) currants

spice (optional)

1 egg

bun wash:

1 lb. sugar (granulated, caster or lump)

1 pint (1¼ pints) water

Add the cleaned currants to the basic bun dough and work well with a little spice if desired. Divide the dough into 16 pieces, mould each into a ball and place them on a lightly greased baking sheet, not too closely together. Wash with egg and let them prove in a warm place until double their size. Cook at 460°F. (238°C.) for approximately 10 minutes. Remove from the oven and brush over immediately with *bun wash*. For this boil together 1 pint (1¼ pints) water with 1 lb. sugar till thick. Bun wash will keep very well.

ORANGE BUNS

These are made the same way as currant buns except that the currants are replaced by 4 oz. crystallised orange peel, not too finely chopped. After dividing and moulding, decorate each bun with a piece of peel. Prove, bake and wash with bun wash and then brush again with orange-flavoured water icing.

RICE BUNS

2 oz. (½ cup) self-raising flour

2 oz. (¼ cup) butter

3 oz. (full ⅓ cup) sugar

3 oz. (¼ cup) ground rice

grated rind of 1 lemon

2 eggs

Cream the butter and sugar together. Add 1 of the eggs, then the ground rice and lemon peel. When blended thoroughly, add the second egg and the flour and mix well. Place in greased patty-pan tins and bake in a moderate oven at 350°F. (177°C.) for 20 minutes.

SWISS BUNS

Divide 1 lb. bun dough into 16 equal portions and mould each into a ball. Leave them for a few minutes and then roll them into finger-lengths (approximately 3½ in.) and leave the ends blunt. Put them on a greased baking sheet, egg-wash them and prove in a warm place until double their size. Bake at 450°F. (233°C.) for approximately 10 minutes and on removal from the oven, brush with warm water icing.

BELGIAN BUNS

Roll out as for Chelsea Buns and spread thinly with almond cream before egg-washing the edges. Divide and place on the tray and flatten slightly with the hand. Wash the tops with egg and sprinkle with flaked almonds. Allow to prove as usual and bake at 450°F. (233°C.) for approximately 10 minutes. Remove from the oven and brush with hot apricot glaze and then with warm water icing.

MISCELLANEOUS RECIPES

BALMORAL BONNETS

½ pint (1¼ cups) water
1 cinnamon stick
peel of 1 lemon
3 tablespoonfuls (3¾ tablespoonfuls) flour
1 walnut of butter
2 yolks of eggs
pinch of salt
fat for deep frying

Pour water into a saucepan, add to it the cinnamon stick and lemon peel. Simmer for 10 minutes then strain. When nearly cold, stir enough into the flour to make a smooth cream, then add the remainder of the water. When blended, cook in a saucepan for 2–3 minutes, stirring all the time, then add the butter. Stir till blended then remove from the heat and leave until cold. Add beaten yolks of eggs and salt, beat until blended then drop into hot deep fat from a dessertspoon. Fry till golden brown turning in the fat as required, then drain on absorbent paper. Serve covered with sifted icing sugar and with lemon slices.

BOILED DOUGHNUTS

2 fl. oz. (¼ cup) water
1 oz. (2 tablespoonfuls) sugar
a very little salt
4 oz. (½ cup) butter
5 oz. (1¼ cups) flour
4 eggs

Mix together with the water, the sugar, salt and butter. Over a low gas bring this to the boil. When it starts to boil add to it the flour, bit by bit, and continue to boil until it becomes thick. Allow to cool and then add the 4 eggs, mixing very well. Take a big, long baking tin and put this mixture on it using a spoon to make small balls; placed 3 in. apart. Bake in a very low oven till golden coloured.

BOSTON BREAKFAST CAKE (U.S.A.)

It is still a very popular breakfast food for leisurely breakfasts, when you have time to enjoy nice, warm breakfast cakes. The recipe is simple.

flour
1½ oz. (3 tablespoonfuls) sugar
½ oz. (¾ cake) yeast
2 eggs
a pinch of salt
2 pints (2½ pints) milk

Use as much white flour as will produce a soft yet firm dough. Make the dough in the evening and let it stand overnight. It should have turned sour by the morning. Then add half a teaspoonful of bicarbonate of soda dissolved in a little milk. Then knead the dough: shape into small tea buns, let them rise for 30 minutes and bake them in a moderate oven for half an hour. Serve them hot.

CHEESE GOMBOC (Hungary)

1 lb. (2 cups) cream or cottage cheese
1 whole egg
2 yolks of eggs
semolina
salt
breadcrumbs

Mix the cheese well with the eggs and add enough semolina to it to bind together. Leave to rest for half an hour. Put on the gas a large saucepan half filled with water, add a little salt and bring to the boil. With the palms of your hands or your fingers form small round balls of the paste and drop them carefully into the boiling water. The paste must be of the right consistency. If it is too soft the balls will break into pieces. More semolina should be added if this happens. It must not be too hard either. When it is just right, boil for 12 or 15 minutes. When they are cooked the balls rise to the surface of the water. Remove and drain well and place in a fireproof dish and mix well with previously buttered and roasted breadcrumbs. If you like sprinkle the top with thick Devonshire cream. Heat in the oven for another 10 minutes and serve very hot.

Here I have to tell you that in my childhood this cheese *gomboc* was my birthday cake.

POTATO CAKES

Very many years ago, during the war, that most wonderful woman, Constance Spry, invited me with my husband for a weekend at her nice house in Orpington. They had very good food in spite of the severe rationing. We found their fellow guests interesting and pleasant people. Her house was pretty, large, spotlessly kept and furnished in excellent taste and she had some beautiful and valuable antiques. Her only help in the large house was a little 14-year-old girl. Her table was most beautifully laid with lovely china and glass and the food, I think, was the best I ever tasted in England. For breakfast we all went into her kitchen where she cooked on a large cooker for all of us; on the table was a large jug of coffee, another jug with hot milk and a big pot of tea and then she cooked eggs and 1 slice of bacon for everybody. Then she made potato cakes which were so good freshly made that I would happily have eaten nothing else. She gave me the recipe, so I pass it on to you.

1½ lb. mashed, freshly boiled, floury potatoes
6 oz. (1½ cups) flour
salt
milk

Crush the potatoes and mix on a floured board. Add salt and work in the flour by degrees, kneading lightly and very quickly. Roll out the paste very thinly, as thinly as possible, in a round shape about 6 in. in diameter. Cook on a rather hot griddle for 7–10 minutes, turning once.

POTATO GOMBOC (Hungary)

1½ oz. (3 tablespoonfuls) butter
a pinch of salt
1½ lb. mashed potato; cooked in salt water and passed through a sieve
4 oz. (1 cup) flour
1 lb. plums
1 cup (1¼ cups) buttered breadcrumbs

Mix all the ingredients together (except the plums and the crumbs). Work quickly because the potato makes the dough very soft. When it is nice and smooth roll it out thinly; not thicker than your little finger. Cut out 2½ in. squares and put in each square a plum, if possible a special sweet plum which we have in Hungary called *squvachen*. If *squvachen* plums are not available you can use prunes. Take the stone out of the plum and replace with a small piece of lump sugar rolled in cinnamon. Place the plum in the square and form a nice round ball. Again, work quickly. When they are ready drop them in salted, boiling water. They should not boil too fiercely. When they are cooked the balls rise to the surface of the water; this takes between 12 and 15 minutes. Drain the water off and roll in previously buttered roasted breadcrumbs. Keep them hot either in the oven or placed on the stove over a pan of boiling hot water. Allow 3 or 4 per person.

You can make the same dumpling with fresh, ripe apricots or with fresh cherries. Of course, with the cherries you have to put about 4 in each dumpling.

POTATO DOUGHNUTS (Hungary)

In Hungary shooting was one of the most entertaining of sports. It depended on the time of the year whether the guns went out and took with them a picnic or came back to the house and had a hearty lunch. One of the lunch favourites was potato doughnuts. The recipe is:

$7\frac{1}{4}$ oz. ($1\frac{3}{4}$ cups) flour
$7\frac{1}{4}$ oz. (1 cup) boiled,
    mashed potato
salt according to taste
$2\frac{1}{2}$ oz. (5 tablespoonfuls)
    butter
$\frac{1}{2}$ oz. ($\frac{3}{4}$ cake) yeast
milk
3 yolks of eggs
3 lb. (6 cups) lard
Parmesan cheese

Dissolve the yeast in a little warm milk; then add to the mixture of the flour, potato, salt and butter. Add the 3 yolks of egg. Mix these all together and let the mixture rest for an hour or so. Then put it on a pastry board and roll it out thinner than $\frac{1}{2}$ in. and cut out with a small $1\frac{1}{2}$ in. diameter cutter, then let it rest for another good hour or so. When it has risen enough, put in a deep frying pan 3 lb. lard. When this is hot, drop in the little doughnuts. Cover the pan with a lid just for a few minutes. Turn the doughnuts over and allow to cook another minute. Then quickly take out and place on absorbent paper. Before serving sprinkle on it grated Parmesan cheese and serve it with hot tomato sauce.

YEAST GOMBOC (Hungary)

2 eggs
2 oz. ($\frac{1}{4}$ cup) butter
$1\frac{1}{2}$ oz. (3 tablespoonfuls)
    sugar
a pinch of salt
$\frac{1}{2}$ oz. ($\frac{3}{4}$ cake) yeast
1 teaspoonful ($1\frac{1}{4}$ tea-
    spoonfuls) rum
a little grated lemon
enough flour to make
    a soft dough

Dissolve the yeast in 3 or 4 teaspoonfuls of warm milk. Mix it into the ingredients and allow to rest. After the rest knead it very well. Take the dough and roll it out on a floured pastry board. Then cut out small squares and put in each a plum or plum jam. Form them into round balls and cook for 15 minutes in boiling salted water. Then drain and roll in butter roasted crumbs and put in the oven for 10 minutes. Serve very hot with melted butter.

If you like you can put extra sugar on the top of the dumplings.

CRUMPETS

I give you another completely English recipe – crumpets. I am afraid I am not such a friend of crumpets as I am of muffins because when for the first time in my life I met the English crumpet it was a sad disappointment and you know that if we are once disappointed we can never feel the same again. When I first saw a crumpet I was delighted and I thought this is a lovely something made of potato and that it would taste like the potato pancakes which belong to my childhood memories. I tasted the first crumpets cold; oh, how I disliked them. Later on I tasted them nice and hot and buttered so I feel that they deserve to be written about, and therefore I give you the recipe:

1 lb. (4 cups) flour
salt
a little sugar
½ oz. (¾ cake) yeast
¾ pint (2 cups) warm water
a pinch bicarbonate of soda dissolved in ¼ pint (⅓ pint) cold water

Dissolve the yeast in the warm water. Then mix all the ingredients together and make a soft, smooth dough. It must be almost liquid. Allow to ferment for 1 hour and then dissolve a pinch of bicarbonate of soda in ¼ pint (⅓ pint) water and add this to the dough. Beat thoroughly the whole time.

Crumpets are cooked in the same way as muffins (*see* p. 65) on a hot griddle inside greased rings, but with this recipe the mixture is so soft that you have to use a ladle to pour it by spoonfuls into the rings. Turn the crumpets over and cook on both sides till golden coloured. Before serving put a pat of butter on top and warm them thoroughly. Serve in a heated covered dish.

Sultana scones 1; scone round 2; muffins 3; drop scones 4

MUFFINS

'How English can you get?' I wonder whether any of you who will read my book are interested in making this very nice, very ordinary and very traditional English tea bun. Can you call a muffin a tea bun? I hope the muffin will not be offended! I like muffins and I feel very English when I eat one. So I give you the recipe:

1 lb. (4 cups) flour
1 teaspoonful (1¼ tea-
    spoonfuls) salt
sugar
1 oz. (1½ cakes) yeast
½ pint (1¼ cups) water

Dissolve the yeast in the water which should be warm. Then mix all the ingredients in and continue mixing until soft, and smooth. Allow this dough to stand about an hour and then knead it very well. The dough should now rest for another half an hour and then it should be shaped into round pieces; each piece should weigh about 3 oz. Put them on a lightly floured board and cover with a cloth and allow to rise. The muffins should be cooked on a hot girdle or hotplate which should be slightly greased. Turn onto the other side when they are a nice golden-brown colour.

MUFFINS (U.S.A.)

7 oz. (1¾ cups) flour
2 oz. (¼ cup) sugar
a good pinch bicar-
    bonate of soda
salt
2 eggs
2 oz. (¼ cup) butter
5⅓ oz. (⅔ cup) milk

Sift the measured dry ingredients together. Melt the butter very slowly and set it aside to cool a little. Beat the eggs and add to them the milk and butter. Add the egg mixture to the dry ingredients and blend quickly – but just enough to incorporate the flour. The batter must be lumpy. Fill greased muffin tins a little less than three-quarters full and bake at 400°F. (205°C.) for about 25 minutes. Serve hot with butter and jam.

OATCAKES

½ lb. (1⅓ cups) oatmeal
salt
1 oz. (1 tablespoonful)
    melted fat
pinch of bicarbonate of
    soda
approximately ½ tea-
    cupful hot water

Heat a griddle slowly (if you have no griddle a strong frying pan may be used). Mix the oatmeal with salt and bicarbonate of soda. Make a well in the centre and pour in the melted fat (this should be either bacon, ham or dripping), then stir in as much hot water as is needed to make a very stiff dough. Place on a board rubbed with plenty of medium oatmeal. Knead very well. Divide into 2 equal pieces, and knead into 2 smooth balls, then shape into 2 rounds. Press out a little and roll to $\frac{1}{8}$-$\frac{1}{4}$ in. thickness depending on your taste. Cut out neatly with a plate and rub with oatmeal. You now have 2 oatcakes if you rolled the dough to $\frac{1}{4}$ in. thickness or if you made them $\frac{1}{8}$ in. thick you should cut them into 4 triangles. Using a spatula, slip the oatcakes onto the griddle, smooth side uppermost. Bake over moderate heat until the edges of the cake or cakes begin to curl. Remove carefully to a board. Rub smooth side with oatmeal and either toast them in front of a fire, in a moderate oven or under the grill till crisp and slightly brown.

PEANUT BUTTER KISSES (U.S.A.)

In America I ate and liked several cakes and petits fours made with peanut butter. This recipe comes from a very kind friend of mine; she wishes that I should use it in my book, so I do, and would be very happy if you like it.

4 oz. ($\frac{1}{2}$ cup) butter
6 oz. ($\frac{1}{2}$ cup) peanut butter
3$\frac{1}{2}$ oz. ($\frac{1}{3}$ cup) white sugar
3$\frac{1}{2}$ oz. ($\frac{1}{3}$ cup) brown sugar
4 oz. (1 cup) flour
1 egg
$\frac{1}{2}$ vanilla pod, scraped
salt
pinch of bicarbonate of soda

Mix the butter with a wooden spoon till white and creamy. Then add the sugar and slowly add the other ingredients and enough flour to make a firm dough. If 4 oz. (1 cup) flour is not enough add a little more. Take a baking tin, butter it and flour it and with a tablespoon put in little bundles and flatten with a fork. Mark the top with a fork and bake in a moderate oven about 350°F. (177°C.). It is ready when it is nice and firm.

RUSKS

1 lb. (4 cups) flour
2 oz. ($\frac{1}{4}$ cup) butter
$\frac{1}{4}$ pint ($\frac{1}{3}$ pint) milk
2 oz. ($\frac{1}{4}$ cup) sugar
3 eggs
$\frac{1}{2}$ oz. ($\frac{3}{4}$ cake) yeast

Put the milk and butter in a saucepan and shake it around until the latter is melted. Put the flour and sugar into a bowl and mix. Beat the eggs, stir them with the yeast, then add to the milk and butter; work into the flour to make a smooth dough. Leave this to rise in a warm place. Knead, and divide into 12 pieces; bake for about 20 minutes in a hot oven at 400 °F. (205 °C.). Remove the rusks, break them in half and then set them in the oven to get crisp on the other side.

When cold they should be kept in tins to keep them dry. If they are to be used for cheese the sugar should be omitted.

POPPYSEED AND WALNUT BEIGLE (Hungary)

1 lb. (4 cups) flour
½ lb. (1 cup) butter
2 yolks of eggs
1 whole egg
4 oz. (½ cup) caster
  sugar
milk
cream (optional)
1 oz. (1½ cakes) yeast
salt
filling:
1 tablespoonful (1¼
  tablespoonfuls) rum
vanilla essence
  (optional)
walnuts or poppyseed,
  and sugar (total
  weight equal to that
  of the paste)
milk
sultanas (optional)

Mix the paste, using enough milk or cream to make it smooth; the yeast should be dissolved in a little warm milk. Mix well until smooth, and you can add a little vanilla essence. Put it into the refrigerator for use the next day then make your filling.

Weigh the paste and mix together sugar and walnut or poppyseed so that these equal the weight of the paste. Mix together with milk, boil it up and let it cool. Add to it as many well-washed sultanas as you like. The pastry and filling should be the same weight. Roll out the pastry, which should have rested in the refrigerator for 12–14 hours, until it is approximately ⅛ in. thick, and spread the walnut or poppyseed filling over it, also ⅛ in. thick. You have to be careful with the sugar; if there is too much, the paste will be breakable. Roll it up as you would a 'roly poly'; put it on a well-greased baking tray. Take 1 or 2 yolks of eggs, mix in half a teaspoonful of icing sugar and brush this over the roly poly. Allow it to rest for 10 minutes and wash over again. Repeat after another 15 minutes. Leave it to rest for another 15 minutes and then bake it in a moderate oven until it is a nice golden brown.

CAKES

Nothing worries me more than to make, bake or cook very English food, cakes, pastry, crumpets or muffins, things that I have not seen before I came to this country. Of course, this was long ago; that was the time when I made the birthday cakes of the greatest Englishman, according to me the greatest man in the world. I made birthday cakes for Sir Winston Churchill for many, many years; a very special mixture which I will give you later. But from the first one to the last one, they were all great successes and I got the most beautiful letters of appreciation from this great man. Of course, this helped enormously and gave me confidence and daring. I miss this wonderful job I did for so many years. I planned the design of his cake the whole year and this gave me more pleasure than anything else; I can't do it any more. I have a little consolation that I still have the opportunity to make Lady Churchill's birthday cake. I have done this, too, for very many years.

In Hungary we did not have birthday cakes, not traditional ones as in England. Anybody in a family had their favourite food on his or her birthday and at the end of the meal their favourite gâteau or pastry.

My favourite was – don't laugh, please – a savoury cream-cheese *gomboc* or dumpling. I still like it better than any cakes or gâteaux. When I first visited England about 40 years ago, one of my greatest interests was looking at the windows of bakers' shops. I admired some of the round and heavily decorated cakes, which had written on them 'Happy Birthday'.

I think, in my whole life nothing has given me so much pleasure as to plan and make cakes for Sir Winston Churchill. These cakes have given me the unearned reputation of being able to design just the right birthday cake for anybody. That is not true. He gave me the ideas for his own birthday cakes from his very varied activities. My favourite was a cake in the form of a spiral, decorated with 32 models of his famous hats. I suppose it is very wrong on my part to call that cake a masterpiece, that is if we can call a cake a masterpiece at all, but I do, and I do more. I called it 'Churchill's life story in hats'.

I had an amusing episode with this cake. A picture of the cake appeared in a newspaper and the next day a little man, very modest, came up to see me. My secretary guarded me like a prize pig – as friends said – and tried to find out from him what his business was. He said: 'The fact is that I am a colleague of hers and therefore I must see her in person.' Since my secretary knew that I did not like to refuse anybody who insisted on seeing me, she showed him into my office. Coming in, he greeted me very jovially: 'You know, we are colleagues. I have a fruit-stand in Covent Garden.'

I told him, I felt very honoured and asked, what I could do for him. Then he told me that he was the proud father of a six-year-old boy whose birthday it was in ten days time. So he wanted, whatever the cost, the same cake that Sir Winston Churchill had just had.

I replied to him that while I did regret it very deeply, unluckily the man who had done the actual work had gone for a fortnight's very well-deserved holiday. So, I could not make the same cake, but I could make another very nice cake. He would not hear of it – a Churchill cake or nothing. Very likely I lost a very important customer!

I worked and planned the Churchill cake from the beginning of December till the following November. I planned it, I dreamt of it and I have to admit, so did my whole family – everybody had ideas. We pooled them and we enjoyed discussing them. Now I miss the whole procedure more than I can tell. . . .

The mixing of the Churchill cake was also special, according to Lady Churchill's wish. She is a most exacting woman, always knowing what she wants. She liked only light fruit cakes with specially chosen raw materials. We used the very best fruit which was soaked in the best brandy for days. The success I had with these cakes, the most wonderful appreciation I got from his letters was so rewarding that it made worth while the many bitter, sad and nasty experiences which come your way, if you work for a long time in this kind of business.

On his 80th birthday, which was celebrated at No. 10 Downing Street, my husband and I were invited. He greeted me, took my hand between his two hands and said: 'How nice to see you, Madame Floris. You've played such a big part in my life'.

What is a knighthood or any other reward equal to this?

Cake and pastry tins: 1. *Guglhupf* tin; 2. sponge sandwich or open tart tin; 3. *Savarin*; 4. honey cake tin; 5. petit four or tart ring tins

ANGEL CAKE

Just before the Second World War we heard more and more of two very able American ladies working in England. They made three kinds of cakes, nothing else but these three cakes. They were most successful. I wonder now, where and how I heard of them, but I had. And then I had the opportunity to taste all the three cakes; they were threatening competitors of mine. I had to admit that the cakes were first class. They looked very well and tasted just as good.

The ladies made one very large yellow sponge cake, about 5 or 6 in. high and about 10 or 12 in. in diameter. The sponge was very plain, but the best I've ever tasted. There was also a very large angel cake, snow white and very light, and a chocolate devil cake.

I have to admit that I tried, but I could not copy them. With my very long experience I can generally copy anything, food or cakes. Most of the times I have a good idea of what are the ingredients and how to do it. But I just could not make these cakes, at least not so well as they did.

But, as luck had it, I heard that the two American ladies had left England. They did not want to be involved with our war. With the same luck I heard that two English girls who had worked with the American ladies were looking for similar jobs. Of course, I jumped at the opportunity and engaged them both. They worked for me for very many years. They made in my bakery angel cakes, devil cakes and sponge cakes.

The angel cake was quite good – but not the same. It seems that the American ladies had taken the important secrets with them back to America. What a pity. The Americans have so much more wealth in every way than we have here. But perhaps they will hear my cry and send me back the secret. If they do, I promise here and now, I will share it with you. In the meantime, you and I have to be satisfied with the next best, the recipe the girls made for me.

12 whites of eggs
10½ oz. (1½ cups) fine caster sugar
1 good teaspoonful (1¼ teaspoonfuls) cream of tartar
salt
2 oz. (⅓ cup) finely-ground almonds
½ vanilla pod
4 oz. (⅞ cup) cake flour

Beat the whites of eggs till very stiff; the mixture must remain moist and fluffy. Add the cream of tartar and salt, finally fold in the flour very slowly. Be very careful not to break the stiff egg white, and make the mixture smooth and even. Pour into a large buttered and floured cake tin about 10 or 12 in. diameter and bake it for 50 minutes in a slow oven at about 300°F. (149°C.). It should be very high, nice golden-brown. Then turn off the heat and leave the cake in the oven for another 8 or 10 minutes. Take out and turn out of the tin.

ALMOND CAKE (1)

I was once invited to visit a very old lady, who insisted that I should come and have tea with her. I tried to persuade her to come to me instead, but she told me I had to come and taste her almond cake. I went, I found her charming and delightful. Her small tea table was beautifully laid, and her little almond cake, as she had suggested, was very good indeed.

What touched my heart most was that the recipe of the cake had already been written down on her very elegant writing-paper. I have to mention that the old lady was French. As my son George explained it to me just now, we don't fulfil our existence if we don't do something for humanity, so I hand over the French lady's recipe to you.

7 eggs
2 yolks of eggs
9 oz. (1 full cup) sugar
6 oz. ($\frac{3}{4}$ cup) flour
5 oz. ($\frac{3}{4}$ cup) ground almonds
$\frac{1}{2}$ vanilla pod
5 oz. ($\frac{2}{3}$ cup) butter
2 oz. ($\frac{1}{2}$ cup) chopped almonds

Break the eggs in a saucepan. Add the yolks and sugar. Beat these very well together and then put on a very low heat. Whip with a wire whisk until the mixture starts to thicken. Then take it off the flame and blend in the flour, the ground almonds and the vanilla. Melt the butter and add to the batter. Then take small moulds, like *brioche* moulds. Butter them and put in the bottom of each a few chopped almonds. Fill the little moulds two-thirds full and bake them in a cool oven for 45 minutes.

ALMOND CAKE (2)

A useful everyday cake for you for tea.

10 oz. ($1\frac{1}{4}$ cups) butter
2 yolks of eggs
1 whole egg
a little cherry brandy
$\frac{1}{2}$ lb. (2 cups) flour
$5\frac{1}{2}$ oz. (scant $\frac{3}{4}$ cup) sugar
7 oz. ($1\frac{1}{4}$ cups) ground almonds
$\frac{1}{2}$ vanilla pod

Cream the butter, which should first be warmed with the sugar till very creamy; add the yolks of eggs, one by one, and then add the whole egg; add the liqueur, but stir it all the time. Put the flour on a pastry board; add the sugar, the ground almonds and the vanilla. Add the creamed butter and work it in thoroughly. When the mixture is smooth and very silky put in a mould; a buttered *savarin* mould is best. Bake for 35 minutes in a medium oven.

BAUMKUCHEN (Germany)

Baumkuchen is a cake shaped like a tree which originated in Germany but has not become popular in other countries. It is very decorative and I think nearly every German household which can afford it has one on the Christmas table.

Baumkuchen is something that a housewife cannot make. It should be a joy for us professionals that this is so, but unluckily *Baumkuchen* is not an everyday 'bread-and-butter' necessity. So we can keep our secret, but it isn't much help.

A *Baumkuchen* is very decorative. I tell you the ingredients in spite of the fact that they are of no use to you – flour, ground almonds, a lot of butter, many yolks and whites of eggs, and sugar. This is all mixed together into a thick batter, something like pancake batter but thicker.

Now comes the problem you cannot solve. To bake a *Baumkuchen* you need a big, clumsy piece of equipment which is neither a tool nor a machine. It is a big sheet of tin with many holes in the back. In the middle it has a $2\frac{1}{2}$ ft wooden tube with a little wheel at one end which one person has to turn like a spit. The gas is lit, the flames come out through the numerous holes and the batter is poured on the big wooden tube with a big spoon. This process is repeated for about an hour or two; it depends, how big the tree cake will ultimately be. When it is big enough, then it is left on the wooden tube to cool. Then we take it off and you can do two things with it. Either cover it with thin white fondant or with chocolate. Either is equally good. When you cut the cake, it looks and tastes layered. The layer effect is from the baking.

BANBURY CAKES
$\frac{1}{4}$ lb. ($\frac{1}{2}$ cup) **butter**
2 oz. ($\frac{1}{4}$ cup) **sugar**
$\frac{1}{2}$ lb. (1 cup) **currants**
$\frac{1}{4}$ lb. (1 cup) **minced mixed peel**
ground cinnamon
some puff pastry
icing:
1 **white of egg**
some caster sugar

Cream the butter and sugar; add fruits and mix together very well. Add the ground cinnamon.

Roll out the puff pastry for its final time and make into 2 diamond shapes. Place the mixture on one diamond and cover with the second. Wet the edges so that they stick together. Bake in a hot oven at 420°F. (216°C.).

Whisk a white of egg stiffly and add some caster sugar. Place on the Banbury cake when cooked and allow to set in a cool oven.

BIRTHDAY CAKE
$\frac{1}{2}$ lb. (1 cup) **vegetable fat**
$\frac{1}{2}$ lb. (1 cup) **butter**
1 lb. (2 cups) **sugar**
8 large **eggs**
1 lb. 2 oz. ($4\frac{1}{2}$ cups) **flour**
3 lb. **sultanas**
1 lb. **glacé cherries**

Beat the vegetable fat, the butter and sugar together until light and creamy. Now beat the eggs in, one at a time, and continue to beat until the mixture is light and fluffy. Now gently fold in the flour but do not over-mix at this stage. Finally add the sultanas and glacé cherries, which have been thoroughly washed and dried. Fill 6 in. cake tins with the mixture, about 1 lb. of it in each one. Bake at 380°F. (194°C.) for 1 hour.

BASIC FRUIT CAKE

6 oz. ($\frac{3}{4}$ cup) butter

6 oz. ($\frac{3}{4}$ cup) sugar

4 eggs

9 oz. ($2\frac{1}{4}$ cups) flour

2 oz. ($\frac{1}{3}$ cup) ground almonds

10 oz. ($1\frac{1}{2}$ cups) sultanas

6 oz. ($\frac{3}{4}$ cup) currants

3 oz. ($\frac{3}{4}$ cup) mixed peel

3 oz. ($\frac{3}{4}$ cup) chopped glacé cherries

1 lemon (juice and the grated rind)

pinch of baking powder

a little sweetened milk

Mix butter till creamy; add the sugar and then add the eggs, one by one. Fold the flour in a little at a time. Then mix in the almond and all the dry fruit and then add the baking powder. Mix all well together and then pour into a greased baking tin 7 in. by 3 in. and bake in a medium slow oven for about 2 hours. Approximately 1 hour before the cake is cooked remove from the oven and decorate the top of the cake by scattering a few almonds then replace the cake for a further 40 minutes. Then remove it again and brush over the top with the sweetened milk. This is a very good cake and will keep well in a sealed cake tin.

BROWN SUGAR CAKE

7 oz. ($1\frac{3}{4}$ cups) flour

1 teaspoonfuls ($1\frac{1}{4}$ teaspoonfuls) cream of tartar

$\frac{1}{2}$ teaspoonful ($\frac{3}{4}$ teaspoonful) bicarbonate of soda

12 oz. ($1\frac{1}{2}$ cups) brown sugar

4 oz. ($\frac{1}{2}$ cup) butter

2 eggs plus 2 egg yolks

$5\frac{1}{3}$ oz. ($\frac{2}{3}$ cup) milk

vanilla

10 oz. ($1\frac{1}{4}$ cups) brown sugar plus 4 oz. ($\frac{1}{2}$ cup) white sugar

$2\frac{2}{3}$ oz. ($\frac{1}{3}$ cup) water

2 whites of eggs

vanilla

Sift together the flour, cream of tartar, bicarbonate of soda and put it to the side. Cream together till very light and fluffy the brown sugar and butter: then add, one by one, the whole eggs and the yolks, blending well after each addition. Now add alternately to the sugar mixture the dry ingredients and the milk in three parts, stirring with each addition till the ingredients are incorporated. Finally, add the vanilla. Pour the batter into a pair of 9-in. layer tins, which have been greased and floured, and bake at 375 °F. (191 °C.) for 25 minutes.

For the icing, dissolve the sugars in the water over medium heat, and then boil quickly till the syrup spins a thread when dropped from a spoon. Cool slightly. Beat the whites of eggs stiffly and fold them into the syrup. Cook in a double boiler till grains begin to form around the edge of the pan. Add vanilla to taste and beat till it is cool and reaches a spreading consistency.

BROWNIES (U.S.A.)

8 oz. (1 cup) butter
1 lb. (2 cups) sugar
4 eggs
4 oz. (4 squares) bitter
  chocolate
4 oz. (1 cup) flour
vanilla essence
½ lb. chopped pecan
  nuts or walnuts
pinch of bicarbonate
  of soda
raisins (optional)

Melt the chocolate and butter in a double boiler. Beat eggs and sugar well together and then mix in the sifted flour and soda. Blend well. Stir in the nuts (and raisins if you are using them) and finally the chocolate mixture and vanilla. Pour onto a greased and floured oblong baking tin. Bake for 45 minutes at 275°F. (133°C.). When cooked remove from the oven and cut into rectangles. Cool on a wire rack. I saw these cakes being eaten many times by children in the U.S.A. They loved them and there were never any left on the plate at the end of tea.

CHEESECAKE (1 – U.S.A.)

Before I went to the United States of America I had always been told that the best cheesecake is made in that country. I ate several and they were really good. Some American cheesecake tops are covered with fresh strawberries, brushed over with orange jelly. Some cheesecakes are covered with large pineapple rings and are brushed over with pineapple jelly.

I was determined to bring home a cheesecake recipe, but I did something even better. I went to classes held by an Italian pastrycook in New York. There for my five dollars fee they showed me how to make cheesecake. I spent altogether fifteen dollars – because you have to have three lessons and pay in advance. I give you the recipe I learnt there.

2 oz. (¼ cup) butter
4½ oz. (full ½ cup) sugar
10 oz. (2½ cups) cream
  cheese
2 oz. (⅓ cup) ground
  almonds
1 grated rind and juice
  of a lemon
2 oz. (⅓ cup) semolina
2 oz. (scant ½ cup) sul-
  tanas (white raisins)
2 eggs

Beat the butter and sugar, then add the sieved cheese. Beat very well, add the almonds, the lemon rind the juice. Mix in the yolks of eggs one by one, add the semolina and beat the whites of eggs very stiff and mix very carefully with the other ingredients. Pour into a tin which is first buttered and floured; put a greaseproof paper at the bottom of the tin – bake the mixture at 325°F. (163°C.) for about an hour.

CHEESECAKE (2 – U.S.A.)

The second cheesecake recipe I learned in America:

1 lb. Philadelphia
   cream cheese
$3\frac{1}{2}$ oz. (7 tablespoonfuls)
   butter
$3\frac{1}{2}$ oz. ($\frac{1}{3}$ cup) sugar
$2\frac{1}{4}$ oz. (full $\frac{1}{2}$ cup) flour
sultanas
4 tablespoonfuls ($\frac{1}{4}$ cup)
   of cream
4 eggs
shortcrust pastry

Pass the cheese through a sieve. Beat the butter and sugar until very creamy. Add the yolks of eggs and the cream, the sultanas and the flour. All these have to be mixed very well. Whip the whites of eggs very stiffly so that they stand up in peaks, then add slowly to the rest of the mixture.

Now line a 8 or 9 in. cake tin with the shortcrust pastry, pour the mixture in the tin and bake it in a hot oven, 400°F. (205°C.) for about an hour.

CHEESECAKE (3 – U.S.A.)

Some American cheesecakes are baked in a baking tin which is first lined with shortcrust pastry. The recipe of that shortcrust pastry is as follows:

6 oz. ($1\frac{1}{2}$ cups) flour
4 oz. ($\frac{1}{2}$ cup) butter
1 egg yolk
2 or 3 tablespoonfuls
   ($2\frac{1}{2}$-$3\frac{3}{4}$ tablespoonfuls)
   of water
1 pinch of salt

Rub the butter into the flour with the fingertips, make a well in the middle, add the yolk of egg, salt and enough cold water to make a light dough.

CHEESECAKE (4)

1 lb. 4 oz. cream cheese
8 oz. (1 cup) sugar
1 pint ($1\frac{1}{4}$ pints) milk
$2\frac{1}{2}$ oz. (5 tablespoonfuls)
   butter
12 whites of eggs
4 oz. rice flour (scant
   cup) or flour (1 cup)
3 yolks of eggs
a little lemon peel

Cream the sugar with the yolks of eggs and add it to the lemon peel. Boil the milk and mix it with the cheese, sugar and yolks of eggs until very thick. Add to the egg mixture. Whip the whites of eggs till very stiff, fold in the rice flour and fold very lightly into the mixture and bake in a 8 or 9 in. cake tin in a moderate oven for 45 minutes.

CHEESECAKE (5)

First make a German sweet pastry as follows:

1¼ lb. (5 cups) pastry
   flour
2 eggs
5 oz. (⅔ cup) butter
a little rum
a very small pinch of
   salt
filling:
8 oz. (1 cup) butter
8 oz. (1 cup) sugar
1 lb. (2 cups) cottage
   cheese
4 eggs
2 fl. oz. (¼ cup) sherry
grated rind of 1 lemon
grated nutmeg

Mix these ingredients very quickly in a cold room. First sieve the flour and put it on a pastry board; add the eggs into the centre of the flour. Add the butter bit by bit and mix well together till smooth add the salt and sugar and enough rum to make a dough. Knead this till smooth. Cover with a bowl and let it stand for an hour or two before rolling out. Line a 9 in. baking tin with this.

Beat the yolks of eggs slightly; add the butter bit by bit, then the sugar and cottage cheese, which has previously been sieved. Add the sherry and the lemon peel; beat the whites of eggs very stiffly and fold into the mixture and pour this into the baking tin lined with the pastry. Bake it in a hot oven at 400°F. (205°C.) for 30 minutes.

CHEESECAKE (6)

1 lb. (2 cups) cream
   cheese
1¼ oz. (5 tablespoon-
   fuls) flour
zest of ½ lemon
¼ pint (⅓ pint) cream
3 eggs
6 oz. (¾ cup) caster
   sugar

Whip together the eggs and sugar until stiff. Beat together cheese, flour and lemon in separate bowl, then add in the cream very slowly. Fold in the egg mixture to the cream mixture (*not* the cream mixture to the egg mixture) and beat for 2 minutes. Place in a medium oven at 350°F. (177°C.).

CHERRY CAKE

This is one of the trickiest cakes to make. It is easy to make it too tough or else too wet and sloppy and then find that after baking all the cherries are at the bottom. Glacé cherries are usually full of heavy syrup, so it is essential to wash and dry them thoroughly, otherwise your cake will not be a success. If your time is limited you can wash the cherries and dust with flour which will soak up the moisture; but before using the flour must be shaken off.

2 oz. ($\frac{1}{4}$ cup) butter
2 oz. ($\frac{1}{4}$ cup) white vegetable fat
4 oz. ($\frac{1}{2}$ cup) sugar
2 eggs
$\frac{1}{2}$ lb. ($1\frac{1}{3}$ cups) glacé cherries
5 oz. ($1\frac{1}{4}$ cups) flour

Beat the butter, fat and sugar until light and creamy. Then beat in the eggs, one at a time. The mixture should become fluffy. Then fold in the flour and finally add the glacé cherries. Bake for $1\frac{1}{4}$ hours at 400°F. (205°C.).

CHESTNUT SLICES

2 eggs
2 oz. ($\frac{1}{4}$ cup) sugar
2 oz. ($\frac{1}{2}$ cup) flour
1 oz. (1 square) chocolate
$\frac{1}{2}$ oz. (1 tablespoonful) butter
sherry or brandy
2 oz. ($\frac{1}{4}$ cup) cream
6 oz. (1 cup) chestnut purée (sweetened)
icing:
chocolate
granulated sugar
a little water
drop of olive oil

Break chocolate into small pieces and place in a bowl with the butter. Allow to soften in a warm place. Put eggs and sugar in a bowl and whisk over hot water till they are thick, remove from the heat and whisk on till they are cool. Fold in flour and finally the butter and chocolate. Place greaseproof paper on a baking sheet and spread the mixture on it to a depth of $\frac{1}{2}$ in. Bake at 410°F. (210°C.) till cooked. Remove the paper while it is still hot, cut into slices 2 in. wide, sprinkle with sherry or brandy. Whip the cream and fold in chestnuts. Put together with this filling.

For the icing, melt the chocolate, equal in quantity to the sugar. Cook sugar with water to 'small thread' then remove from heat and cool. Stir into chocolate and add some olive oil and continue stirring until it thickens enough to spread over the cakes.

CHOCOLATE CAKE (1)

A simple cake, easy to make, not expensive and suitable for everybody. It is not rich; it is very good for people who have delicate stomachs but like chocolate cake and want something sweet. I ate it in an English house well over 30 years ago. Everything around the house was lovely and the food was perfect. Since then I can never stay silent if people say that English food is not good and that the English can't cook. I spent a delightful weekend with these very rich people. A river ran through their beautiful garden and on the river a sizeable yacht was moored. But on Sundays evening after dinner I have seen our host take off his coat, put on an apron and with his son wash up the dinner dishes. Very naturally, smilingly, they say the staff have a day off. Mind you that was 30 years ago. They had two large labrador dogs which I loved. The dining room was all old oak furniture, highly polished, I went on stroking the table which felt like silky velvet; I am sure it had been polished for over 400 years. Our bedrooms were perfect and had everything even a tiny basket hung on the head-board of the bed; I suppose they were for paper handkerchiefs. I was most intrigued by the framed samplers on the walls. I don't know if that is the right name, but they are very English.

But I had better give you the recipe otherwise I can go on and on writing about this house.

I ate this cake 33 years ago and I still remember it.

5 oz. ($\frac{2}{3}$ cup) **butter**

5 oz. ($\frac{2}{3}$ cup) **sugar**

4 oz. **unsweetened (4 squares) chocolate**

4 **yolks of eggs**

$1\frac{1}{2}$ oz. **(6 tablespoonfuls) flour**

$1\frac{1}{2}$ oz. ($\frac{1}{4}$ **cup) ground almonds**

4 **whites of eggs**

$\frac{1}{2}$ **vanilla pod**

Beat the butter till creamy; melt the chocolate and sugar, beat it into the butter until smooth. The best way to melt the chocolate is in a double boiler. Then add the yolks of eggs one by one and go on stirring and then slowly add the flour and ground almonds and the vanilla. In the end add the egg whites very stiffly beaten. Mix very carefully, the mixture must be the same colour all the way through.

Butter two 7 in. gâteau rings, and pour in the mixture; you can also bake it in two small bread tins. Bake in a moderate oven 350°F. (177°C.) for about 30–35 minutes. Test it with a knitting needle; if it comes out clean the cake is cooked. Cool in the tin before turning out. If you use sweetened chocolate you can reduce or leave out the sugar altogether.

CHOCOLATE CAKE (2)

When I was in America, naturally I went round and round looking at bakeries and pastry shops; and the cake and pastry trolleys in restaurants. All, all looked wonderful, beautifully finished and enormously rich decorated with cream, fruit and jellies. Everything looked tempting and appetising. There was everything from apple *strudel*, poppyseed *strudel* to large salt pretzels.

My friends all urged me to come and open a business there. My answer was 'What for? Nobody is waiting for me here, nobody needs me'. When, afterwards, I tasted these wonderful-looking and lovely cakes, I was not so sure!

As you know, America has everything of the very best quality. There fruit looks so lovely, their apples are so beautiful, you could not paint them, they are so beautiful, but they do not have the flavour of the English Cox's Orange Pippins.

I'm afraid the same applies to the pastries. They look very fine, but don't taste so good. I think, one of the troubles there is the 'Food and Drug' laws. These force the pastry-makers and chocolate manufacturers to use the tested essences instead of the real article – the fruits, cream and butter we use here.

I saw there a beautiful chocolate cake and I obtained the recipe from the owner of the restaurant and now I hand it over to you.

6 oz. ($\frac{3}{4}$ cup) unsalted
   butter

6 oz. ($\frac{3}{4}$ cup) caster
   sugar

4 eggs

7 oz. (1$\frac{3}{4}$ cups) plain
   flour

1 teaspoonful (1$\frac{1}{4}$ teaspoonfuls) baking
   powder

3 oz. ($\frac{3}{4}$ cup) cocoa

5 tablespoonfuls ($\frac{1}{4}$ cup)
   milk

1 vanilla pod

1 pinch of salt

icing:

3 whites of eggs

4$\frac{1}{2}$ oz. (1 cup) icing
   sugar

4 oz. ($\frac{1}{2}$ cup) butter

1 vanilla pod

4 oz. (4 squares) plain
   dessert chocolate

chocolate flakes:

2 oz. (2 squares) plain
   dessert chocolate

1 sprinkle of icing
   sugar

First brush the inside of a ring-shaped cake-mould very thoroughly with butter. Preheat oven to 380°F. (194°C.) Then beat the butter to a soft cream, add to it the caster sugar: separate the yolks from the white of eggs, and add one by one to the other ingredients. Slowly add the flour, the baking powder, cocoa and salt and add all this to the cream and mix it very well. Add the vanilla, the milk and finally whip the whites of egg until very stiff. Add this slowly to the cream and carefully mix until it is very smooth and creamy. Then pour all this into the prepared mould and put the mould into the oven, preferably the middle of the oven and let it cook for 40–45 minutes. Then take it out and turn the cake out of the mould on a cake rack and let it cool.

In the meanwhile prepare the butter icing. For this the method is as follows. Put the egg-white into a basin, add to it the sifted icing sugar and stand the basin above a pan in which water is simmering and stir it without allowing the mixture to boil. Don't let the bottom of the basin touch the water. Then whip the mixture for 5 or 8 minutes, until it becomes thick and creamy. Then take it off the heat, but go on beating until it is almost cold. Now slowly add the butter to the cream very gradually. Beat in the remaining egg yolk and mix all this carefully and well together. Add the vanilla.

Now roughly chop the chocolate. Put it on a plate and melt it very slowly over a pan of hot water, stirring all the time with a spoon until it is all melted and smooth. Beat it slowly into the icing. Stand the icing to one side till it is cold and thick and then spread it all over the cake.

Finally, make the chocolate flakes. Chop the chocolate roughly and put it on a large plate. Then put the plate on a pan of water, simmer the chocolate and work it with a spoon until it is melted and smooth. It should be melted but do not overheat. Have ready a clean table, possibly with a marble slab on top; an enamel tray would do as well. Spread the chocolate evenly and thinly on the surface and leave till almost set. Then scrape a knife blade down the chocolate strip by strip, and make it into rolls and flakes. Lift the chocolate flakes on the cake with a palette knife and sprinkle the top of the cake very lightly with a little icing sugar. This is best rubbed through a strainer.

CHOCOLATE CRUNCH

As I said in my first book I have so many kinds and nationalities of pastry cooks and bakers from the whole world that we could make our own United Nations, but, as I said before, they are not always united! When I have a new man I let him loose so that he can do what he likes for a week or so. I have a young man just now who came to me from the U.S.A. but who is a Swiss by birth. He made two very interesting looking cakes. He called the first one chocolate crunch. The recipe is:

6 oz. ($\frac{3}{4}$ cup) butter

6 oz. ($1\frac{1}{2}$ cups) icing sugar

5 oz. ($\frac{1}{2}$ cup) golden syrup

6 level tablespoonfuls ($\frac{1}{2}$ cup) cocoa

small packet of cornflakes

$\frac{1}{2}$ pint ($1\frac{1}{4}$ cups) double cream

2 small whites of eggs

1 large dessert red apple

1 large Granny Smith apple

First grease and line an 8 in. cake tin with greaseproof paper. You need two circles of greaseproof paper for the bottom of the tin. Use corn oil for greasing the tin. Put only one of the circles of greaseproof paper in the tin, and brush it also with corn oil.

Put the butter into a large saucepan and melt over a very gentle heat. Remove from the heat and stir in the icing sugar and then the golden syrup. Mix well and then add the cocoa powder, then very carefully stir in the cornflakes. Try not to break the cornflakes. Pour half of this mixture into the cake tin. Smooth over and cover with the other circle of greaseproof paper. Now pour on the other half of the mixture. Press down carefully to level it and place in the refrigerator overnight. Use a sharp knife and run round the edge of the cake with it and then turn it out. Prepare the filling.

Whisk the whites of egg till very stiff and do the same with the fresh cream. Mix the two together. Pipe a little of the cream onto the centre of the cake, using a star tube. Cover the other half with the cream.

Quarter both the apples, remove the core and peel two of the quarters of the red apple and two of the green. Chop them and sprinkle them over the cream filling. Sandwich the cakes together with the layer of cream filling inside. Slice the remaining red and green apple quarters very thinly and decorate the top of the cake with a ring of the apple slices, alternating red with green.

You can flavour this cake if you like with crystallized ginger or with pineapple which has been well drained and chopped.

CHOCOLATE PINEAPPLE CAKE

This is a very simple cake. Suitable for tea or after dinner with fruit salad or ice cream.

$\frac{3}{4}$ **lb. ($1\frac{1}{2}$ cups) granulated sugar**
$\frac{3}{4}$ **lb. ($1\frac{1}{2}$ cups) butter**
6 oz. best marzipan
4 yolks of eggs
$\frac{1}{4}$ **lb. tinned pineapple
(drained and
chopped)**
$4\frac{1}{2}$ **oz. (full cup) flour**
$4\frac{1}{2}$ **oz. (full cup) cornflour**
grated rind of 1 lemon
**the inside of $\frac{1}{2}$ vanilla
pod**

Beat the sugar, butter and marzipan together; add the yolks one by one and the eggs whole one by one; mix very well. Add the lemon peel and the vanilla and add the two flours slowly stirring all the time. Add the chopped pineapple; mix well and then put it in buttered and floured bread tins. This mixture will make three or four cakes. If you make four they will be about 14 oz. each. If it is three then each one will be about 1 lb.

Bake in a hot oven at 450°F. (233°C.) till slightly coloured; this should take about 15 minutes. Lower the heat to 360°F. (182°C.) bake for another 30–35 minutes.

When cold glaze the tops with hot apricot jam and with water sugar glaze. These cakes are very nice covered with chocolate. Decorate with pieces of pineapple previously boiled in hot syrup. Place a glacé cherry in the middle.

CHOCOLATE ROLL

2 oz. (2 squares) plain chocolate

3 eggs

2 oz. ($\frac{1}{4}$ cup) sugar

1 oz. (3 tablespoonfuls) ground almonds (not blanched)

sweetened whipped cream

Break chocolate into small pieces and put in a warm place to soften. Separate the eggs. Add the yolks and sugar to this; whisk till thick and fluffy. Beat the whites of eggs until stiff and fold into mixture, finally fold in ground almonds. Line a Swiss roll tin with buttered greaseproof paper and spread it with the mixture. Bake at 380-400°F. (194-205°C.). Turn out onto sugared paper, remove paper sticking to pastry. Roll up lightly over sugared paper. When cold unroll, spread with sweetened whipped cream and roll up again. Dust with icing sugar.

CHRISTMAS CAKE

I love Christmas in England. Here Christmas is jolly, gay, it is party time for children and grownups. You give the Christmas presents on Christmas day; we on Christmas Eve. Christmas Eve in Hungary was the most exciting evening of the whole year. Our biggest room, the sitting-room, suddenly was closed, shut and locked, at least 3 or 4 days before; we couldn't go near to it. When we asked why, the answer was, the angels are working and if we disturb them they will go away and there will be no Christmas tree and no Christmas presents. These days were tantalising. I still feel the excitement but the longest day was the 24th; it would not end. At last a faint, heavenly bell rang. I could never forget it; I hear it still; suddenly the big door opened and there was the miracle, from the floor to the ceiling – a huge, huge Christmas tree, decorated and snow painted, I thought there was nothing so beautiful. Hundreds and hundreds of candles, not electric, but real candles, gold angel hair as they called it. Little gold, silver, red and green balls, shining, sparkling, on the top a huge angel with lovely wings and a smiling beautiful face. Under the tree were parcels, beautifully packed. Each parcel was a different colour, green, yellow, red, pink tied with all kinds of coloured ribbons. Even the little cards were home-made and home-painted. Christmas wasn't commercialized then. How I would love to have just one more moment with something of the joy that we experienced then. We did not have Christmas cakes, but the tree was hung with little home-made biscuits and sweets packed in coloured paper, suspended on golden threads. Walnuts and apples too covered with gold hung on the tree, and oranges in hand-crocheted nets. Everybody, everybody had parcels. Dinner on Christmas Eve was not important; really nobody was hungry; the excitement was too much. Anyway the dinner was without meat and included nothing really sweet.

¾ lb. (1½ cups) butter

¾ lb. (1½ cups) sugar

3 oz. (½ cup) ground almonds

3 oz. (¾ cup) roughly chopped almonds

6 oz. (1½ cups) crystallized mixed fruit

1 lb. sultanas

1 lb. stoned raisins

½ cup crystallized glacé cherries

5 whole eggs

¾ lb. (3 cups) flour

1 teaspoonful (1¼ teaspoonfuls) baking powder

2 glasses brandy or rum

Cut some cherries into small pieces, if large, mix these together. Prepare a 9 in. baking tin; line it with greaseproof paper so that it fits the bottom. Cream butter first, then add the sugar and beat well. Add the almonds, the fruit, the cut cherries. Put in the 5 egg yolks and the sieved flour with the baking powder. Beat the whites of the eggs very stiff and fold in very carefully; mix everything together. If you want to be extravagant you can soak your fruit in ½ pint (1¼ cups) brandy or rum, leaving it overnight and draining it the next day to add to the cake. If your mixture turns out too hard, you can always add a little milk. Bake in a slow oven for about 6 hours. Test by inserting a knife; if it comes out clean the cake is ready.

CUPID CAKES

1 oz. ($\frac{1}{4}$ cup) glacé
    cherries
1 oz. ($\frac{1}{4}$ cup) citron peel
2 oz. ($\frac{1}{4}$ cup) butter
3 oz. (full $\frac{1}{3}$ cup) caster
    sugar
2 eggs
4 oz. (1 cup) flour
pinch of baking powder
vanilla essence

Chop the cherries and peel. Cream the butter and then beat in sugar till light and creamy. Sieve the flour with baking powder and add alternately with beaten eggs to the butter. Add cherries, peel, vanilla essence and mix. Fill patty tins three-quarters full and bake in a moderate oven 375°F. (191°C.) for 20 minutes. Cool on a wire rack and ice with water icing flavoured with rum, decorate with a half cherry.

CUMBERLAND FRUIT CAKE

1 lb. (4 cups) flour
$\frac{1}{2}$ lb. (1 cup) lard
1 lb. currants
4 oz. ($\frac{1}{2}$ cup) brown
    sugar
4 oz. ($\frac{1}{2}$ cup) caster
    sugar
pinch of baking powder
salt
2 oz. ($\frac{1}{4}$ cup) butter

Sift the flour, baking powder and salt; then rub in the fat. Mix with cold water to make a dough, not too stiff, but soft enough to roll out. Make 2 rounds. Cover round with the currants which have been mixed with the sugar. Cut butter into little cubes and dot over this mixture. Cover with the second round and bake in a hot oven about 400°F. (205°C.).

CITRON CAKE

5 oz. (1$\frac{1}{4}$ cups) flour
2 oz. (4 tablespoonfuls)
    butter
5 oz. (full $\frac{1}{2}$ cup) sugar
4 eggs
juice of 1 lemon
grated rind of 1 lemon

Put the butter in a dish and cream till soft, then add the eggs, sugar, a pinch of salt and the rind and juice of the lemon. Beat over a very low heat. Work on it till it is very creamy and when it starts to thicken remove from the heat but continue stirring until it is cold. Then slowly add the flour and continue stirring vigorously. When it is very smooth pour it into a buttered cake tin about 9 in. in diameter and bake in a moderate oven, for about half an hour. When the cake is cold, cut it and layer with lemon butter cream. For this use ready-made butter cream in which you should put orange and lemon peel. This should have been very finely shredded and boiled first in a little water then in syrup. It should boil in the syrup for 6–8 minutes. Then add this to your butter cream. Cover the whole cake very thinly with the cream, alternatively use lemon fondant.

DUNDEE CAKE (1)

$\frac{1}{2}$ lb. (1 cup) butter
$\frac{1}{2}$ lb. (1 cup) white vegetable fat
1 lb. (2 cups) sugar
8 eggs
1 lb. (4 cups) plain flour
3 lb. sultanas
$\frac{1}{2}$ lb. (2 cups) currants
$\frac{1}{2}$ lb. (2 cups) mixed peel
$\frac{1}{2}$ lb. (1$\frac{1}{3}$ cups) glacé
  cherries
split almonds

Cut the cherries in half; wash all the dried fruit thoroughly. Beat the butter and vegetable fat with the sugar until light and creamy. Beat into it the eggs, one at a time, and beat it till you have a stiff, fluffy mixture. Now slowly stir in the flour. Here you have to be careful not to over-mix. Finally fold in the sultanas, currants, mixed peel and glacé cherries.

Line cake tins with greaseproof paper on the sides as well as on the bottom. When the mixture is in the tins decorate the top with the split almonds. Bake in the oven at approximately 380°F. (194°C.) allowing 1 hour to 1 lb. of mixture.

Dundee cake

As we are doing cakes or Christmas cakes of other nationalities, I tell you one which I have made for Greeks here in England. This is a yeast dough recipe that they gave to me to make called Easter *kalacs* (*see* p. 150).

DUNDEE CAKE (2)

¾ lb. (1½ cups) butter
¾ lb. (1½ cups) brown sugar
1 lb. (4 cups) flour
pinch of bicarbonate of soda
salt
¾ lb. (2½ cups) cleaned sultanas
½ lb. (2 cups) chopped mixed peel
6 oz. (1 cup) halved glacé cherries
grated rinds of 2 lemons
grated rinds of 2 oranges
3 oz. (½ cup) Jordan almonds (blanched)
8 eggs
vanilla essence
sweet sherry to taste
a few drops browning or 2 fl. oz. (¼ cup) caramel

Beat butter till soft; gradually beat in the sugar and continue beating till fluffy. Add 1 beaten egg with 1 teaspoonful of flour. Add all the eggs in this way. Add remainder of flour sieved with the soda and salt and the fruit, almonds and rinds. Stir in vanilla essence, sherry, browning or caramel. The mixture should be 'dropable', if not, add buttermilk or sour milk. Put in a greased tin 9 in. in diameter lined with 3 layers of greased paper. Make a slight hollow in the centre. Place the tin inside a baking tin thickly lined with kitchen salt and tie a thick fold of brown paper round the outside of the tin. Bake in a slow oven, 300°F. (149°C.) for about 6 hours, or till dry in the centre when tested with a warm skewer.

GERMAN CAKE

A few years back I went to Bad Wörishofen, where I stayed in a hotel in the middle of a beautiful forest. The cure kept everybody busy the whole day long. The food was not particulary good but I was told that was part of the cure, and alcohol was not allowed at all.

But one evening they served us with a cake and we all found it the best thing we ate there. In memory of this great occasion I give you the recipe:

8 eggs

$\frac{1}{2}$ **lb. (1 cup) granulated sugar**

$\frac{1}{2}$ **lb. (1$\frac{1}{3}$ cups) ground walnuts**

$\frac{1}{2}$ **oz. (1 tablespoonful) very finely ground freshly roasted coffee**

3 tablespoonfuls (3$\frac{3}{4}$ tablespoonfuls cake crumbs

cream filling:

5 oz. (full $\frac{1}{2}$ cup) sugar

$\frac{1}{2}$ **lb. (8 squares) chocolate**

4 tablespoonfuls ($\frac{1}{4}$ cup) water

6 oz. ($\frac{3}{4}$ cup) butter

4 yolks of eggs

Beat the eggs and sugar till the mixture becomes very creamy. Add the ground walnuts, the cake crumbs and the coffee powder. Mix very thoroughly, turn the mixture into two 7 in. buttered and floured baking tins. Bake in moderate oven 320°F. (149°C.) for 30 minutes. When done, cool and meantime make the cream filling.

Put the sugar and chopped chocolate into a bowl; add 4 tablespoonfuls of hot water and place the bowl over a pan of boiling water and stir without stopping until the mixture is creamy. Take it off the heat and go on mixing it until it becomes cold. Mix the butter with the yolks of eggs and add to the chocolate mixture. Continue stirring this until it is smooth and silky.

Spread one-third of this cream on one of the cake sponges. Smooth it lightly with a palette knife. Do this neatly, seeing to it that the cream is evenly spread. Now put more of this cream on the other cake sponge, then put the two sponges together and cover the whole cake with the remainder of the cream. Finish the cake with chocolate powder or cake crumbs.

GUGLHUPF (1 – Germany)

$\frac{2}{3}$ **oz. (1 cake) yeast**

3 yolks of eggs

6 oz. ($\frac{3}{4}$ cup) butter

4 oz. ($\frac{1}{2}$ cup) sugar

1 lb. (4 cups) flour

$\frac{1}{2}$ **pint (1$\frac{1}{4}$ cups) milk**

grated rind of 1 lemon

2$\frac{1}{2}$ oz. ($\frac{1}{2}$ cup) washed and dried raisins

6 oz. ($\frac{1}{2}$ cup) blanched almonds

$\frac{1}{2}$ **oz. (1 tablespoonful) sugar**

Cream yeast with $\frac{1}{2}$ oz. sugar, warm the milk till tepid and add a little to creamed yeast. Stand in a warm place to prove. Butter cake tin well (a *Guglhupf* tin is a type of fluted *savarin* tin made in copper, aluminium or enamel or ideally fireproof pottery, and can be obtained from most shops specialising in continental kitchen ware); sprinkle with blanched almonds cut in thin strips and dust lightly with flour (ground almonds instead of flour add greatly to the flavour). Cream the butter (some cooks prefer to use a mixture of lard, butter and margarine or again a mixture of only two of these fats, or just margarine) with the sugar and add yolks of eggs. Add a little of the flour then the proved yeast. Now the remainder of the flour should be added alternately with the milk. Beat well until the dough leaves spoon and sides of bowl clean. Add raisins and lemon rind. Put dough in tin and allow to rise in a warm place. The tin should be about three-quarters filled and left to rise till dough reaches to $\frac{1}{2}$ in. of rim. Bake cake in hot oven 440°F. (228°C.) for 6 minutes, lower the heat to 410°F. (210°C.) and a little later to 375°F. (191°C.). Cover with buttered greaseproof paper if the cake becomes too brown while still baking. When cooked turn out of the tin and allow the *Guglhupf* to cool a little before sprinkling it generously with vanilla sugar. Store *Guglhupf* in a cake tin, where it will keep quite well, although it is such a good cake that it will probably be eaten very quickly. It is not only a delicious teacake, but it is beautiful to look at as well.

GUGLHUPF (2 – Germany)

Guglhupf can also be made with baking powder instead of yeast. I give you a recipe to make it in this way.

Guglhupf

4 oz. ($\frac{1}{2}$ cup) butter

6 oz. ($\frac{3}{4}$ cup) sugar

5 eggs

10 oz. ($2\frac{1}{2}$ cups) flour

2 teaspoonfuls ($2\frac{1}{2}$ teaspoonfuls) baking
   powder

a little milk

grated rind of $\frac{1}{2}$ lemon

blanched almonds

3 oz. ($\frac{1}{2}$ cup) raisins

Make ready a *Guglhupf* mould as given above. Cream together the butter and sugar. Sift the flour and baking powder. Add well-beaten eggs to butter alternately with flour and milk. Fold in grated lemon rind and the raisins which have been washed and dried. Bake at 375°F. (191°C.) for about 1 hour. Dust with icing sugar.

RUSSIAN EASTER CAKE

2 lb. (8 cups) flour

2 oz. (3 cakes) yeast

4 oz. ($\frac{1}{2}$ cup) sugar

$\frac{1}{2}$ pint ($1\frac{1}{4}$ cups) milk

6 eggs

salt

$\frac{3}{4}$ lb. ($1\frac{1}{2}$ cups) butter

6 oz. (1 cup) seedless
   raisins

2 oz. ($\frac{1}{2}$ cup) chopped
   candied peel

2 oz. ($\frac{2}{3}$ cup) roughly-
   chopped almonds

2 tablespoonfuls ($2\frac{1}{2}$
   tablespoonfuls) rum

2 tablespoonfuls
   ($2\frac{1}{2}$ tablespoonfuls)
   breadcrumbs

1 egg

few scraps of saffron
   soaked in a little
   water

Cream the yeast with a little sugar and dilute it with warm milk. Put it into a mixing bowl and add half the flour. Mix well and leave to rise in a warm place. Then separate the eggs, and cream the yolks with the sugar. Add this egg mixture, salt and melted butter to the yeast mixture. Mix well again and slowly bit by bit add the flour to it. Then beat the whites of eggs till they are very stiff and carefully fold into the dough. Knead well and then leave it in a warm place to rise for about 1 hour. Then add the raisins, peel and chopped almonds and the saffron water. The saffron should be soaked merely and you should use only the water coloured by the saffron. When everything is well mixed then leave the mixture for a further 30 minutes to rise. This Russian Easter cake has a very original shape like a bishop's mitre. It is high and about 6 or 7 in. in diameter. If you happen to have a deep enough mould it is very good to use it, but if not build up your usual cake tin with greaseproof paper.

For children the Russians make tiny cakes about 2 in. in diameter and very high. Cocoa tins were commonly used as moulds. Bake in a warm oven. Paint the top with beaten egg. Bake for 1 hour or more at 450°F. (233°C.). When cold pour white fondant on the top which should run down the sides.

SACHER GUGLHUPF (Austria)

5 oz. ($\frac{3}{4}$ cup) butter

3 yolks of eggs

1 whole egg

5 oz. (1$\frac{1}{3}$ cups) icing sugar

5 tablespoonfuls (6 tablespoonfuls) milk

a little rum

pinch of baking powder

10 oz. (2$\frac{1}{2}$ cups) flour

jam

4 oz. (4 squares) plain chocolate

4 oz. ($\frac{1}{2}$ cup) sugar

$\frac{1}{4}$ pint ($\frac{1}{3}$ pint) water

drop of olive oil

Butter a *Guglhupf* mould, sprinkle with flour (almonds should not be used for this recipe). Cream the butter and add the yolks of eggs and whole egg alternately with the sugar. Beat very well, add the milk, rum and flour which should have been sieved with the baking powder; take care that the mixture does not curdle. Bake for 45 minutes at 375 °F. (191 °C.). Allow to cool.

Melt the chocolate. Dissolve sugar in water and heat to 'small thread' consistency. Remove from heat and cool to lukewarm then stir into chocolate and add a drop of good olive oil. Continue stirring till mixture is thick enough to spread over the cake, which has first been spread with the jam.

HAZELNUT ROULADE

6 yolks of eggs

6 whites of eggs

4 oz. ($\frac{1}{2}$ cup) sugar

4 oz. ($\frac{2}{3}$ cup) ground hazelnuts

sweetened fresh whipped cream

liquid chocolate

Whip together the yolks of eggs and the sugar. Add the ground hazelnuts and the whites of eggs which have been previously whipped. Spread this mixture on a big baking sheet $\frac{1}{2}$ in. thick and bake for 15 minutes in a slow oven. When cooked, quickly remove from the tray and place on a fairly damp teacloth; cover it with the whipped cream and quickly roll it up; when cold cover it with the thick liquid chocolate.

ISCHLER GUGLHUPF (Austria)

1 oz. ($\frac{2}{3}$ cake) yeast with a little sugar

8 oz. (1 cup) butter

4 yolks of eggs

1 whole egg

2$\frac{1}{2}$ oz. ($\frac{1}{3}$ cup) sugar

a little rum

1 lb. (4 cups) flour

2 oz. ($\frac{1}{3}$ cup) sultanas

Melt the yeast in a little sugared milk, and leave aside for a few minutes. Cream the butter well and add to the yeast. Then add the egg yolks one by one, mixing well all the time. Then add the other egg, the sugar, the rum and then slowly add the flour. Finally add the very well washed sultanas. Work all these ingredients well together until very smooth and silky. Allow to rise until double its original size. Place into a well-buttered and floured *Guglhupf* mould. Let it rise again for a good half an hour and then bake it in a moderate oven for 1 hour.

This is a yeast dough which in Austria and Vienna in the good olden days was never missed from a coffee table. If I remember well, it was not served with morning coffee, but in the afternoon – which was coffee time, not tea time, there.

I gave you other *Guglhupf* recipes (*see* pp. 88, 89, 91), but I feel you ought to know how *Guglhupf* was made in Ischl, its original home deep in the Austrian Alps.

JULIA SPONGE CAKE

We had a cook in my childhood home, a charming woman but very fat. She was not round, she was almost square, as broad as she was tall. She always wore a huge white apron which covered her enormous body. To us children she was very old, but now I think she could not have been more than 35 or 40 years old. She was always cross, always grumbling, but she did everything for everybody, and especially for us. I remember one occasion very vividly. My mother was very much annoyed with her. We three children smelled a very exciting aroma coming out of the kitchen and we stormed in wanting to see Julia and what she was cooking. 'Oh', she said very gruffly, 'we have guests again for lunch, guests, guests, always guests!' She grumbled but she worked quickly; nobody could have done it so beautifully in such a short time.

When we arrived in the kitchen she took out from the sizzling fat a beautifully fried, rosy chicken leg. At home the chicken leg was the important part of the chicken and one that was offered to the guest; not like the breast here. She gave each of us a big chicken leg, beautifully fried and still hot. But bad luck, at this moment my mother came into the kitchen to see how lunch was progressing. Seeing us each having a big piece of chicken, she asked Julia, annoyed, 'What will you serve to the guests?' Julia said a not very nice word, and what should happen to the guests and for me, she said, the children come first. Of course, I think secretly my mother agreed with her, but poor Julia had to go quickly and get another chicken; that meant to kill it quickly and cook it quickly but of course very well. In our yard the chickens wandered about. No great harm was done then and we all kept Julia in our memory and think of her with great love.

She always had in reserve some pastries, and biscuits in the big larder which was next to the kitchen. Her speciality was a very nice sponge cake which was layered sometimes with jam, sometimes with chocolate cream and sometimes with fresh whipped cream. My favourite was when it was layered with red currant jam or jelly. Julia's sponge sandwich recipe is a very simple one.

6 oz. ($\frac{3}{4}$ cup) butter
6 oz. ($\frac{3}{4}$ cup) sugar
3 eggs
4 oz. (1 cup) flour
**2 oz. ($\frac{1}{3}$ cup) finely-
    grated almonds**
a very little milk
a little caster sugar

Cream the butter and then slowly add the sugar. Work it till smooth and then add the yolks of eggs, one by one and work till very creamy and silky. Add slowly the flour with just a very little milk to make it a little lighter. Add the almond slowly and mix well. Then whip the whites of eggs very stiffly and fold in very carefully. Bake it in two 7 in. sponge tins at 375°F. (191°C.) for 25–28 minutes. When cold sandwich with cream, butter cream or red currant jam. Put the two together and dust over with very fine vanilla-flavoured sugar.

Sponge sandwich cake

A VERY LIGHT SPONGE CAKE

3 large eggs
6 oz. (¾ cup) caster
sugar
4 oz. (1 cup) flour
flavouring:
orange, lemon, vanilla
or almond

First grease and flour a cake tin, which should be 7 in. × 3 in. deep. Whisk the eggs in a warm bowl. When they are frothy and creamy add the sugar, which should be very slightly warmed. Continue to whisk for 10 minutes, then fold in the flour and flavouring pour the mixture into the tin and bake for 1 hour at a temperature of 275°F. (133°C.). Leave your cake in the tin before carefully removing it. It can be covered with water icing, or butter cream, or split and filled with whipped cream, coffee cream or jam. In summer you cannot imagine how delicious this cake can be filled with fresh strawberries or raspberries and whipped cream. Then it should be merely dusted with sifted icing sugar. You will never have any of this cake left over for the next time, I promise you.

MADEIRA CAKE

Madeira cake must be light and short, otherwise it is the dullest cake you could possibly eat.

In contrast to cherry cake in which we increase the amount of flour in proportion to the fat, in a madeira cake it can be decreased slightly, possibly by 10 per cent.

The flavour of madeira cake can be greatly enhanced by the addition of the centre of half a vanilla pod, which really gives it a most gentle and satisfying flavour.

The following recipe is very successful.

2 oz. (¼ cup) butter
2 oz. (¼ cup) vegetable
fat
4 oz. (½ cup) caster
sugar
2 large eggs
the centre of ½ vanilla
pod
4 oz. (1 cup) flour

Beat the butter, vegetable fat and the sugar till light and creamy. Then beat in the eggs, one at a time and add the vanilla and continue beating till the mixture is fluffy. Now fold in very gently the flour until your mixture is smooth. Take great care not to overmix and after placing in a greased and floured cake tin, bake at 400°F. (205°C.) for 45 minutes.

As readers can see I am using the same basic recipe for the batter of all these cakes. I mention this simply because it is the most successful and easily followed by the average housewife. If it is not possible for any of my readers to obtain vanilla pods (which are fairly expensive) they can use a few drops of vanilla essence which is obtainable at most good class grocers or any chemist's shop.

NUT ROLL

4 oz. ($\frac{2}{3}$ cup) ground almonds, walnuts or hazelnuts
3 eggs
fine breadcrumbs or cake crumbs
3$\frac{1}{2}$ oz. (1 cup) icing sugar
filling:
cream
dash of kirsch
small wild strawberries

Separate the eggs. Whisk the yolks with the sugar till pale and creamy. Fold in ground nuts alternately with stiffly beaten whites of eggs. Butter a baking sheet and spread with the fine breadcrumbs or cake crumbs then spread the mixture on this. Bake for 15 minutes at 370°F. (189°C.). Remove from the oven and roll carefully and lightly over sugared paper. When it is cold unroll and fill with the filling then roll it up again.

To make the filling, whip the cream and fold in the kirsch and strawberries.

ORANGE CAKE (1)

Years ago I went with my son to North Africa where we had a lot of fun mostly because we then had hardly any money. It was the time when foreign allowances for holidays were very restricted. Poverty is quite enjoyable, even a little hunger, if it is not real, but just temporary. We made a lot of silly mistakes with our travelling arrangements; we did not buy all the tickets here but used our meagre allowance on fares. We went first to Tangier, from there to Casablanca, Fez, Rabat and finally to Marrakesh. Of course we booked in the most expensive hotels, which we enjoyed enormously except for the bill; but as my holiday was a busman's holiday because I went to see and taste food, I had to go to the best places. It annoyed us very much that the beautiful hotel was surrounded with orange and lemon orchards which were heavily guarded. We had bed and breakfast in the hotel. The breakfast consisted of tea, one French *croissant*, two pieces of toast, a very small piece of butter and a very tiny portion of marmalade. Such a tiny bit of marmalade in the middle of a huge orange orchard! Lunch we had to skip but we went to all the most expensive restaurants for dinner. We could never afford a drink so we were strictly teetotal. I had and still have a very nice antique ring and I put my hand in such a position that everyone could see it and I waited for an American millionaire to fall in love with it and offer me a fantastic sum. Of course, things like that only happen in a fairy tale. It was all disastrous. In the hotel the food was outstanding; the portions elegantly small and my son, then very young, was not very satisfied with the good food, he wanted much more. It was all very amusing. Nothing tickled us more than the ridiculous portion of marmalade which we compared with any small English hotel where they serve ten times more marmalade. We stayed for tea in our hotel, which was again most elegant. They served tiny sandwiches and very nice plain cakes; one of these was an orange and the other a lemon cake.

3 eggs
7 oz. (scant cup) sugar
7 oz. (1¾ cups) flour
1 teaspoonful (1¼ tea-
spoonfuls) baking
powder
1 whole orange minced

Whip the yolks. Add to the flour the baking powder and a pinch of salt; then the minced orange; add the sugar and mix these ingredients till they are smooth and creamy. Now add the yolks of eggs. Beat very well together and then add the whites of eggs, which have been stiffly beaten. Fold the whites in very carefully trying not to break them up too much. Pour into a rectangular cake tin which you should first butter and flour, and bake till nice and golden brown. It needs about half an hour in a medium oven, about 375°F. (191°C.). When it is cold you can serve it as it is, or layer it with butter cream to which should be added the grated rind of an orange. You can cover the cake with the butter cream and decorate with candied orange slices.

ORANGE CAKE (2)

As a young girl I visited an uncle who had a young wife. He was good looking and he became a very successful solicitor, and the pride of my mother's whole family. He was the youngest of my grandmother's nine children and so naturally he was the apple of her eye. He was quite a nice man before he became successful and rich. The richer he was the harder and more heartless he grew. He started his career as a lawyer in a provincial town in Hungary, and as such he very soon married the richest girl in the town. She was tiny, plain and dull and really a poor, sad, little rich girl. She was kind to me and liked me and continually worried my parents to let me stay with her, as she was lonely when I was not there. I was about 15 years old and understood only too well what it was to be lonely. I never minded being there in my school holidays. It was a great change from my own home life. My uncle too, liked my company. I brought young girls and boys to the house. Once my uncle told me very sadly: 'You know it is very good for you to stay with us, you can learn how a marriage should not be'. It was fascinating for me to stay in this house; I could have learned a lot about life, but I suppose I did not have the inclination to learn how to be as economical as they were. I say economical because I do not want to use the nasty word, mean, but in fact they were terribly mean. The set-up of the family was amusing and could have been very pleasant. My uncle and aunt built themselves a very nice home in the most modern style of the time with a beautiful garden which an efficient gardener kept in order. In Hungary men have never known what gardening is. Next to my uncle's house lived his wife's parents. Also a brand new and then ultra-modern villa. I thought it was the most elegant house existing. Next to the villa was the old house where the old people used to live but now one of the other sons lived there with his charming wife, whom I liked very much, and who was equally astonished by the terrible economy of the whole surroundings. In the next house the other brother lived with his wife. The next house again was lived in by the very youngest brother of my aunt, again with a young wife. All of them were unbelievably petty in every way. It was really just amusing, we made jokes of it but we were sorry underneath; what is the good of being rich and living like this? I think all of them wanted to outdo the others; from saving a piece of bread to saving anything that they could save. All the lights would be switched off; it was lucky that we did not all break our necks, because stairs or no stairs, the light was switched off. Opposite my uncle's house lived my aunt's cousin who was married also to a solicitor and his delightful, gay and charming wife was madly in love with him. He lived on his wife's money, ate well and enjoyed their life; I suppose just because they could watch their relatives on the other side of the road counting the pennies day and night. I loved to go over to them and I have to admit that I went over there for the same good food that I was used to at home. There I ate for the first time an orange cake that was always in readiness. They called this Young Ladies' Cake, here we call it Orange Cake.

YOUNG LADIES' CAKE OR ORANGE CAKE

4 eggs
7 oz. (scant cup) caster sugar
4 oz. (1 cup) flour
2 oz. (½ cup) cornflour
7 oz. (scant cup) melted butter
½ vanilla pod, scraped out
½ lb. minced oranges

Beat the eggs and sugar until fairly thick and then gently fold in the flour, which has been sieved in advance. Then add the cornflour. Stir in the melted butter, which should be warm but not hot. Add the vanilla and lastly the oranges. Pour this mixture into a cake tin lined with greaseproof paper and bake in the oven at 380°F. (194°C.) for about 45 minutes. When it is quite cold dust with icing sugar.

It is always useful to keep your flour dry and before using, to warm it up. If you like vanilla flavouring keep one or two vanilla pods in a jar with the icing sugar.

Pineapple cake

PINEAPPLE CAKE

3 oz. (6 tablespoonfuls) butter
½ oz. (¼ pkt) marzipan
3 oz. (full ⅓ cup) sugar
2 eggs
1¼ oz. (scant ⅓ cup) flour
1¼ oz. (scant ⅓ cup) cornflour
1½ rings chopped pineapple
jam
white fondant
cherries, pineapple

Beat the butter, sugar and marzipan together till smooth. Add the eggs one at a time. Beat until light. Add the chopped pineapple and then the flour and the cornflour previously sieved together. Bake in a moderate oven for about 1 hour. When cold spread jam on the top and then cover with fondant and decorate with pineapple and cherries.

PUNCH CAKE (Hungary)

Here is a very old-fashioned recipe, but very popular, especially with men. I think it is most important to please our men with our cooking; think of the lovely mink coat you would like for a Christmas present!

3 eggs

5 oz. ($\frac{2}{3}$ cup) butter

5 oz. (full $\frac{1}{2}$ cup) sugar

6 oz. ($1\frac{1}{2}$ cups) flour

6 oz. (1 cup) sultanas

1 lemon

a little less than $\frac{1}{4}$ pint ($\frac{1}{3}$ pint) rum

1 teaspoonful ($1\frac{1}{4}$ teaspoonfuls) baking powder

Shred the lemon peel very thinly and place it with the lemon juice into a tumbler. Pour the rum into the tumbler and allow this to stand for 12 hours.

Cream the butter with the sugar till it is fine and creamy; then add the 3 egg yolks, one at a time. Bit by bit add the flour, beating very well all the time. Mix the sultanas with the rum and mix into the other ingredients. Then whip the egg whites very stiff and fold into the mixture. Add the baking powder and then turn it onto a baking tin and bake in a moderate oven for $1\frac{1}{2}$ hours.

PRINCESS ALEXANDRA CAKE

3 eggs

5 oz. ($\frac{2}{3}$ cup) butter

5 oz. (full $\frac{1}{2}$ cup) sugar

6 oz. ($1\frac{1}{2}$ cups) flour

$1\frac{1}{2}$ teaspoonfuls (2 teaspoonfuls) baking powder

red currant jam

fresh cream (optional)

icing sugar (optional)

lemon water icing

Cream the butter till very creamy and light. Add the sugar and beat well together. Add the eggs, one by one, adding a little flour with each egg. Beat well together and then add the baking powder and the rest of the flour. Mix well together. Pour into a well-buttered and floured cake tin and bake in a moderate oven for 25–30 minutes. Allow to cool. Cut in half horizontally and layer with jam. If you like you can also layer it with a little whipped fresh cream.

You can either cover the top with fresh cream, dust it over with icing sugar or cover with lemon water icing.

SIMNEL CAKE

The traditional Easter Simnel cake is surrounded by legends. It was originally not so much an Easter cake as a Mothering Sunday cake and one story attributed to it, is that servant girls in the large and stately homes were permitted to go home once a year on Mothering Sunday and the more progressive or liberally minded mistresses would give them the raw materials with which to make a cake to take to their mothers. This cake was usually of a rather solid consistency, perhaps because of the lack of skill on the part of the girls; perhaps because it would keep better that way and also it is said that on their sometimes lengthy walk to their homes on Mothering Sunday, they could rest on their journey by sitting on the cake.

The name of the cake is variously claimed to have derived from a husband and wife, bakers both, who developed the recipe and were called respectively 'Simon and Nelly'. It is alternatively said that it is named after Lambert Simnel who had been duped into impersonating Edward, Earl of Warwick (who was in fact a prisoner in the Tower) with a view to overthrowing Henry VII. However, Henry's armies defeated the rebels with their leader at Stoke-on-Trent on 16 June, 1518 and it is said that Lambert Simnel, the impostor, was shown mercy by the King and was given a job as a scullion in the Royal kitchens, that he progressed to become a cake baker and developed the recipe for the cake which now bears his name.

The most scientific idea about the derivation of the name is that it comes from Old French derived from a late Latin word *siminellus* – meaning fine bread, or from the Latin, *siminela* – meaning the finest wheat flour. For myself I like the story about Lambert Simnel best.

Would you take this story from me as I took it from books – a little here and a little there. It is just as good as anything else and will you please accept it.

½ lb. (1 cup) vegetable fat
½ lb. (1 cup) butter
1 lb. (2 cups) demerara sugar
8 large eggs
1 lb. (4 cups) flour
4 oz. (¾ cup) ground almonds
pinch of mixed spice
2 lb. currants
2 lb. sultanas
½ lb. (2 cups) cut mixed peel
4 oz. (1 pkt) marzipan
gum arabic solution

Beat the vegetable fat, the butter and the sugar together until light and creamy. Beat in the eggs, one at a time until the mixture becomes fluffy and light. Now sieve together the flour, ground almonds and mixed spice; fold in taking care not to overmix. Now add the currants, sultanas and mixed peel.

Unlike all other cakes the Simnel cake is baked with a layer of marzipan baked through the middle. To do this take a 6 in. cake hoop lined with greaseproof paper. Weigh off 6 oz. of cake mixture and place in the hoop. Now take 4 oz. marzipan, roll it into a 6 in. circle and place on top of the cake. Now weigh another 6 oz. of the cake mixture and place it on top of the marzipan. Level the top and bake for 1 hour at 380°F. (194°C.).

When the cake is baked and cooled, the edge should be decorated with marzipan, which can be moulded by hand and placed round the cake or the marzipan can be softened with egg, placed in a bag with a star tube and piped. When the edges have been decorated, the cake is returned to a hot oven, 500°F. (261°C.) and left till the marzipan edging is golden brown. Remove from the oven and glaze the marzipan edging with the gum arabic solution. The centre of the cake should now be flooded with pastel shaded fondant and decorated with chickens, rabbits, birds' eggs and sugar flowers.

SATURDAY CAKE

8 yolks of eggs
4 whites of eggs
12 oz. ($1\frac{1}{2}$ cups) butter
12 oz. ($1\frac{1}{2}$ cups) sugar
1 oz. ($\frac{1}{4}$ cup) glacé
cherries
2 oz. ($\frac{1}{4}$ cup) chopped
almonds
2 oz. ($\frac{1}{2}$ cup) orange peel
angelica
4 oz. ($\frac{2}{3}$ cup) ground rice
$\frac{1}{4}$ glass rum
8 oz. (2 cups) flour

Mix the yolks of eggs and the butter till very creamy. Cut the cherries, peel and angelica finely and add to the mixture. Then add all the other ingredients, except the whites of eggs, one by one. Then add the whites of eggs, very stiffly whipped, folding them in very carefully. Pour into a baking tin lined with greaseproof paper and bake in a moderate oven for about $1\frac{1}{2}$ hours.

SPICE AND SEED CAKES

ANISE (*Pimpinella anisum*). Aniseed originally came from Egypt, but it is now cultivated in Europe as well. It is the seed of the anise and is greyish-brown in colour. It contains a volatile oil, most commonly used in the preparation of cordials and in confectionery.

CARAWAY (*Carum carvi*). Caraway seed is a great friend of mine. I use it widely and find the flavour very pleasant in food, in bread, cheese, even in cakes. Caraway is native to Europe.

CINNAMON (*Cinnamomum zeylanicum*). The cinnamon is a native of Ceylon and is the bark of a tree, a member of the laurel family. The crops are gathered from May till September and two-year shoots are stripped of their bark. Cinnamon comes on the market in long, cylinder-shaped rolls, yellow-brown in colour. It is expensive, therefore cassia is sometimes added which is the bark of *cinnamon cassia* which comes from China and India. Cassia in appearance is similar to cinnamon, but coarser. It is about four times as thick and darker in colour.

CLOVES (*Eugenia aromatica*). They are the dried flower buds of an evergreen shrub, grown in Zanzibar and from the West Indies. The buds are gathered and soon turn reddish in colour, they are then spread out in the sun to dry, when the colour changes to a deep brown. Cloves possess a strong, hot flavour. Because of their strong flavour, I don't like them, despite my fancy for Zanzibar's exotic name.

GINGER (*Zingiber officinale*). This is the root of the herb, a native of India and China, but now cultivated in America, Africa and Australia. Black ginger, which I have never met before, but will search for now, is said to be the most expensive. Green or French ginger is much used in China.

NUTMEG and MACE (*Myristica fragrans*). Did you know that the two come from the same tree? They are the nut and the aril or sheath of the nutmeg tree, which grows in Malaya and the Archipelago.

VANILLA (*Vanilla fragrans*). Vanilla is the pod of a climbing orchid, and comes from South America and the West Indies. Mexican Vanilla is the most highly priced. Modern bakers and confectioners use it a great deal. The highest-priced vanilla has the smallest content of *vanillin*, this being the Mexican variety; Bourbon has more *vanillin*, while Java has nearly double. I tell you, too, that vanilla pods contain a notable amount of gum, resin and sugar, all of which contribute to the final flavour. *Vanilla fragrans* is the most common species of vanilla used today though most vanilla is artificial.

Now I promise I won't bore you any more with seeds or herbs, only if I have to use them for some recipe.

GINGERBREAD

4 oz. ($\frac{1}{2}$ cup) butter
4 oz. ($\frac{1}{2}$ cup) sugar
10 oz. (2$\frac{1}{2}$ cups) flour
$\frac{1}{2}$ oz. (2 teaspoonfuls) ground ginger
a pinch of bicarbonate of soda
2 eggs
$\frac{1}{2}$ lb. ($\frac{2}{3}$ cup) golden syrup
$\frac{1}{4}$ pint ($\frac{1}{3}$ pint) milk
$\frac{1}{4}$ lb. stem ginger

Cream the butter and sugar, add the flour, ground ginger and bicarbonate of soda. Mix this mixture with the eggs, syrup, milk and stem ginger (chopped or finely sliced), then pour into a well-buttered and floured tin. Cover the top with flaked almonds and bake for 45 minutes in a medium oven about 360°F. (182°C.).

GINGER CAKE (1)
Ginger cake is very popular in this country, so I give you a simple recipe:

2 lb. (8 cups) flour
8 oz. (1 cup) butter
7 large eggs
mixed spice
6 oz. (1½ cups) chopped ginger
10 oz. (1¼ cups) sugar
1¼ lb. (2 cups) golden syrup
2 oz. (¼ cup) baking powder
ground ginger
split almonds

Mix well and bake it in baking tins in a moderate oven, about 400°F. (204°C.). It should still rise during the baking. When mixing you should add the syrup very slowly and the flour should also be added bit by bit. The tins have to be greased, and I like them greased with butter. Dust with flour and put the split almonds in the bottom of the tin so that when you turn it out, they should be on the top of the cake. Fill the tin only three-quarters full to leave space for the mixture to rise.

GINGER CAKE (2)

4 oz. (½ cup) butter
4 oz. (½ cup) sugar
10 oz. (1 cup) golden syrup
1 lb. (4 cups) flour
pinch of baking powder
ground ginger
mixed spice
¼ pint (⅓ pint) milk
1 egg
a little ginger-root
flaked almonds

Cream the butter and sugar. Add the syrup, flour and spices and baking powder. Beat until the mixture becomes a smooth batter. Moisten with the milk and egg. Add the ginger, thinly sliced. Butter and flour a baking tin and sprinkle flaked almonds to cover the whole tin. Bake for 45 minutes at 300°F. (149°C.). After baking turn upside down; the flaked almonds will now be on the top of the cake.

HONEY CAKE
Honey cake in Hungary was not a 'cake', not a biscuit, not a pastry, not a food at all. It was something romantic, something heart-warming, something heart-breaking. In Hungary, on the big markets there used to be rows of stands full of all kinds of honey cakes. There were beautiful and very expensive ones on the bigger stands; the more modest ones were on the smaller stands. But all of them had messages to take to sweethearts.

Large heart-shaped biscuits were made from honey cake covered with pillar-box red fondant. In the middle a little *real* mirror, underneath it a little love poem, shorter or longer depending on the size of the heart.

Beautifully dressed Hungarian peasant boys in their navy-blue or black suits, with bow ties of long, black ribbon, shiny-shiny black boots reaching up to the knee, boys with round, black hats on which they had a little bouquet of flowers – these boys bought heart-shaped honey biscuits for their girls. The message, the form of the little verse on the heart, told them of the boys' feelings.

All kinds of shapes were made from honey cakes – whose manufacture was, by the way, a very big village industry – some of them were thin, the shape of plates and beautifully designed. They made from honey cake little dolls which were then coloured, and beads which the boys bought to hang round their sweethearts' necks.

I personally used to buy the thin, flat, crisp biscuits: here is the recipe.

4 oz. ($\frac{1}{2}$ cup) **butter**
7 oz. (scant cup) **brown sugar**
1 **whole beaten egg**
6 oz. ($\frac{3}{4}$ cup) **honey**
12 oz. (3 cups) **brown or rye flour**
salt
a little cinnamon
pinch of bicarbonate soda
pinch of allspice
a few cloves
4 fl. oz. ($\frac{1}{2}$ cup) **sour milk**
3 oz. ($\frac{1}{2}$ cup) **raisins**
5 oz. ($1\frac{1}{4}$ cups) **chopped nuts**
2 oz. ($\frac{1}{3}$ cup) **shredded coconut**
4 oz. (1 cup) **icing sugar**

Beat all these ingredients together except the icing sugar and work into a smooth mixture; then spread it onto a greased baking tin $\frac{1}{2}$ in. thick; bake in a moderately warm oven at 375 °F. (191 °C.) for 20 minutes. When cool spread with a very thin layer of icing made by thinning 1 cup of icing sugar with water. When the cake is iced and dried cut it into thin bars.

SEED CAKE

This is a cake which I am afraid will not be to everybody's taste, but you can never tell and perhaps I will find a few people who will like it. It is seed cake. If you don't like it please forgive me, I do like caraway seed cake myself.

8 oz. (2 cups) flour
8 oz. (1 cup) butter
8 oz. (1 cup) sugar
5 eggs
3 oz. ($\frac{3}{4}$ cup) chopped
   orange peel
a little nutmeg
   (optional)
grated or crushed
   caraway seed
$\frac{1}{4}$ glass rum

Cream the butter till smooth and creamy. Add the sugar and mix well. Add the yolks of eggs one by one, adding at the same time a little of the flour. Then add the caraway seed, orange peel and nutmeg. Beat well together and then very carefully add the very stiffly beaten whites of eggs and very slowly add the rest of the flour. Finally stir in the rum. Then pour into a cake tin and bake in a slow oven, about 350°F. (177°C.) for about 1 hour. The cake may be sprinkled with a little brandy when it is cooked.

SAFFRON CAKE (recipe dated 1805)

$4\frac{1}{2}$ lb. (18 cups) flour
1 oz. ($1\frac{1}{2}$ cakes) yeast
12 oz. (2 cups) currants
12 oz. (2 cups) sultanas
1 lb. (2 cups) lard
$\frac{1}{2}$ lb. (1 cup) butter
4 eggs
saffron
4 oz. (1 cup) lemon peel
$\frac{1}{2}$ lb. (1 cup) caster
   sugar

Cut the saffron very finely and infuse in a cup of boiling water for 12 minutes. Rub fat thoroughly into the flour, then add the sugar and add a little warm milk, which should be a little hotter than tepid. When the yeast rises in the cup, make a pit in the flour and pour the yeast in and sprinkle a little flour over it. When this cracks and the yeast shows through then mix it all into a soft dough with the hand using a little warm milk if required. Beat the eggs, add to the dough.

Add the saffron, including the water in which it has been steeped – warm this before using. Then add the fruit. Put a warm plate on top of the bowl and stand in a warm place until the mixture doubles in bulk and appears light and spongy. Put into tins and allow to rise for a short time before baking. Allow 45 minutes –1 hour for baking cakes according to size using a moderate oven heat. This mixture can be made into buns, for which allow approximately 15–20 minutes baking time.

STOLLEN

The Germans have a very famous Christmas cake which is not really a cake at all but rather a very rich, very expensive and very good bun. It is oval in shape; known the world over. The most famous of these German Christmas *Stollen* were those from Dresden. It was the proud boast of the people of Dresden that Germans sent them to their friends throughout the world. I used often to be in Dresden. It was one of the most delightful of German cities, its architecture was beautiful and the atmosphere of culture was felt wherever you went. The people were very friendly, very hospitable, cultured and musical. Music making was the pastime of all. Middle-class families always had a music room with two pianos and other musical instruments, and very often held musical evenings after coming back from their shops or offices. I had a friend who had a big grocery business and who sent *Stollen* all over the world. After the Second World War, Dresden was still occupied and he started a very small bakery which has now grown large and very well known.

I give you one of his recipes which he kindly gave to me many years ago. I exchanged it for my English Christmas cake recipe!

2 lb. 2 oz. (8½ cups) flour
3 oz. (4½ cakes) yeast
2 fl. oz. (¼ cup) milk
6 oz. (¾ cup) sugar
12 oz. (1½ cups) butter
1 lb. (2⅔ cups) sultanas
9 oz. (2¼ cups) candied lemon peel
9 oz. (1½ cups) roughly chopped almonds
3 oz. (¾ cup) candied orange peel
3 eggs
1 glassful rum
8 pieces chopped bitter almonds
2 oz. (½ cup) flour
2 oz. (¼ cup) butter
rose water

First make a little dough with the milk and 2 oz. (½ cup) of the flour. Mix with the yeast which you have to soak in a little warm milk. Prove. When this dough has risen mix all the other ingredients slowly together and work into the dough till it is all very smooth and silky. Then mould and make a flat round piece and fold it once over into an oval-shaped bun. Bake it in a moderate oven till nice and brown. Let it cool and when not quite cold sprinkle it with the melted butter and some rose oil or water. When dry dust over generously with icing sugar. When it is cold pack it in cellophane and then you can keep it for weeks.

STREUSEL KUCHEN (Germany)
I feel that I have to give you this popular, very German bun. It is so popular in England that I think you should have the recipe and make it at home; it is very easy. Make it in two parts. First you make the *Kuchen* which is a light, yeast dough made as follows:

½ lb. (2 cups) flour
a pinch of salt
about ½ oz. (¾ cake) yeast
1 oz. (2 tablespoonfuls)
    sugar
1 egg
2 oz. (¼ cup) butter
¼ pint (⅓ pint) luke-
    warm milk
Streusel:
2 oz. (½ cup) flour
2 oz. (¼ cup) sugar
2 oz. (¼ cup) butter

Sift the flour, mix the sugar with the yeast, add this to the flour; then the egg, the milk and the slightly warmed butter. Mix this very well till it is very smooth and put in a warm place to rise. It has to be about double its original size. Take a floured pastry board, put the dough on it and knead it and shape like a loaf. Put it in a biggish bread tin; the dough should only be a quarter of the tin. The *Streusel* will fill up the rest of the tin. To make this; take a bowl and mix the flour, sugar and butter. Mix the. flour and sugar together first; melt the butter till warm and pour it on the mixture: stir till crumbly. Pour on the top of the *Kuchen* and bake it for 35-40 minutes at 360°F. (182°C.).

SOLIMÈNE

12 oz. (3 cups) flour
½ oz. (¾ cake) yeast
¼ lb. (½ cup) butter
2½ teaspoonfuls oil
2½ oz. (⅓ cup) sugar
8 fl. oz. (1 cup) cream
4 eggs
salt

With a quarter of the flour, the yeast and a very little warm water, make the first small amount of paste. Leave this to rise in a warm place for 30 minutes. Now add to this paste 2 eggs, half of the cream, the rest of the flour and knead the dough. Then add the butter and the rest of the cream and the eggs, little by little. Beat the dough until it is very smooth, and quite soft. If it is too firm add a little more cream. Do not make the paste firm. Take a deep cake tin, grease it with butter and half fill it with the dough. Leave it again to rise for 15-20 minutes then bake it in a medium oven until it is nicely browned. Turn it out from the tin and cut it into two layers. Sprinkle each layer with hot melted butter. If you prefer it, the butter can be slightly salted. Then put the layers together and serve hot. This is quite a good cake, pleasant with coffee or tea.

SWISS ROLL (1)

I am sure everybody knows how to make a Swiss roll. I am sure you know it better than I do because it is so very English. I give you the recipe because Swiss roll is such a useful stand by. It keeps well; it is easy to make, it is not expensive and can be varied with a variety of fillings – jam, very many kinds of jam; chocolate or coffee cream, *crème patissière*, chestnut purée or whipped cream.

4 eggs
pinch of salt
6½ oz. (full ¾ cup) caster sugar
1 tablespoonful (1¼ tablespoonfuls) water
a little lemon extract
3 oz. (¾ cup) flour
1 tablespoonful (1¼ tablespoonfuls) corn-flour
1½ teaspoonfuls (1¾ teaspoonfuls) baking powder
jam for filling

Prepare oven sheet with greased paper turned up at edges to form a tray. Sift mixed flours and baking powder. Separate the eggs. Sift sugar and set aside 4 tablespoonfuls to beat with the whites of eggs. Beat whites of eggs with salt till stiff, incorporate 3 tablespoonfuls of the sugar and add fourth at the last, folding it in. Beat yolks to a ribbon, adding the water mixed with the lemon extract, add the remaining sugar. Fold the whites into the yolks. Fold in flour. Pour on tin moderately thinly; spread evenly. Bake about 12 minutes in a moderate oven, 350°F. (177°C.). Prepare the filling. Turn sponge onto paper or cloth sprinkled with sugar. Remove greaseproof paper quickly. Spread filling over it and roll up.

SWISS ROLL (2)

4 oz. (½ cup) sugar
3 oz. (¾ cup) flour
3 large eggs
1 tablespoonful (1¼ tablespoonfuls) tepid water
pinch of baking powder
jam for filling

Method as above.

SWISS ROLL (3)

2 whites of eggs
3 yolks of eggs
5 oz. (scant ⅔ cup) sugar
4 oz. (1 cup) flour
¼ pint (⅓ pint) cold water
jam for filling

Put the sugar in a saucepan with the cold water. Bring this to the boil and boil very hard for 5 minutes. Cool for 5 minutes, then pour the syrup onto the whites and yolks of eggs that have previously been well whisked. Whisk for 15 minutes or until the mixture thickens. Sieve the flour and then fold into mixture as lightly as possible. When blended pour into a tin which has been lined with greased greaseproof paper. Bake in an oven

375°F. (191°C.) for 10 minutes then lower temperature to 350°F. (177°C.) till the cake is golden-brown and firm to the touch.

Sprinkle a damp teacloth with caster sugar. Remove the cake by turning it upside down. Trim the edges and spread with warm jam. Roll up tightly with the aid of the cloth; leave for a few minutes in the cloth then place on a wire cake rack.

TWELFTH NIGHT CAKE

In France this cake is called the *gâteau des rois*, as Twelfth night is Epiphany, the feast of the three kings. It used to be the last of the Christmas celebrations, and perhaps the symbolic cake represented the gifts of the Magi to the infant Jesus. There used to be a charming custom that this cake would be shared among the guests and family all except for three pieces which the host would keep. These were for the baby Jesus, his mother and the Magi. Then these pieces would be given to the poor. A silver token was always baked in the cake and the person who found this in his or her portion would be the king of the feast, and would have to give another party in return.

There are, it seems, different cakes in different parts of France; in some provinces it is a kind of flat pastry *galette*, a sort of biscuit wafer. In others it is a kind of *brioche* dough shaped like a crown. You may use whichever of my *brioche* recipes you find the most successful but you will need 1 lb. (4 cups) of flour and the other ingredients in proportion. When the dough is ready for the final shaping, make into the form of a crown and leave it to rise in a warm place. Allow the crown to cool and then brush over with yolk of egg and put crystallized sugar and candied slices of lemon carefully round the crown like jewels, before baking in a medium oven. Don't forget your silver coin or token.

WALNUT CAKE (1)

For years and years I went to Tangier for my holidays where I had friends with whom I stayed. They were a delightful couple, artistic and artists both of them. I have never met so many interesting people as I met there.

The food was good, I could say perfect, and as simple as their way of life. They had an Arab chef, who moved quietly and slowly in the kitchen. I thought he would never finish a lunch, dinner or whatever it was he was preparing, with his leisurely quiet way of working. But every meal was on time, whether we were alone, or, as was very frequently the case, there were several guests.

For tea we used to have tiny sandwiches and a very simple walnut cake which I liked very much. In memory of my lovely Tangier days I set down the recipe of that walnut cake.

½ lb. (2 cups) flour
1 pinch baking powder (a very small coffee-spoonful)
3 oz. (full ⅓ cup) sugar
¼ pint (⅓ pint) milk
¼ pint (½ cup) golden syrup
3 oz. (full ½ cup) roughly chopped walnuts
2 eggs
2 oz. (⅓ cup) sultanas

Sieve the flour and the baking powder, add the milk, sugar and golden syrup. Add the roughly-chopped walnuts and the sultanas. Beat the eggs well together, add them to the mixture, mix once more all together lightly. Pour it in a buttered and floured baking tin – a breadbaking tin – and then bake it in a moderate oven, 350°F. (177°C.) for about 45 minutes. Afterwards leave it in the tin until it becomes cool.

WALNUT CAKE (2)
8 eggs
½ lb. (1 cup) caster sugar
2 tablespoonfuls (2½ tablespoonfuls) white cake crumbs
½ lb. (1½ cups) ground walnuts
grated rind of ½ lemon
a little rum
3 oz. plain (3 squares) chocolate
4 oz. (½ cup) butter
4 oz. (½ cup) sugar
1 egg

Cream the yolks of eggs and sugar well. Add the cake crumbs, ground walnuts, grated lemon rind and rum. Mix it very well, then fold in the stiffly whipped whites of eggs. Turn the mixture into two buttered sandwich tins and bake in a moderate oven for about 20–25 Do not open the oven door for the first 15 minutes, because your cake will collapse if you do so. When it is baked, cool it and prepare your cream thus: melt the chocolate, mix it with the butter, sugar and whole egg until it is smooth. Spread a thick layer of filling on one of the cakes and cover with the other cake. Spread the remaining chocolate cream evenly on the top and the sides of the cake. Then sprinkle with coarsely-chopped walnuts. Put in the refrigerator to cool properly. Roast the walnuts, then chop them very finely, and sprinkle over and round the cake.

WEDDING CAKES
Once upon a time I would not have believed that I would make these very strange white cakes, which resembled buildings, the reason for which I have never under-

stood. Now as I look back at thirty years of work in this country I cannot remember how many of these strange objects I have made.

I made hundreds and hundreds, perhaps thousands, during these thirty years. I made all of them during the twenty-one years I supplied Fortnum and Mason. Fortnum and Mason had then a very important clientèle. But for many years now these people have come direct to me. One of my favourite cakes was the one which I made for the then Sir Anthony Eden's marriage to Miss Clarissa Churchill.

The reception at 10 Downing Street was very small. The cake too was small, but most elegant. Just a cake covered with white roses. Nothing could be simpler, nicer and more elegant than that wedding cake. Nothing at all like a building about that one!

I have made very many conventional wedding cakes, if the customer insisted. This mostly happened when I had nothing to do with the order. Countess Eszterhazy's mother came to me with a set idea. She wanted a wedding cake in the shape of a rabbit, because the young Countess's name – or nickname – happened to be Bunny. I just would not agree. An erect bunny would look clumsy and not at all interesting, a sitting or lying one even worse. So we agreed that I would make a very beautiful three-tier wedding cake, decorated like a forest with rabbits running round it. On the top to finish the cake, was a large erect rabbit.

I also made the Duke of Bedford's wedding cake. The cake was unbelievably beautiful. The Duke brought me a sample of a rare lily, a fresh flower which was a beautiful specimen. Only ours made of sugar looked even better.

I had, again, great pleasure and joy making the Duke's son's wedding cake which had to match the first present the young bridegroom had given his beautiful fiancée. So the cake was decorated with blue. In spite of this, it looked very beautiful, just as the bride did.

Of the many, many wedding cakes I made, I liked most the one I made for Princess Margaret. I designed it myself. Do you know where I have taken my idea from? I had just returned from Geneva where I had seen an umbrella-shaped rose tree in one of the parks. I walked there for a long time, because the park fascinated me with its unusual flower beds and those beautiful rose trees. I kept those rose trees in my memory.

When Princess Margaret became engaged, I thought that this was my opportunity to utilise my idea: the rose tree. You would not believe how badly I draw, but I do draw if I have to. So I drew a seven-tier wedding cake, covered with white rosebuds and white marguerites and on top of the cake a white umbrella of white rosebuds. Hanging from the umbrella were long sprays of white rosebuds and marguerites. When I entered my office I saw the decorations with the initials 'A' and 'M' and I

Hungarian wedding cake

put these on the top of the umbrella. It was just a dream! I gladly showed my design
to everybody who came into my office. Some people became quite excited about the
beauty of the cake.

    If I make a wedding cake, I have to see the bride. I like to make each wedding cake
just the cake for that one girl, for it will be her wedding, her day.

As I said before, we in Hungary don't have wedding cakes. The rich Hungarian peasants, however – or at least in my time – made a very big wedding gâteau, three or four feet high, covered with white icing and decorated with *crockant* (ground almonds and sugar caramelized till light brown and bent into 'S'-shaped ribbons). A four-foot column of *crockant* was erected in the middle of the cake and decorated like a tower. Orange blossoms or white roses completed the decoration.

I have also made French wedding cakes – those tall towers made of *profiteroles*, filled with *crème parisienne* and built up with caramel sugar. It is a beautiful cake, but tends to suffer if made on a very humid day.

WEDDING CAKE (1)

½ lb. marzipan with a little white of egg
½ lb. (1 cup) vegetable fat
½ lb. (1 cup) butter
1 lb. barbados or demerara sugar
little burnt sugar or caramel
8 large eggs
1 lb. 2 oz. (4½ cups) flour
4 lb. currants
1 lb. sultanas
¼ lb. (1 cup) cut mixed peel
½ lb. (2 cups) glacé cherries

Soften the marzipan with a little white of egg and then cream with the vegetable fat, the butter and the barbados or demerara sugar till creamy and light. Now to ensure the right colour add the burnt sugar or caramel. Beat in the eggs, one at a time, till the mixture becomes light and fluffy. Now fold in the flour, but take care not to overmix at this stage. Finally, add the currants, sultanas, cut mixed peel and the glacé cherries. Owing to the very rich nature of this mixture with so much fruit and sugar it is advisable to bake at a slightly lower temperature than for fruit cake. The oven should be at 280–300°F. (126–150°C.) and 1 lb. cakes should be left in the oven for 1 hour and 10 minutes. The flavour of the wedding cake is greatly enhanced if it is sprinkled with a mixture of rum and rose water as soon as it comes out of the oven.

WOMAN'S MOOD CAKE

8 oz. (2 cups) flour
5 oz. (⅔ cup) butter
1 whole egg
2½ oz. (scant ⅓ cup) sugar
1 lb. fresh red currants or raspberries
10 whites of eggs

Beat till smooth the flour, butter and the egg. Roll out the pastry very thinly and bake for 10 minutes in a slow oven. Then take the red currants or raspberries and spread on the pastry. Spread on top of this the very stiffly beaten whites of eggs. Sprinkle over with sugar, according to taste. Put back in the oven and bake till golden-brown. When it is cold cut it into square slices.

WEDDING CAKE (2)

3 lb. butter
**3 lb. sugar ($1\frac{1}{2}$ lb. bar-
    bados, $1\frac{1}{2}$ lb. demerara**
3 oz. ($\frac{1}{2}$ cup) caramel
24 eggs
6 fl. oz. ($\frac{3}{4}$ cup) rum
**1 oz. (2 tablespoonfuls)
    cinnamon**
**$\frac{1}{2}$ oz. (1 tablespoonful)
    mace**
1 grated lemon peel
3 lb. (12 cups) flour
1 lb. ground almonds
$6\frac{1}{2}$ lb. currants
3 lb. sultanas
1 lb. minced peel
$1\frac{1}{2}$ lb. glacé cherries

Cream the butter, sugar and caramel till light, add the eggs, slightly warmed, one at a time. Add the mace, cinnamon, grated lemon peel and stir in the flour. Then add the ground almonds, dried fruit and cherries and, finally, the rum. It is preferable to soak the fruit in the rum before adding to the mixture. Bake at 325–350 °F. (163–177 °C.) till cooked. Test this by inserting a knife. When it comes out clean, the cake is ready. This will take about 8 hours.

WALNUT SLICE

7 oz. ($\frac{7}{8}$ cup) butter
10 oz. ($2\frac{1}{2}$ cups) flour
2 yolks of eggs
very small pinch of salt
a little sugar
filling:
5 yolks of eggs
**4 tablespoonfuls (5
    tablespoonfuls) sugar**
**1 oz. (2 tablespoonfuls)
    chocolate powder**
7 whites of eggs
**10 oz. (2 cups) chopped
    walnuts**

Mix all the ingredients together into a dough. Divide the dough in half. Roll both pieces out thinly and cut into 2 rounds. Bake 1 piece for a few minutes and then make the following filling.

Whisk together 4 yolks of eggs and sugar till thick and creamy. Add the chocolate powder. Whip the whites of eggs till very stiff and fold into this mixture; then add the chopped walnuts. When all mixed together spread onto the cooked layer of pastry and cover it with the other sheet of pastry. Prick with a fork and wash over with the yolk of an egg mixed with a very little sugar.

Cook for 18–20 minutes at 470 °F. (246 °C.)

GÂTEAUX

You may well wonder what the difference is between a cake and a gâteau, why I separate them. It is hard to define sometimes, but the difference is a matter of degree rather than of kind. A gâteau is commonly richer than a cake though basically the ingredients are the same. A gâteau should be richer, more elaborate and often more expensive, I am afraid. Whipped cream, nuts, chocolate will all add to the decoration and the taste. A gâteau will not always keep well, but must be used fresh. For your dessert you would naturally think of using a gâteau, especially when you are having guests. While you might have a slice of gâteau with your coffee or tea, especially when you want to celebrate a special occasion or wish to spoil yourself, your husband or children, you would never think of offering a slice of plain cake as a dinner dessert.

In many countries I have known, the gâteau for a dinner or a party would be chosen and ordered for the event from a good patisserie. But it is quite possible and much nicer to make your own and I hope you will try some of the recipes.

BOHEMIAN GÂTEAU
Bohemian gâteau is a most useful and very beautiful cake. It is a great joy that it can be kept for a week or 10 days. It is very good to eat. It is not difficult to cut if you have a really sharp knife which you should first dip in hot water. The easiest method is to cut the cake in two, and then into slices. This mixture can also be made as a long rectangular cake from which you can cut slices, decorating it exactly as the round gâteau.

10 **whites of eggs**
½ **lb. (1 cup) sugar**
3 **oz. (¾ cup) flour**
3 **oz. ground (⅔ cup) hazelnuts**
3 **oz. (3 squares) grated chocolate**
chocolate butter cream
praline butter cream (see p. 139)
melted chocolate
chocolate vermicelli

Whisk the whites of eggs and the sugar stiffly; then add the dry ingredients. Spread about ¼ in. thick on greased and floured trays and bake in a moderate oven till lightly browned, then cut into 8 in. circles while still warm. Leave till cold. Build up the gâteau with alternate layers of butter cream between each cake layer. Keep the butter cream layers approximately the same thickness as the gâteau. Finish with a layer of gâteau on top. Mask the sides with butter cream; either pipe the remainder of the butter cream on the top or coat with melted chocolate and cover the sides with chocolate vermicelli.

CHOCOLATE GÂTEAU (1)

This is one of the best-known and most delicious chocolate gâteaux and was the first gâteau I made in this country. The recipe is as follows:

8 **eggs**
8 **oz. (1 cup) sugar**
2½ **oz. (2½ squares) chocolate**
3½ **oz. (3½ squares) unsweetened chocolate**
5 **oz. (1¼ cup) plain flour**
the inside of ½ a vanilla pod
chocolate cream:
3 **oz. (full ⅓ cup) sugar**
a little water
2 **yolks of eggs**
2 **oz. (4 tablespoonfuls) melted butter**
3 **oz. (3 squares) melted chocolate**

Put the chocolate in a bowl and melt it over warm water. Put the eggs in another bowl – whisk them with the sugar till thick. The easiest way to do this is over warm water. Go on beating and slowly add the flour. Afterwards add the chocolate, mix everything quickly together and do it very carefully so that it is evenly mixed. Have ready a 7 or 8 in. tin with the bottom lined with wax paper and the tin greased and floured. Then pour in the mixture and bake for 35–40 minutes in a moderate oven. When the cake is out of the oven let it cool, cut in two and fill with chocolate butter cream. Cover the top and side of the cake with the same cream. Finish the gâteau with chocolate vermicelli or chocolate powder and pipe little chocolate shells from the chocolate cream round it.

The chocolate cream is made by mixing the 3 oz. sugar with a very little water, say about 2½ fl. oz. (¼ cup)), 2 yolks of eggs, 2 oz. melted butter and 3 oz. melted chocolate. Dissolve the sugar in warm water and boil it till you can 'thread' it. When it is thick and syrupy take off the heat, but go on stirring. Add the yolks one by one very slowly, mix very thoroughly and go on stirring till it is really thick. It should look like a mousse. Cream the butter till very creamy and white and whip it very firmly and add to the egg and sugar mixture. Then add the melted chocolate and, if you like, a little very strong coffee essence.

CHOCOLATE GÂTEAU (2)

3 oz. (¾ cup) flour
a pinch of salt
5 oz. (scant ⅔ cup) sugar
2½ oz. (2½ squares) bitter chocolate
4 eggs
7 oz. (7 squares) bitter chocolate for the butter cream filling
butter cream (see p. 137)

Melt the chocolate with a little water and stir till creamy and then put it aside to cool. Beat the sugar with the eggs and put over a low heat. Stir all the time till it is nice and creamy, then take off the heat but continue stirring till it is nearly cold. Add the flour with the salt, bit by bit and finally the melted chocolate. Mix thoroughly and pour into a baking tin 8 or 9 in. in diameter and bake in a moderate oven, 370°F. (191°C.) approximately, 50 minutes. Now I suggest you should sit down and have a cigarette with a cup of coffee. Then take the chocolate and melt in a bowl and beat it into the butter cream. When your chocolate sponge is cold cut it into two or three layers. Spread each layer with butter cream, put the layers together and spread the remainder of the butter cream on the sides and on the top. Round the sides put chopped almonds or chocolate vermicelli. You can decorate the top with fresh cream or shredded chocolate.

CHOCOLATE PINEAPPLE GÂTEAU

2 rounds white sponge
1 round shortcrust pastry
marzipan
chocolate whipped cream
whipped cream
chopped pineapple
chocolate vermicelli

Sandwich a white sponge cake and a short pastry base with softened marzipan, build on it a pyramid of chocolate and fresh cream and bring up level with the top and sides with fresh cream to which has been added small pieces of chopped pineapple. Place chocolate sponge on top, thinly cover with fresh cream, place chocolate vermicelli around the base, dusted with cocoa powder, work into portions and place small sections of pineapple on each portion with a small blob of cream.

CHESTNUT GÂTEAU

6 yolks of eggs
11 oz. (1⅓ cups) sugar
2 lb. chestnuts
2 oz. (⅓ cup) grated hazelnuts
a little vanilla
6 whites of eggs
fresh whipped cream flavoured with a little vanilla
decoration:
pieces of chestnut or marron glacé

Whisk the yolks of eggs and the sugar. Then add the chestnuts which have been previously boiled and sieved. Add the grated hazelnuts and the vanilla. Whisk the whites of eggs till stiff and fluffy and add carefully to the mixture. Pour into a round cake tin and bake in a low oven. Take out when cooked and allow to cool; then cut in two and layer with the fresh cream. Then decorate the top with pieces of chestnut or marrons glacés if liked.

COFFEE CREAM GÂTEAU

An old-fashioned coffee cream gâteau that everybody enjoyed at Gerbeaud's – the best patisserie in Budapest.

8 eggs
9 oz. (full cup) caster sugar
5 oz. (1 cup) finely chopped almonds
5 oz. (1¼ cups) flour
cream filling:
6 yolks of eggs
9 oz. (full cup) sugar
½ cup very strong black coffee or 1 oz. (2 tablespoonfuls) Continental Nescafé powder in ½ cup water
6 oz. (¾ cup) butter
½ pod vanilla (the inside)
chocolate coffee beans

Whisk the yolks and sugar till very creamy; add the finely chopped almonds, the flour and the whites of eggs whipped very stiff. Turn the mixture into a buttered and floured gâteau tin and bake it in a moderate oven which is about 350–360°F. (177–182°C.). Bake it for 30 minutes. When it is ready, put it on a wire tray and let it cool.

For the cream; mix the yolks of eggs and sugar till very smooth; add the black coffee or Nescafé and put it on a pan of boiling water and go on stirring till it is smooth and creamy. Take it off the heat then and go on stirring till it is cool. Beat the butter; when it is smooth and white add to the mixture, also the vanilla. When the cake sponge is cold, cut it in two and spread half of the cream on the bottom half of the sponge. Put on it the other half of the sponge and spread the remaining cream on the top and the sides of the cake so smoothly and neatly that you only need the chocolate coffee beans for decoration.

HOT CHOCOLATE GÂTEAU

6 eggs
8 oz. (1 cup) butter
5 tablespoonfuls (full
  ¼ cup) sugar
4 slices chocolate
2 oz. (½ cup) flour
chocolate sauce:
4 fl. oz. (½ cup) liquid
  chocolate
5 tablespoonfuls (6¼
  tablespoonfuls) sugar
a little water
vanilla pod
1 pat of butter

Beat together the yolks of eggs, the butter and the sugar. Add the slices of chocolate after having softened them. Add gradually – and alternately – the whites of eggs (beaten stiff) and the flour; 1 spoonful of flour, then 1 spoonful of white of egg and so on.

Put the mixture into a greased and floured cake tin – the centre should be soft and creamy. Bake for approximately 10 minutes.

For the sauce, cook the chocolate, the sugar, the water and the vanilla together till it thickens. When it is ready, add the butter. Pour this hot creamy sauce over the gâteau and serve while hot.

DATE GÂTEAU

4 yolks of eggs
4 oz. (½ cup) sugar
5 oz. (2 cups) shredded
  almonds
5 oz. (scant cup)
  chopped dates
4 whites of eggs
filling:
vanilla-flavoured
  whipped cream with
  a little sugar

Beat the yolks and the sugar very well together. Add the shredded almonds and the dates. Whip the whites of eggs very stiff, and add them carefully to the mixture. Pour into a cake tin and cook till nice and golden-brown at 375°F. (191°C.). When cold cut in two and layer with the cream.

DOBOS GÂTEAU (Hungary)

In Hungary every gâteau has a story behind it. This one was made for a duchess, that one for a lovely little countess; another was made for a princess and one perhaps for a gypsy band leader, but all of them have a happy or a sad romance behind them. The princess fell in love and the gypsy ran away with her; this was the Princess Stephanie and the gâteau was named after her. This *Dobos* gâteau, I am afraid, has no romance behind it, only an excellent and famous pastrycook called Dobos. It is a good gâteau and it is not very difficult to make. When I first came to England and before I had my own business, I could not buy one, and so I had to make it

myself as it was my son's favourite birthday cake. I admit that the first one gave me
one or two sleepless nights. To make a big *Dobos* gâteau presents some problems.
But after my first effort I found that it was not really so very difficult. You can make
anything if you want to very much and I wanted my cake to be as good as the ones
my son was accustomed to in Budapest, when it had been made by professional
pastry-cooks. I believe that everything can be successfully achieved. I believe that
you can achieve anything if you want to please someone you love very much. I give
you the recipe:

2 oz. ($\frac{1}{2}$ cup) flour

**2 oz. ($\frac{1}{4}$ cup) granu-
lated sugar**

3 eggs

filling:

**6 oz. ($\frac{3}{4}$ cup) caster
sugar**

**6 oz. ($\frac{3}{4}$ cup) unsalted
butter**

**6 oz. (6 squares) bitter
chocolate**

topping:

**3 oz. (full $\frac{1}{3}$ cup) granu-
lated sugar**

Separate the eggs. Whisk the yolks with the sugar.
Whisk the whites very stiffly and add to the egg mixture.
Fold in the flour. Butter and flour a sandwich tin and
spread one-sixth of the cake mixture onto it very thinly.
Bake in a moderate oven for 6–8 minutes. Remove
from the tin with the help of a spatula. Place the cake
round on a flat surface to cool. Meanwhile butter and
flour another baking tin and repeat the above process
till you have 6 rounds of wafer-thin layers. Of course,
if you have several tins of equal size you can bake more
than one layer at a time. While your cakes are cooling
prepare the filling.

To do this, cream the butter and sugar; melt the
chocolate over a very low heat adding 3 teaspoonfuls
of water to the chocolate and stirring all the while. Then
stir into it the creamed butter and sugar. Spread some
of the cream on the first layer, cover with the second
layer and repeat, finishing with a layer of biscuit. Now
comes the trickiest part. Prepare the top as follows.

Melt 3 oz. (scant $\frac{1}{3}$ cup) sugar on a low heat, stirring
till golden-brown. Be careful because in a minute the
sugar will burn and become useless. But when it is a
nice golden-brown pour the thick caramel on the top
of the round biscuit; even it with a wide knife which
you must first dip in a little oil. Mark it with your knife
into 10 or 12 slices. Do not cut it right through, only
mark it; you have to do this when the sugar is still hot.
Decorate the cake with chopped almonds, cocoa powder or chocolate vermicelli.

DELICIOUS GÂTEAU

7 eggs
9 oz. (full cup) sugar
**9 oz. (1¾ cups) ground
    walnuts**
**25 roasted coffee beans
    grated finely**
a little vanilla
filling:
5 oz. (⅔ cups) butter
**6 oz. (6 squares) melted
    chocolate**
3 oz. (full ⅓ cup) sugar
3 yolks of eggs

Beat the eggs and sugar till very creamy and fluffy. Use the whisk to do this. Add the walnut, coffee beans and vanilla. Pour into an 8 in. gâteau tin and bake in a slow oven 350°F. (177°C.) for 40 minutes. Leave to cool and split.

If the chocolate for the filling is bitter than add the 3 oz. sugar; if not bitter then just add sugar to taste. Put the chocolate and butter in a dish and place the dish in a bowl of hot water and heat up. Slowly add the yolks of eggs and continue to heat till the mixture becomes thick. Allow to cool, spread the mixture between the layers of the cake and cover it with the same mixture. Finish with a little almond or cake crumbs.

FOURRIE GÂTEAU

½ lb. (1 cup) sugar
¼ lb. marzipan
5 eggs
6 oz. (1½ cups) flour
**1 oz. (¼ cup) glacé
    cherries**
2½ oz. (½ cup) sultanas
2 nips of rum
¼ pint (⅓ pint) custard
**1 pint (1¼ pints) whipped
    cream, sweetened
    with 1 oz. (2 table-
    spoonfuls) sugar**
jam
white fondant
roasted flaked almonds

Soften the marzipan with a very little water. Add the sugar and the eggs and then whip till light and fluffy. Gently add the flour. Split the mixture into two 9 in. sandwich tins and bake in a moderate oven for 30 minutes. Soak the cherries and the sultanas in the rum, preferably overnight. Keep 3 cherries and a dozen sultanas separate for decoration. Gently mix the fresh cream into the cold custard and then add the soaked fruits. Cut one sponge into two (one half for the base and one for the top). Cut a 7 in. ring out of the other sponge. Place this ring on the base and then fill the centre with the cream mixture – keeping a little back for masking the sides. Put the top half on with the cut side next to the cream. Mask the sides. Then spread jam on the top and ice over with white fondant. Sprinkle the sultanas and the cherries, previously cut, over the fondant while it is still soft. Put the roasted flaked almonds round the sides.

It is best to soak the fruit in the rum in advance and leave overnight before mixing into the ingredients. It does give you a little trouble to make but in the end you will be pleased that you took the trouble. It will keep for 1 or 2 days in a refrigerator.

GÂTEAU ÉDOUARD

I read, many years ago, a recipe in an old book which went like this:

5 oz. (scant $\frac{2}{3}$ cup)
  sugar
5 eggs
4 oz. (4 squares)
  chocolate
1 teaspoonful ($1\frac{1}{4}$ teaspoonfuls) bread-
  crumbs
2 oz. ($\frac{1}{3}$ cup) ground
  almonds
1 teaspoonful ($1\frac{1}{4}$ teaspoonfuls) finely
  ground coffee
cream filling:
3 yolks of eggs
3 teaspoonfuls ($3\frac{3}{4}$ teaspoonfuls) sugar
$\frac{1}{4}$ pint ($\frac{1}{3}$ pint) strong
  black coffee, fresh or
  instant
5 oz. ($\frac{2}{3}$ cup) butter

Cream the yolks of eggs and sugar; melt the chocolate; add the breadcrumbs, the ground almonds and the ground coffee. Fold in the stiffly beaten whites of eggs. Turn into a buttered and floured cake tin and bake in a moderate oven for 25–28 minutes. Let it cool, split into three.

Mix the cream filling, put the mixture into a bowl and put the bowl into slowly boiling water, and mix the cream till it starts to be smooth and thick. Take the bowl off the hot water and continue stirring till the cream cools. Add 5 oz. softened butter and mix it well with the cream between the layers of the cake, cover the top of the cake with the thick whipped cream. Sprinkle it with roasted chopped almonds.

GENOESE GÂTEAU

14 oz. ($1\frac{3}{4}$ cups) fine
  sugar
16 eggs
pinch of salt
good piece of vanilla
  pod
15 oz. ($3\frac{3}{4}$ cups) plain
  flour
1 lb. (2 cups) butter

Place the sugar, eggs, salt and the vanilla in a copper basin. Set the pan on the stove over a very gentle heat and whisk the ingredients. You can do this in a double boiler if you find it easier. When the mixture begins to foam or rise remove from the stove but continue whisking till it is cold. Still beating the mixture add the flour slowly and then bit by bit the butter. It is better to melt the butter a little. Pour this mixture into a sloping sided baking tin or in a deep square tin. Bake at 375°F. (191°C.) for 40–45 minutes. This mixture will give you 3 or 4 cakes or gâteaux depending on how big you want them.

HAZELNUT GÂTEAU

a white sponge cake
praline buttercream
   (see p. 139)
roasted hazelnuts

Cut the sponge in half and sandwich with a praline buttercream. Put praline buttercream on the top and sides and then put roasted hazelnuts round the sides. The top can be piped with praline buttercream and decorated with hazelnuts. Then, using a spatula, shake some hot liquid sugar over the hazelnuts in thin filaments.

ISCHLER GÂTEAU (Austria)

As a young girl I spent some years at school in Vienna. That was in the happy era of the Emperor Franz-Josef. For me Vienna was then the top of the world and I could not dream of anything better than to have lived in Vienna. I am sure that I was right. One saw and felt Vienna as a most cultured city, full of music. Every shop girl, any young hairdressers' assistant talked of music and literature.

From Vienna as a schoolgirl, I was taken on an outing to Ischl, a small summer resort in the mountains south of Salzburg, which became famous, because the Emperor Franz-Josef went there once a year.

In that very small Austrian town there was a small pastry shop which became world famous because Franz-Josef patronized it. I give you a very simple pastry recipe which is still fashionable and very much liked in eastern Europe. This is a little chocolate pastry, we could really call it a biscuit, known as *Ischler*. We, in my bakery, still make it and the public, even in England, still likes it. If you have the recipe it is very easy to make.

5 oz. ($\frac{2}{3}$ cup) butter
3$\frac{1}{2}$ oz. (scant cup) flour
3 oz. ($\frac{1}{2}$ cup) grated
   almonds, walnuts or
   hazelnuts
2$\frac{3}{4}$ oz. ($\frac{1}{3}$ cup) sugar
pinch of cinnamon
vanilla
raspberry or red
   currant jam
8-10 oz. (8-10 squares)
   chocolate

Mix all the ingredients together into a very smooth little dough. Leave it for an hour to rest and put it on a floured pastry board and roll it out to less than a $\frac{1}{4}$ in. thick. Then with a 2$\frac{1}{2}$ in. or 3 in. pastry cutter, cut out round little biscuits and bake them in a moderate oven for 10-15 minutes till they are firm and crisp. When cool paste 2 biscuits together with raspberry or red currant jam.

Take the chocolate and melt it very carefully. Put the biscuits on a wire rack and pour the liquid chocolate over them. Let them dry. They can be kept for several days.

Linzer Torte

LINZER TORTE (Austria)

As we are discussing Austria, I would like to tell you about a very famous Austrian gâteau, mostly favoured by men, because it is neither sweet, rich nor creamy.

I wonder, how it is that certain articles, food or other materials, spread over the whole world. I am sure they are no better, or worse than the *Sacher*, the *Linzer* or the *Dobos* gâteaux. And yet they all have become internationally known.

Eventually I understood the *Sacher* gâteau. This came originally from Vienna, from the world famous Sacher Hotel which was then managed by the equally famous Madame Sacher. She was unique! Kings, archdukes, dukes, the whole world of geniuses, authors, poets, musicians went to her hotel and not only paid high prices, but also homage, to her. She commanded respect from everybody around her. She also created the famous *Sacher Torte*. Why is just the *Sacher Torte* still alive, very much alive? You have two *Sacher Torte* recipes, because there are several recipes for this. The same is the case with *Linzer* gâteau or *Torte*, therefore I am giving you two recipes for this as well.

LINZER TORTE (1)

1 lb. (2 cups) butter
½ lb. (1 cup) sugar
1 lb. (4 cups) flour
½ lb. (1½ cups) ground walnuts
2 eggs
2 yolks of eggs

Cream the butter till it is very light and creamy. Add the sugar and ground walnuts to it. Add the 2 eggs one by one and the 2 yolks of eggs also one by one. Mix all this together with the flour, make a nice round ball and leave it for half an hour or so to rest. Cut about a quarter of it and put it aside. Roll out the rest to ½ in. thickness and cut out of it two round shapes

7 or 8 in. in diameter. Bake the two rounds for 10 minutes; for they have only to be partly baked. Then cover the first round biscuit with raspberry jam, put the other biscuit on it, cover it all with raspberry jam. Now, using the remainder of the original paste; place a trellis across the top of the cake, fill each division with a little raspberry jam. Then bake at 390°F. (200°C.) for about 20 minutes. After baking dust lightly with icing sugar.

LINZER TORTE (2)

6 oz. (1½ cups) flour
4 oz. (½ cup) butter
4 oz. (½ cup) caster sugar
1 whole egg
1 yolk of egg
4 oz. (⅔ cup) almonds or walnuts grated but not blanched
1 grated lemon rind
raspberry jam
extra yolk of egg
red currant jelly

Put the sieved flour on a pastry board with a pinch of salt and cinnamon, according to your taste. Make a well in the middle and place in the butter, sugar, egg and lemon rind and then add the walnuts or almonds. Mix these all well together till smooth and then roll the mixture into a ball and allow to rest for about 1 hour in a cool place. Roll out the paste ½ in. thick and line a flan ring, first putting aside a small amount. Pour into the lined flan raspberry jam or fresh raspberry pulp sweetened in advance with sugar. Roll out the remaining paste very thinly and cut into thin strips; decorate the top of the flan in a criss-cross pattern. Brush over with yolk of egg and bake in a moderate oven for 25–30 minutes. When cool wash over with warm red currant jelly.

MOCHA GÂTEAU

Mocha is a variety of coffee bean grown in Arabia. The beans are roasted; the roasting is a very important part of the coffee process. Coffee can be ruined by over-roasting or by under-roasting. Coffee made from pure Mocha is generally served in special cups, smaller than those used for ordinary coffee. These little differences are important; people are pleased and impressed with them. This gâteau is made by covering round or square layers of cake made from the best genoese paste (*see* p. 122) with butter cream, flavoured with mocha. A layer of genoese paste is spread with the butter cream and another layer of cake placed on top, till the cake is two or three layers deep. Then the top is iced with mocha-flavoured fondant. Or it can be covered with the mocha-flavoured butter cream and decorated with butter cream piped through a fluted tube. Finish with roasted or chopped almonds or any other nuts.

MOCHA GÂTEAU (Austria)

6 oz. (¾ cup) caster sugar
6 eggs
5 oz. (5 squares) plain
chocolate
4 oz. (⅔ cup) ground
almonds
finely ground coffee or
Continental Nescafé
to taste
cream filling:
4 yolks of eggs
4 tablespoonfuls (¼ cup)
caster sugar
¼ pint (⅓ pint) strong
black coffee or 1 oz.
(2 tablespoonfuls)
Continental Nescafé
mixed in same
quantity water
6 oz. (¾ cup) butter
¾ pint (1 pint) cream

Beat the yolks of egg with the sugar, soften the chocolate and add to this. Add the ground almonds and the coffee. Beat the whites of eggs very stiff and fold into the mixture very carefully. Have an 8 in. gâteau tin, buttered and floured, put the mixture in it and bake in a moderate oven 360°F. (182°C.) for 25–28 minutes. Take out of the oven put on a wire tray and let it cool. Then split the cake into 3 pieces.

To make the cream, mix the yolks of egg and sugar, add the Nescafé and place your bowl over boiling water and stir all the time till the yolks and sugar are thick and smooth. Take off the heat and go on stirring till the mixture is cool. Add the butter to it bit by bit and mix it very thoroughly. Spread this filling between the cake layers and cover the top and sides thickly with the whipped cream. Put some of the whipped cream in a piping bag and pipe round the top very neatly.

NOUGATINE GÂTEAU

5 oz. (scant ⅔ cup) sugar
¼ lb. (1½ cups) flaked
almonds
a white sponge cake
coffee buttercream
roasted flaked almonds
icing sugar

For the nougatine, gently melt the sugar, stirring with a wooden spatula till lightly browned. Add ¼ lb. almonds. Mix thoroughly. Roll out with a rolling pin on a greased marble slab. Cut a circle 7 in. in diameter and cut into 12 pie-shaped slices. Place 6 on the rolling pin while still warm and curve them round it. (This quantity of mixture makes 2 rounds.)

Cut the sponge in half and sandwich with the buttercream and a few nougatine pieces. Cover top and side with the buttercream, and put roasted flaked almonds or crushed nougatine around the side. Place the 6 flat pieces of nougatine on top – points meeting in the centre. Dust with icing sugar, then placed the curved pieces alternately between the flat ones.

LOG CAKE

6 yolks of eggs
2 oz. ($\frac{1}{4}$ cup) sugar
2 oz. ($\frac{1}{2}$ cup) flour
6 whites of eggs
5 oz. ($\frac{7}{8}$ cup) grated
  walnuts
a little milk
a little grated lemon
  peel
2 oz. ($\frac{1}{4}$ cup) butter
decoration:
2 oz. ($\frac{1}{4}$ cup) butter
2 oz. ($\frac{1}{4}$ cup) sugar
1 yolk of egg
3 oz. (3 squares) melted
  chocolate

Mix the yolks of eggs, sugar and flour well together and then add the stiffly beaten whites of eggs. Pour into a baking tin so that the tin is covered with a thin layer of the cake mixture. Bake for 15–20 minutes at 410°F. (208°C.). While it cools, make the filling by softening the butter and milk and adding the grated walnuts and lemon peel, spread over the cake and then roll it up like a swiss roll. Cover the log with the decoration mixture.

MORELLO CHERRY GÂTEAU

3 eggs
3 oz. (6 tablespoonfuls)
  melted butter
3 oz. (3 squares)
  chocolate
3 oz. ($\frac{1}{3}$ cup) sugar
2 oz. ($\frac{1}{2}$ cup) flour
filling:
1 yolk of egg
3$\frac{1}{2}$ oz. (scant $\frac{1}{2}$ cup)
  sugar
4 oz. ($\frac{1}{2}$ cup) butter
1 oz. (1 square)
  chocolate
drop of brandy or rum
stewed morello cherries,
  chopped and stoned

Grate chocolate and melt in a warm place. Separate the eggs. Whisk the yolks of eggs with half the sugar. Whip the whites of eggs stiffly; whisk the rest of the sugar into the whites then fold mixture into the yolks. Fold in the flour and finally add melted butter and chocolate. Put in a buttered and floured cake tin and bake for 40 minutes at 375°F. (191°C.).

To make the filling, whisk yolk of egg with the sugar over steaming hot water till thick. Add melted chocolate, butter and rum. Divide the mixture into two. Into one half fold the morello cherries and having cut the cake in half, fill it with this cream. Spread the remainder of the cream over the top and sides of the cake and decorate with stoned morello cherries.

NURNBERGI TORTA (Hungary)

6 oz. (¾ cup) sugar
5 oz. (⅞ cup) walnuts
8 oz. (8 squares) chocolate
2 oz. (⅔ cup) cake crumbs
8 whites of eggs
sweetened cream
covering:
chocolate
milk

Mix all the ingredients together. The whites of eggs are not whipped. Bake in shallow baking sheets at a low temperature. Bake till a golden-pink colour, cool and fill the layers with sweetened fresh whipped cream; cover the cake with chocolate previously diluted with milk so that it will pour easily.

ORANGE GÂTEAU (Tangier)

In Tangier where we were surrounded by orange trees – we naturally had oranges to eat – orange salads, orange sauce – and orange cakes. One of the recipes I hand over to you.

6 eggs
6 oz. (¾ cup) sugar
8 oz. (1⅓ cups) ground almonds
grated rind of 3 oranges
juice of 1½ oranges
3 teaspoonfuls (3¾ teaspoonfuls) cake crumbs
cream filling:
9 oz. (1⅛ cups) butter
6 oz. (¾ cups) sugar
grated peel of 2 oranges
3 yolks of eggs

Whisk the sugar and yolks of egg till they become very creamy. Add the almonds, orange juice and grated peel, and the cake crumbs. Whip the whites of eggs very stiffly and fold into the cake mixture very carefully. Bake this mixture in 3 layers, in 3 separate tins. Bake in a moderate oven 350°F. (177°C.) for 15–18 minutes. When they are baked, let them cool on a cake rack. Then prepare the cream.

Beat the butter and sugar till very creamy; add the yolks of eggs and continue stirring. Slowly add the grated peel and mix till it is stiff and hard. Then spread the cream between the 3 layers and on the side as well. Decorate the cake with pieces of orange; you can cover it with orange jelly and nicely-cut orange rinds.

PISTACHIO GÂTEAU

Pistachio is one of the most delicate of flavours – as a matter of fact it has hardly any flavour. But it adds to the other ingredients something elegant and something very good. I love to use it, just because of that and the lovely pale, fine-green colour. I use it a lot for decoration, I use it in cooking. Here I give you a pistachio gâteau.

6 oz. ($\frac{3}{4}$ cup) **granulated sugar**
5 **eggs**
3$\frac{1}{2}$ oz. (scant cup) **flour**
6 oz. (1 cup) **ground almonds**
1 oz. ($\frac{1}{4}$ cup) **finely chopped mixed peel**
grated rind of 1 lemon
4 oz. ($\frac{2}{3}$ cups) **blanched pistachio nuts**
cream filling:
4 **yolks of eggs**
juice and grated rind of 2 oranges
grated rind of 1 lemon
4 oz. ($\frac{1}{2}$ cup) **caster sugar**
1 pint (2$\frac{1}{2}$ cups) **fresh cream**

Whisk the yolks of eggs and sugar till it becomes creamy. Then add the ground almonds, the mixed peel and the grated lemon peel, fold in the flour, then add the stiffly whipped whites of eggs. Have a 7 in. buttered and floured cake tin and bake in a moderate oven 350°F. (177°C.) for 30 minutes. When it is ready, let it cool before turning out of the tin and cut it in two.

To make the cream, mix the yolks of eggs and sugar, add the orange juice and orange peel, and lemon peel. Put the mixture in a bowl over boiling water, stir all the time till it thickens. Then let it cool; then mix in the cream, very stiffly whipped. Sandwich the gâteau with half of the cream; spread the other half on the top and the sides. Decorate the top with chopped and whole pistachio nuts. Remember to blanch the pistachio nuts. In blanching put a good pinch of salt in the hot water; this gives the nuts their green colour.

PANAMA ISCHLER GÂTEAU (Austria)

One of the gâteaux that I remember from my earliest childhood so very many years ago.

4$\frac{1}{2}$ oz. (full $\frac{1}{2}$ cup) **sugar**
9 **eggs**
3 oz. (3 squares) **melted chocolate**
5 oz. ($\frac{7}{8}$ cup) **grated almonds**
6 oz. ($\frac{3}{4}$ cup) **butter**
6 oz. ($\frac{3}{4}$ cup) **sugar**
vanilla
3 oz. (3 squares) **melted chocolate**
3 oz. ($\frac{1}{2}$ cup) **blanched, grated almonds**

Separate 7 of the eggs and whisk the whites till very stiff. Whisk together the sugar, yolks, grated almonds, melted chocolate and finally the whites of eggs. Butter a cake tin and pour the mixture into it. Bake for 45 minutes in a moderate oven. Leave it to cool, then cut it into 3 layers.

For the cream filling mix together the butter, sugar, vanilla, melted chocolate and the remaining 2 eggs. Mix till it becomes very creamy and light. Spread the cream on two of the layers and sandwich them together. Then cover the whole cake with the rest of the cream. Sprinkle the entire cake with the almonds.

PRAVENIER GÂTEAU (Hungary)
A delicate and delicious gâteau.

10 oz. ($1\frac{1}{4}$ cup) sugar
10 oz. ($1\frac{2}{3}$ cups) blanched ground almonds
10 whites of eggs
filling:
8 oz. (1 cup) butter
8 oz. ($1\frac{2}{3}$ cups) icing sugar
6 oz. (1 cup) roasted and ground almonds
1 oz. (2 tablespoonfuls) coffee
roasted almonds

Mix the ingredients well together and divide into 3 cake rings. Bake till crisp in a low oven. Allow to cool before removing the rings.

Mix the butter and icing sugar till creamy and add the ground almonds and the coffee. Layer the 3 cakes and sandwich together. Cover the whole gâteau with this mixture and then sprinkle it with the roast almonds, roughly pounded.

RIGO JANCSI (Hungary)

5 yolks of eggs
$2\frac{1}{2}$ oz. (scant $\frac{1}{3}$ cup) sugar
2 small spoonfuls cocoa
a little rum
$1\frac{1}{2}$ oz. (full $\frac{1}{3}$ cup) flour
5 whites of egg
$\frac{1}{2}$ pint ($1\frac{1}{4}$ cups) whipped cream
liquid chocolate

Whisk the yolks of eggs and sugar till very creamy. Whisk the whites of eggs till stiff and fluffy. Mix the yolks and sugar with the whites of eggs, flour and cocoa. Divide into 2 square baking tins and bake in a cool oven 360°F. (182°C.). When cold split and layer with the whipped fresh cream which should have as much melted chocolate added to it as it will take. Sandwich and cover with liquid melted chocolate.

RIVIERA GÂTEAU

1 lb. marzipan
3 oz. (full $\frac{1}{3}$ cup) water
5 whites of eggs
5 oz. (scant $\frac{2}{3}$ cup) sugar
whipped cream
mixed fresh fruit

Soften the marzipan with the water and mix together till smooth. Whisk the whites of eggs and sugar into a stiff meringue and then gradually blend into marzipan. Pipe onto a baking sheet lined with greaseproof paper in triangles approximately 8 in. base; using $\frac{1}{2}$ in. plain tube. Dust over with icing sugar and bake in a moderate oven for 30 minutes. Build up into a gâteau by layering with the whipped cream and the mixed fruit.

This is one of the most useful gâteaux. It is usually made in a triangle. It is good because it is different from any other gâteau. I would call this a very useful cake for parties. You can add to the fresh cream chocolate, raspberry, or any other fruit. It is easy to decorate because it has only to be dusted over with vanilla-flavoured icing sugar. I always serve this gâteau with a punch sauce.

punch sauce:

a little custard
whipped cream
sugar
curaçao or rum
raspberry juice
  (optional)

Mix all these ingredients together. If you want the sauce to be pink, add the raspberry juice. The sauce must be ice cold when you serve it.

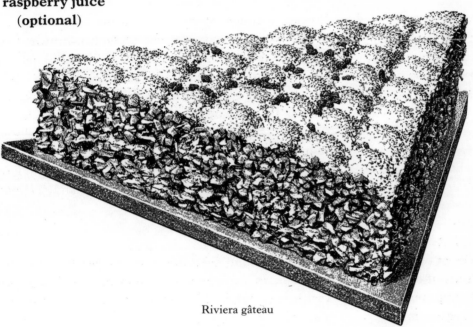

Riviera gâteau

GÂTEAU ST HONORÉ (France)

For over 40 years I have been grumbling – ever since I have owned a bakery and cake business – grumbling and rebelling, that God and man neglect my trade, my fellow-workers, pastrycooks and bakers. It is one of the most demanding kinds of work, day and night: but people don't appreciate it, they demand fresh and perfect pastries, rolls and bread. Sometimes they are quite indignant that we are not open on Sunday. As a matter of fact we do work on Sunday. We work every day of the week except on Saturday night.

I hope now you will sympathize with me and my colleagues. You can imagine how thrilled I was to read that the bakers and pastrycooks have their own patron saint. And what a lovely one – Saint Honoré.

I make hundreds of these very good, very decorative gâteaux, but I never knew that the name comes from Saint Honoré, who was Bishop of Amiens about 560 A.D. His cult began to spread in France in the middle of the eleventh century, and the Faubourg Saint-Honoré in Paris is named after him. His feast is celebrated on May 16. He is the patron saint of pastrycooks and bakers, though nothing in his life connects him with the food industry. I am, however, sure that he was a very nice bishop and now I know if I need help whom to ask; I am sure that my prayer will be answered. I will give you a very precise recipe for a gâteau St Honoré.

1 lb. choux paste
1 pint (1¼ pints) whipped
    vanilla cream
glacé cherries
angelica

Prepare a round of choux paste not less than 1 in. thick. Bake in a moderate oven till golden-brown. This should take about 15 minutes. Also pipe tiny balls of paste on a greased baking tin and bake on a lower shelf than the cake round. Prick these with a fork after removing from the oven to allow steam to escape. Leave the round and the balls to cool. Now stick the balls all round the base with a little vanilla cream, like a coronet and pile the remainder of the cream in the hollow. Decorate with glacé cherries cut in half and chopped angelica.

SACHER TORTE (1 – Austria)

10 yolks of eggs
10 whites of eggs
½ lb. (1 cup) butter
½ lb. (8 squares)
    chocolate
12 oz. (1½ cups) sugar
4 oz. (1 cup) plain flour
4 oz. (⅔ cup) ground
    almonds
apricot jam
decoration:
fondant
block chocolate

Prepare 3 round cake tins 1 in. in depth and either 7 or 10 in. in diameter in the following way: first grease very lightly and then flour, till all the fat is covered with a light layer of flour.

    Cream the yolks and sugar together till light and pale in colour. Add to this 6 oz. of melted chocolate. Sieve together the flour and the almonds and add 2 oz. grated chocolate. Beat the whites till stiff. Fold the whites and dry ingredients alternately into the mixture. Melt the butter and gently fold into the mixture taking care not to spoil the aeration. Divide equally into the 3 prepared moulds. Bake in a fairly moderate oven (approx. 300°F. (149°C.) till firm – this will take about

40 minutes. Allow to cool, and when cool, sandwich with apricot jam.

Melt together fondant and unsweetened block chocolate. Mask the cake with this mixture till completely covered. On the top pipe the word *Sacher* with the fondant mixture.

SACHER TORTE (2 – Austria)

5 oz. ($\frac{2}{3}$ **cup**) **butter**
5$\frac{3}{4}$ **oz.** (**full cup**) **icing sugar**
6 oz. (6 squares) **plain chocolate**
8 **yolks of eggs**
8 **whites of eggs**
3$\frac{1}{2}$ **oz.** (**scant cup**) **flour**
chocolate glaze coating:
1 **lb. 4 oz.** (2$\frac{1}{2}$ **cups**) **sugar**
4 oz. (4 squares) **un- sweetened chocolate**

Melt the chocolate at blood heat. Cream together the butter, yolks of eggs, $\frac{1}{3}$ of the sugar and the melted chocolate; warm slightly. Beat the whites of eggs and the rest of the sugar into a stiff meringue. Fold in the flour last of all.

Divide into two 10 in. baking rings and bake at 390°F. (200°C.) for 45 minutes.

On leaving the oven, dust with icing sugar and turn over onto a tray while still in the hoops.

Leave the cake for 24 hours before glazing – to do this, boil the sugar to thread degree and pour slowly into the melted chocolate and continue stirring till it is lukewarm. Brush the top and sides of the gâteau with apricot jam and pour the glaze over the top. Slip the cake in a warm oven for a very *few* seconds to dry the glaze.

SPITZBUB (Austria)

3$\frac{3}{4}$ **oz.** ($\frac{2}{3}$ **cup**) **ground walnuts**
4 oz. ($\frac{1}{2}$ **cup**) **butter**
5 **oz.** (**scant** $\frac{2}{3}$ **cup**) **sugar**
5 **oz.** (1$\frac{1}{4}$ **cups**) **flour**
1 **whole egg**
a little cinnamon
a little grated lemon peel
raspberry jam

Cream the walnuts and butter, add the sugar; mix well, then add the flour, egg, cinnamon and lemon peel. Divide the paste into two, one piece being bigger than the other. Line a baking tin with the bigger half and cover the paste with raspberry jam; bake till nice and golden-brown. Roll out the remainder of the pastry very thin and cut into long strips and criss-cross over the gâteau in a trellis fashion. Bake again till it has coloured a little then dust over with sugar.

TUTTI FRUTTI TORTA (Hungary)

10 oz. (1¼ cups) sugar
9 eggs
10 oz. (1⅔ cups) ground walnuts
4 oz. (1 cup) chopped dates
4 oz. (⅞ cups) sultanas
4 oz. (1 cup) chopped figs and lemon peel
4 oz. (4 squares) melted chocolate

Beat the yolks of eggs and the sugar together. Then add to it the walnuts, dates, sultanas, figs and melted chocolate. Stiffly whip the whites of eggs and add these to the mixture. Pour this in a shallow baking tin and bake in the oven at 300°F. (149°C.) for about 30 minutes. When it is cold decorate with sweetened whipped cream piped all round the cake and finish off with crystallized fruit.

WALNUT GÂTEAU (1)

I return now to my childhood – to a friend's birthday party. That friend is now living in London, and we see each other from time to time. A few weeks ago she came to see me and we talked, as usual, 'You remember . . .'. That, I think, makes a real friendship, things in common to remember.

She mentioned her birthday party and I remembered that I ate my first anchovy butter and caviar there. Her mother was very modern, much more advanced than any other mothers in those days and her own parties and those of her little daughter's were always different from everybody else's. For tea we had tea – not drinking chocolate or milk – but tea. We felt so grown-up. At each cup there was a plate with two half rolls. One had anchovy butter and the other caviar. After the rolls came the sweets. There was a walnut gâteau which I remember well. After this there came a chestnut purée with fresh cream. That was a sweet never missing from any party – and never failing at any party! Here is the gâteau:

6 oz. (¾ cup) sugar
4 yolks of eggs
4 whites of eggs
2 oz. (½ cup) flour
4 oz. (⅔ cup) ground walnuts
apricot jam
1 tablespoonful (1¼ tablespoonfuls) rum

Beat the yolks and 4 oz. sugar thoroughly, and gradually add the flour and ground walnuts. Finally carefully add 2 very stiffly beaten whites of eggs. Pour into a buttered and floured 8 in. cake tin, and bake at 350–360°F. (177–182°C.) for 25–30 minutes. Take out of the oven, cool, and then split in two.

Now mix the jam and rum and spread a third of this mixture on the bottom round. Put the other cake round on top and spread the remainder of the jam and rum mixture on the top and sides of the cake.

Put the other whites of eggs in a bowl and, with the remaining sugar whisk till very stiff. Put your bowl over hot water and cool till the cream thickens stirring all the time. Cool and pour over the entire top of the cake, and roughen with a fork. That's all.

WALNUT GÂTEAU (2)

12 oz. (3 cups) flour
10 oz. (1¼ cups) butter
6 oz. (⅔ cup) sugar
5 yolks of eggs
1 pinch of salt
¼ pint (⅓ pint) sour cream or cream
cream filling:
5 yolks of eggs
7 whites of egg
8 oz. (1 cup) caster sugar
9 oz. (1½ cups) ground walnuts

Rub the butter into the flour, add the sugar and the yolks one by one. Add the pinch of salt and the sour cream (or cream). Beat this mixture till smooth and silky, then knead it into a very smooth dough. Divide into two, then roll out one half to ¼ in. Place it on an oblong baking tin and bake it in a medium oven for about 12-15 minutes. Meanwhile prepare the cream.

Beat the whites very stiff and add the yolks one by one. Stir in the sugar and add, very slowly and carefully, the ground walnuts. Spread this cream over the baked half of the paste which has meanwhile been cooled. Then cover this with the other half of the mixture; prick with a fork and bake in a medium oven for about 15-20 minutes. When cool cut the cake into slices.

WALNUT GÂTEAU (3)

7 eggs
5 oz. (scant ⅔ cup) sugar
6 oz. (1 cup) roasted, pounded walnuts
5 oz. (5 squares) melted chocolate
cake crumbs
5 oz. (⅔ cup) melted butter
filling:
5 oz. (⅞ cup) walnuts
5 oz. (scant ⅔ cup) sugar
rum
½ pint (1¼ cups) cream

Separate the eggs; whisk the yolks and the sugar; add the butter slowly, then the walnuts and as much of the crumbs as necessary. Beat the whites of eggs till stiff and fold in very carefully. Butter an 8 or 9 in. cake tin and pour in the mixture; bake in a moderate oven at about 375-400°F. (191-205°C.) for 20-25 minutes. Take out of the oven and cool. Split the gâteau in two and then mix your filling. Spread the filling on one of the rounds and cover with the other one. You can ice this gâteau with chocolate. For this melt sweetened chocolate in a bowl over hot water till it is liquid, let it cool just a little and pour it over the cake. If you like you can roast walnuts and chop roughly and scatter over the cake or decorate with shelled walnuts.

STRAWBERRY GÂTEAU

2 oz. ($\frac{1}{3}$ cup) blanched ground almonds
3 oz. ($\frac{1}{4}$ cup) butter
3 oz. (full $\frac{1}{3}$ cup) sugar
3 eggs
1$\frac{1}{2}$ oz. (full $\frac{1}{3}$ cup) flour
biscuit or cake crumbs
filling:
1 lb. strawberries (wild ones preferably)
$\frac{1}{4}$ lb. (scant cup) icing sugar
few drops maraschino and lemon juice
red currant jelly
glacé fruits
thin water icing (see p. 140)

Separate the eggs. Cream the butter and sugar and add the yolks of eggs. Beat the whites stiffly and fold into the yolks with the almonds, flour and crumbs. Bake in a well-buttered and floured cake tin at 375°F. (191°C.). Remove from tin while warm and allow to cool.

Dust the strawberries with icing sugar and put through a sieve. Add maraschino and lemon juice, bind with red currant jelly. Fill the cake with two-thirds of this purée; pile the remaining third on top of the cake. Sprinkle with the chopped glacé fruit and then cover the whole cake with thin water icing.

Another way is to arrange a layer of halved strawberries on the top of the purée and to mix the icing with lemon juice instead of water which gives a lovely sharp taste to it.

WALNUT RUM GÂTEAU

6 eggs
$\frac{1}{4}$ lb. ($\frac{1}{2}$ cup) sugar
$\frac{1}{4}$ lb. ($\frac{1}{2}$ cup) butter
$\frac{1}{4}$ lb. ($\frac{2}{3}$ cup) ground, roasted walnuts
$\frac{1}{4}$ lb. (2 cups) fine toasted cake crumbs
filling:
$\frac{1}{4}$ lb. roasted, chopped walnuts
$\frac{1}{4}$ lb. ($\frac{1}{2}$ cup) sugar
rum
$\frac{1}{4}$ pint ($\frac{1}{3}$ pint) fresh cream
covering:
chocolate fondant

Separate the eggs. Whisk the yolks, sugar, and butter till creamy; add the walnut and the cake crumbs. Add the whites of egg very stiffly beaten. Pour into a buttered cake tin and bake for 20–25 minutes at 360°F. (182°C.). When baked let it cool, cut in two and layer with the filling. Ice with chocolate fondant (*see* p. 207).

FILLINGS AND ICINGS

The best filling of all for cakes and gâteaux is fresh cream; the next best is butter cream, which is good for layering and decorating. There are very many kinds of butter cream and I give you several recipes which I hope will be useful.

BUTTER CREAM (1)

3 oz. (full ⅓ cup) granulated sugar
¼ pint (⅓ pint) water
2 yolks of eggs
4–6 oz. (½–¾ cup) unsalted butter
a little sweetened chocolate or coffee or the rind of an orange or lemon

Boil the water and sugar to a temperature of between 220–250°F. (191°C.) till it becomes like a thread. To test this put your fingers in very cold water and then very quickly dip into the boiling sugar mixture. Take a pinch of the mixture between finger and thumb and if the mixture cracks or breaks it is ready; it should look like a piece of glass. Then take the mixture from the heat, whisk the yolks of eggs and pour the syrup into them. Pour in a steady stream, stirring vigorously and then continue whisking till it is thick, smooth and silky. Now work your butter with a wooden spoon till it is creamy and white and go on working it into the syrup till the cream becomes like a good mousse. You can flavour it to your taste with melted chocolate, sweet chocolate, Nescafé, or very strong fresh coffee. You can use fresh sieved raspberries or flavour it with the rind of lemon and a little lemon juice.

BUTTER CREAM (2)

¼ lb. (½ cup) granulated sugar
¼ pint (⅓ pint) water
4 yolks of eggs
½ lb. (1 cup) unsalted butter

Melt the sugar in the water and boil till it starts to become sticky. Then quickly test it by first putting your finger and thumb in cold water and then quickly putting them into the syrup. If the sugar 'pulls' when stretched and breaks like a piece of glass then it is ready. If it is thick take off and put the syrup in the dish with the yolks of eggs. Beat the syrup with the yolks till thick. Cream the butter in a separate dish till creamy and then add to the egg and syrup mixture beating all the ingredients are thick, creamy and silky. You can use this cream with any flavour you like.

BUTTER CREAM (3)

$\frac{1}{4}$ pint ($\frac{1}{3}$ pint) milk
4 oz. ($\frac{1}{2}$ cup) caster
  sugar
2 yolks of eggs
$\frac{1}{2}$ lb. (1 cup) unsalted
  butter

Put the milk in a saucepan with half of the sugar and warm it slowly. Mix the yolks of eggs in a bowl with the other half of the sugar and the butter. Whisk this mixture till light and creamy and then slowly add the hot milk and stir all the time. Add to this some Nescafé; quantity according to taste. I found Continental Nescafé the best; it has the strongest coffee flavour; instead of coffee you can add chocolate.

BUTTER CREAM (4)

$\frac{1}{4}$ pint ($\frac{1}{3}$ pint) milk
2 oz. ($\frac{1}{4}$ cup) caster sugar
2 yolks of eggs
2 oz. ($\frac{1}{4}$ cup) sugar
$\frac{1}{2}$ lb. (1 cup) unsalted
  butter

Put the milk and sugar in a saucepan and heat slowly. Mix another 2 oz. sugar with the yolks of eggs and cream till light and then add to it the hot milk very carefully and put the pan back on the heat, mixing all the time till the mixture starts to thicken. Remove from the stove. Continue to stir till the mixture is cool, then add the already creamed butter, beating all the time. Continue till thick. Put aside and flavour it with anything you like; the butter cream will keep till you require to use it.

CHOCOLATE BUTTER CREAM

1 lb. ($3\frac{1}{2}$ cups) icing
  sugar
1 lb. (2 cups) unsalted
  butter
4 oz. (1 cup) cocoa
  powder

Whip the butter and the icing sugar till light and fluffy. Finally, blend in cocoa powder and mix thoroughly. More or less cocoa can be added according to your taste.

MERINGUE BUTTER CREAM

2 whites of eggs
$\frac{1}{4}$ lb. ($\frac{1}{2}$ cup) caster sugar
$\frac{1}{2}$ lb. (1 cup) unsalted
  butter

Put the whites of eggs in a china bowl and place in a saucepan of water on the stove. Add the sugar and whisk vigorously till it starts to thicken. Cream the butter and add to the meringue, and continue stirring over the hot water till the mixture is very thick and creamy.

Any flavouring you like can be added.

MOCHA BUTTER CREAM

4 oz. (½ cup) butter
2 oz. (¼ cup) caster sugar
coffee essence

Cream the butter, add the sugar and a little coffee essence. Beat well together till smooth and light.

PRALINE BUTTER CREAM

1 lb. (2 cups) butter
1 lb. (2 cups) icing sugar
praline paste

Whip the butter and sugar; add praline paste and whip till absorbed.

For praline paste heat brown sugar, ground almonds and vanilla; cool and press together.

ICING A WEDDING CAKE

I think that the English way of icing wedding cakes and birthday cakes is a very big subject and I am sure several people have written books about it. It is an art and a very nice art. I want to give you one way of icing a wedding cake. It is simple and easy, and, if you are very artistic you can do anything with the decoration.

Take a 5 lb. wedding cake; cover it with marzipan and put it aside and make the icing. This is one recipe:

1¼ lb. (4⅓ cups) icing sugar
8 whites of eggs
juice of 1½ lemons

Sift the sugar and then very slowly add the whites of eggs beating all the time; the icing should be stiff and firm. Mix in the lemon juice, very little at a time. Beat it till very light and white and smooth. Take your cake and put the icing on it with a spoon and a palette knife, smoothly and neatly; have a jug of hot water ready and dip the spoon and palette knife in this each time before using. Leave it to dry and if you have some icing left over put it in a forcing bag and decorate the cake as your mood dictates.

LEMON ICING

1 lb. (3½ cups) icing sugar
2 whites of eggs
1 lemon rind, juice and the oil from the skin

The oil from the lemon skin should first be squeezed onto your icing sugar. Mix the sugar with the whites of eggs till it starts to thicken. Then mix in the lemon juice and the rind and continue beating till the mixture will stand up in peaks by itself. You will find it very useful for petits fours or for covering gâteaux.

FRANGIPANE

Frangipane is a tasty filling for flans, tarts and sponge cakes.

4 oz. (½ cup) unsalted butter
4 oz. (½ cup) sugar
2 eggs
4 oz. (⅔ cup) ground almonds
1 oz. (¼ cup) flour
a little lemon juice
a little vanilla pod

Cream the butter and the sugar. Beat in the eggs one at a time, then the ground almonds, lemon juice and vanilla and, finally, the flour. Pour into pastry shells or cases, either individual ones or rounds, and bake in a moderate oven till the mixture is firm to the touch.

ROYAL ICING

½ lb. (1¾ cups) icing sugar
a little lemon juice
1 white of egg

Add sugar to the white of egg and beat till smooth. Add the lemon juice and use.

SUGAR ICING

1 lb. (4 cups) cube sugar
4 whites of eggs
1 oz. (2 tablespoonfuls) fine starch

Pound the sugar and add to whites of eggs which should have been beaten till frothy. Then add starch, also finely sifted; beat well.

Ice the cakes as required, then place them in a cool oven and allow the icing to dry and harden but not to colour. You can colour the icing if you like with cochineal, strawberry or red currant juice.

If you ice the cakes straight from the oven when still hot the icing will become firm as they cool.

On rich cakes such as wedding and christening cakes, etc., a layer of almond paste is spread underneath the sugar icing.

WATER ICING

1 lb. (3½ cups) icing sugar
¼ pint (⅓ pint) water

Add the water to the icing sugar, which has been well sieved, and mix well together. Flavour with lemon or orange juice, etc., or just colour with cochineal.

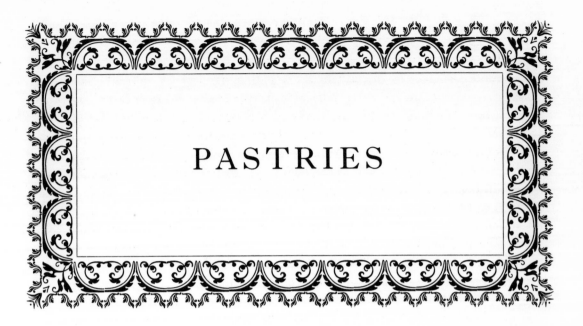

PASTRIES

PUFF PASTRY

For the last two hundred years, the most popular of all pastries has been puff pastry. In my childhood in Hungary we had cream slices with yellow vanilla cream mixed with egg yolks, sugar and fresh cream. The flavour was unforgettable and very difficult to repeat. I wonder whether they were really so good or that my childhood appetite added to the flavour. Very likely the famous Hungarian flour had something to do with it. Of course, the eggs were different; the chickens were different – they were all very happy chickens: no batteries, not enclosed in little prisons; they wandered about in the yard or the fields and three times a day their mistress threw maize to them with love and care.

Another important ingredient in the making of continental cream slices is vanilla pod. There are many kinds of vanilla; very good thin pods, with an especially good flavour; much thicker ones, much cheaper and with less flavour. Hungarian importers bought the very best kind of vanilla, tea or coffee because the duty was the same. The differences in the prices didn't matter very much, therefore the Hungarian coffee was always good. As long as I can remember, I drank only Darjeeling tea in Hungary, because the price was hardly different from that of the poorer quality.

For forty years I have fought actively for better food, better pastry, better everything. But to go back to puff pastry, I want to tell you how many kinds of pastries you can make out of it. First the cream slice of which there are at least three kinds: one is the famous *millefeuille*; another is a coffee slice filled with whipped cream and coffee cream, again in three layers; and lastly whipped cream and chocolate cream.

Of course, only fresh cream is used – that wonderful Jersey cream is best. You can make hundreds of kinds of pastries from puff pastry: sweet ones and savouries, vol-au-vents, pie cases and tarts, sausage rolls, pie crusts and fruit tarts, large ones and tiny ones. To make really good puff pastry is not one of the easiest things to do. I remember at home, when we engaged a cook, one of the most important questions was 'Can you make puff pastry?' It is a difficult procedure because the temperature of your hand plays a part as well. A cook with a naturally warm hard can seldom make good puff pastry, as everything should be kept cool, including utensils and ingredients. I will try to give you a recipe for the making of puff pastry which is interesting because it is not so much different from that which pastrycooks made in 1760, over two hundred years ago.

I like everything in the puff pastry line made with butter. I do not know whether I am right in sticking so much to butter but what can you do with your upbringing? It is difficult to shake it off. I was born into a farmer's family, and in Hungary butter was taken for granted, being an agricultural country. In my youth, which was a long, long time ago, the margarine was not good – I only suppose so, because I never tasted it, to be truthful. There were margarine factories in my time but we never used it either at home or in the business. I have even had arguments in Hungary with margarine-factory owners who wanted to convert me, but without success. I am still a butter believer. Making puff pastry needs precision. As with most things you cannot take short cuts in the pastry kitchen; of course, there are daily routines and so it is very simple. In making puff pastry it is very important to have the best pastry flour, I was told by my miller. This flour is called pastry flour everywhere.

As a general rule in the making of puff pastry it is very important that your water should be ice cold and you should use the lemon juice with the water. You make the pastry by first mixing the flour with the water and lemon juice. The pastry should not be soft and not hard. But it must be hard enough to hold your butter. It often happens that the pastry is too soft when you roll it out and so the butter is squeezed out. It is important that when you add the butter to the pastry the butter should be firm, but again not too hard and not too soft. I am afraid these things have to be learnt by practice and experience. The pastry and the butter should be the same consistency. If you can achieve this then the mixing will not be difficult. If it is reasonably firm it is easy to roll out. Where most experience is needed is in the technique of rolling out the pastry. This must be done firmly using a big, heavy rolling pin. Then roll backwards and forwards, repeating the movement several times. Again experience is far more helpful than any recipe. If you press too much you will push out the butter and then the pastry will not rise properly. You have to be pretty careful for the first two or three turns because the butter must not come through the pastry, which would make it sticky; if this happens you have to use more flour and you have to be very sparing with extra flour. Too much flour ruins the pastry. I must warn you, if I have not done so before, that it is difficult to make puff pastry if you happen to have very warm hands. Let us assume however that you have mastered the art because I would like to give you a few recipes made with puff pastry.

PUFF PASTRY (1)

1 lb. (4 cups) flour
1 egg
½ lb. (1 cup) butter
water

Beat the egg hard, work ¾ lb. flour in gradually and add as much water as the flour will absorb. The result should be a pretty stiff paste. Roll out very thin. Lay about 2½ oz. butter, cut into very small pieces, on the paste. Dredge it with the remaining flour. Roll it up tight, and then with your rolling pin, roll it out again. Repeat till all your ½ lb. butter is mixed with the flour. Roll it out and fold one-third over and the other third of the pastry on top, then repeat this three times folding the other way. Put it into the refrigerator to rest for 1 or 2 hours. Make out of it whatever you like. You can make a sheet of pastry from which you can make cream slices; you can make 'horns' filled with fresh cream, vol-au-vents, or *palmiers*. Always bake puff pastry in a very hot oven 500–525°F. (261–275°C.).

PUFF PASTRY (2)

8 oz. (2 cups) flour
6 oz. (¾ cup) unsalted butter
2 yolks of eggs
a little vanilla pod

(The method is as above.) From this pastry you can make a good cream slice or anything else. Put it on a baking sheet and bake quickly in a very hot oven till it is a nice rosy-brown. You will need 4 of these round pieces to make cream slices. Let them cool and then layer with *crème patissière*, or any other filling you like.

PALMIER (France)

puff pastry
caster sugar

The pastry for *palmiers* is rolled out very thinly, tightly rolled up and then cut across into slices, which can be either thick or thin. They are then put on a greased baking tray, sprinkled with caster sugar, and baked for 10 minutes in a medium oven. They are then turned onto the other side, sprinkled with sugar again and baked for approximately another 10 minutes till crisp and golden. You can eat them as they are or put two together, layered with fresh cream.

CREAM SLICES

Cream slices are one of the most tempting of puff pastries. I remember that as a child I stopped at every shop window where I saw these lovely cream slices. I just never could understand how any man or woman who had enough money in their pocket or purse could pass a shop and not go in and buy and take one home or eat it there and then. Where are these lovely young years when these little things were such a temptation? I give you one kind of cream slice recipe:

millefeuille pastry (see below)

13 oz. (full 1½ cups) milk

½ vanilla pod

1 oz. (1 tablespoonful) cornflour

3 eggs

5 oz. (⅔ cup) sugar

Boil the milk with the vanilla pod and add to it very slowly the yolks of eggs which have been slightly whipped with ⅓ of the sugar, and cornflour; bring these very slowly to the boil. Stir till it is thick. Add to this, while it is still cooking, the whites of eggs which have been whipped very firm with ⅔ of the sugar and continue cooking for another minute. Now pour this cream when it is cool enough on a sheet of previously cooked *millefeuille* puff pastry; the cream should not be less than 1½ in. thick. Put another well-baked puff pastry sheet on the top of the cream and cut through into slices with a very sharp knife dipped into boiling water. Dust with icing sugar and the cream slices are now ready to serve. And they are very good, too!

CARLTON MILLEFEUILLE GÂTEAU

Many years ago I went to Cannes and stayed in the Carlton Hotel. The Managing Director and his wife were most kind and good to me and I never felt lonely there. I learned much and tasted wonderful food, very specially pastries and gâteaux. The *millefeuille* gâteau, the recipe for which I want to give you, was the best I have ever tasted. The puff pastry from which the gâteau was made was a different puff pastry from the English one or, indeed, from any other puff pastry I have tasted before. I suppose it was so good because it was made differently. It was very light, and tasted heavenly. The chef told me that the most important factor was the very careful mixing of materials and a light touch. In the Carlton Hotel the pastrycooks, all very young men, were quite outstanding. This was their method.

The chef sifted the flour on a marble slab, and made a well in the flour; he then put the butter, which was very fresh and unsalted, in the well. Next he added the sugar and eggs, and at this point no more liquid. In this way the pastry will not shrink and will not loose shape during the cooking. He told me he preferred icing sugar as this made the pastry lighter. He mixed the butter, sugar and eggs together, blended the mixture well, very slightly drawing the flour to it. He used only his finger-tips and very gently, little by little, he mixed the whole dough. It was a joy to see him working, his hand was not sticky, not even floury. He worked only with one hand and only the finger-tips. When the dough was ready and the flour was used slowly, his finger-tips were quite clean, then he used the heel of his palm and kneaded the whole dough together. He said you should not work the pastry too long or too much because the pastry then will be sticky and it will be difficult to turn. If you work it too hard and long you have to use more flour and that would spoil your whole pastry. When the pastry is formed, shape it into a nice square piece, pack it in a greaseproof paper and set aside in a cool place or keep it in the refrigerator overnight and use it the next day. Here are the ingredients.

4 oz. (1 cup) plain flour	Mix the ingredients as shown above. Cut 4 rounds,
2 oz. ($\frac{1}{4}$ cup) butter	bake in a hot oven. Cool. Put a layer of *crème patissière*
2 eggs	between each round or use whipped cream. Vanilla
a little icing sugar	flavouring may be added if liked.

You can eat this with whipped cream which can be sweetened to your taste. You can flavour it with very strong coffee; nowadays you use Nescafé. You can cover it with water icing and ring your gâteau with fresh cream and very finely-chopped roasted almonds or hazelnuts. Alternatively, you can leave it plain and eat it dry or put two together with fresh whipped cream.

You can also make puff pastry horns, which again you fill with fresh whipped cream. I think these are very popular in England. Roll the puff pastry on little round wooden or steel cones. Bake the pastry on these, let them cool and fill with fresh whipped cream; you can also use chocolate or coffee cream.

Flaky pastry and puff pastry are both made in the same way, but all my pastry-cooks – in Hungary, in Vienna, Prague, Berlin and London – made them a little bit differently. Old-fashioned puff pastry contained eggs. But in modern puff pastry we no longer use them. We used to start with the flour, a very small piece of butter, a pinch of salt, 2 yolks of eggs and about 3 fl. oz. ($\frac{1}{3}$ cup) of water. This was made into a very silky dough, neither too hard, nor too soft.

In contrast, a modern puff pastry contains no eggs, but plenty of butter. You can, indeed, have in a puff pastry the same amount of butter as flour; in such a case, ice-cold water is needed. Proportions should be 6 oz. flour ($1\frac{1}{2}$ cups) the same of butter to $\frac{1}{4}$ pint ($\frac{1}{3}$ pint) water. Sieve the flour in a bowl. Take about $\frac{1}{2}$ oz. of butter and mix a $\frac{1}{4}$ pint ($\frac{1}{3}$ pint) cold water and make a soft dough from this. Then roll it out on a pastry board to about $\frac{1}{2}$ in. thickness. Then flatten the butter with your rolling pin, put it in the middle of the pastry and pack the butter into the dough as if making a parcel. Put the pastry in a cold place or in a refrigerator, then roll it out again and fold it six times. Then put it back in the cold place or the refrigerator for another hour. Repeat the operation once more. Then yet once again – three times altogether.

You can make really hundreds and hundreds of different kinds of savouries and sweets from puff pastry. You can also make the famous *rissoles* used to garnish soups. These *rissoles* are three cornered and filled with mushrooms which are first fried with a little onion and chopped mushrooms. These are then fried in deep fat. You can make the filling with cream cheese; for a sweet add sugar and a yolk of egg, and fill your little three-cornered pastry. If it is savoury you add to cream cheese, salt and quite a bit of chopped dill. You can put with the cream cheese chopped chives and salt; you can also fill the savoury puff pastry with ham, anchovy or with any other meat or fish.

I have already given you several puff pastry recipes, but one night – not able to sleep because my troubles and bad conscience – I started to read a very, very heavy book, which is difficult in bed. I thought my arm would break, but I went on reading till I found a passage about puff pastry. There it was said that puff pastry was one of the most fashionable and most popular culinary products very many years ago. There was a lot of discussion as to who had been the first maker of this delicacy. Somebody said in France that a very famous painter in the seventeenth century was the original founder. The other party said that it was a very famous pastrycook. But the historian said that the Greeks and the Romans had already made this pastry.

I read and read in the night. I was so tired in the end that I could not make any notes and decided to look up the passage again next morning. Of course, the 'next morning' for me means to get up and rush to my office. But puff pastry was in my mind during the whole day. I came home earlier than usual in the afternoon, sat at my desk surrounded by books and started to look for the interesting story about puff pastry. You would not believe it, but for four solid hours I looked through all the heavy books and could not find the piece about puff pastry.

In the end from irritation I got a headache and left the books and came out to watch television. I hardly believe that this is the best medicine for headache. Anyway, I watched for a while and then went back and looked for another half-hour, but without result. Angry I went to bed and read a little, then went to sleep.

The next morning I woke up, still annoyed. I looked at all the books, especially at one which I had suspected the most, and I said aloud: 'I look for you once more and . . .'. In that moment I opened the book – a huge book – exactly on the page where my puff pastry was. Yet it was not called 'puff pastry', but *flaky* pastry. That was the silly reason why I could not find it before.

For Jewish pastries use the same method, the only difference being that instead of butter, use oil. In that case the 'packing' must take the form of ordinary mixing of the oil with the flour.

MILLEFEUILLE GÂTEAU (France)

A few years ago *millefeuille* was very fashionable and very popular. I do not think people could buy *millefeuille* in many places, so we found we had to make much more than I ever reckoned with, but slowly it has become less and less popular. I think this is inevitable as people will always want something new. People in our shop sometimes look round and ask if that is all we have. We never have less than two or three hundred different cakes, buns, pastries and gâteaux. So sometimes I ask the customer 'Oh, what do you want, if there is not enough here?' 'Oh, I only want one or two'. What can we do but smile! I find in any difficulty a smile helps you, and the customer, perhaps, goes out a satisfied one. But let me deal now with the *millefeuille* gâteau.

To make this, roll out puff pastry thinly and cut out six rounds 7 in. in diameter. Prick them well with a fork. Put them on a damp baking sheet and bake them in a hot oven, till they are a light-golden colour. Let them cool and then layer one round with fresh, sugared, whipped cream. Cover the next round of puff pastry with raspberry jam, and alternate the rounds with fresh cream and jam and repeat till the rounds are used up and then cover them with lemon icing.

SAVOURY FLORENTINE

Take $\frac{1}{2}$ lb. puff pastry, roll out very thin. Cut with a 2 in. cutter and wash with the yolk of an egg. Sprinkle some of the centres with a little salt, some with grated cheese, some with caraway seed and some with poppyseed. Bake in a warm oven till golden-brown.

Millefeuille gâteau

VANILLA CUSTARD SLICES

½ lb. puff pastry
crème patissière
raspberry jam
whipped cream
6 oz. (¾ cup) lemon
   icing
pistachio nuts

Roll out the pastry into a rectangle about ¼ in. thick. Cut into strips 2½ × 1 in. Bake in a hot oven 500°F. (261°C.) till pastry has risen and set then lower to 350°F. (177°C.) till it is crisp and golden in colour. When cool sandwich in 4 layers in this way.

Spread 1 layer with the crème patissière and cover with a layer of pastry, spread this with the jam, cover and spread with whipped cream, then put on the fourth layer. Spread the lemon icing on this and decorate with chopped blanched pistachio nuts.

DANISH PASTRY

Danish pastries were introduced into England about fifteen years ago. I went to Copenhagen where I think I visited all the existing bakeries. These are mostly small businesses. The biggest, which holds the Royal Warrant, employed sixteen pastrycooks; the others were all family businesses where parents and children worked together. They were all delightful people, the bakeries were small, spotlessly clean and tidy, but oh my poor legs, they still hurt me because I had to toil up the stairs in the three- or four-storied houses in which the bakeries were housed; all of them showed me round everything very thoroughly and I did this for eight solid days. In each establishment I tasted their products which were extremely good, but must be eaten fresh from the oven: the pastries were sold in small shops throughout the day and one small boy does nothing else but carry the freshly baked pastries to the shops, still on the baking trays, puts them in the window and they are sold then and there.

Every day we make thousands of Danish pastries. I really do not know why we call them Danish as I have never seen pastries like these in Denmark. What we call Danish pastry does not resemble the true rich Danish pastry at all but is more a kind of flaky pastry. However, I give you our recipe and here it is:

$1\frac{1}{2}$ oz. ($2\frac{1}{4}$ cakes) yeast
$2\frac{1}{2}$ oz. (scant $\frac{1}{3}$ cup) sugar
2 eggs
2 tablespoonfuls ($2\frac{1}{2}$ tablespoonfuls) warm milk
8 oz. (1 cup) butter
1 lb. (4 cups) flour
pinch of salt

Put the yeast and sugar into a wooden bowl and mix with a spoon till this is smooth and creamy. Add the eggs, milk and flour, and mix thoroughly. Add 3 oz. butter and a pinch of salt, and work with your hand till the dough is smooth and silky. Cover the bowl with a cloth and put it in a fairly warm place for about 1 hour to rise. The dough should double its size.

Flour a board and roll out the dough and put on it 5 oz. ($\frac{2}{3}$ cup) butter cut in pieces. This should have been cooled in the refrigerator. Fold the dough three times, roll it out again, put in the rest of the butter treated in the same way; now fold the pastry three times again, roll out, fold in three for the second time and let it rest for 20 minutes. Then roll again once more and rest for another 20 minutes. After the third rolling and folding put in the refrigerator for some 20 minutes or so. It must be firm before it is finally rolled out for shaping or cutting. The pastry may be cut and rolled in a variety of ways, stars, envelopes long or round, triangles, buns. Different fillings may be used, custard, almond paste, any dried fruit, cherries, sultanas, raisins, or any combination of fruits. Almonds paste filling is one of the most popular and here is the recipe:

almond paste filling:

3 oz. ($\frac{1}{2}$ cup) ground almonds
1 well-beaten egg
3 tablespoonfuls ($3\frac{3}{4}$ tablespoonfuls) sugar
grated peel of lemon

Mix the almonds with the sugar, work in the egg, then work till it is firm and paste-like. Fill your dough with this. Add a little vanilla flavouring if liked.

Variations

1. *Bun :* you can make several different shapes; cut out a piece and roll it very thin and narrow. Brush it over with melted butter; mix cinnamon, chocolate and sugar together and sprinkle it over the paste. Fold over once and roll up like a Chelsea bun.
2. *Square :* cut out squares 2 in. in diameter, put softened marzipan in the middle and roll up like a *croissant*.
3. *Envelopes :* have ready a pretty stiff custard and place into a pastry which should be cut in a square and then folded like an envelope.
4. *Rectangle :* cut a rectangle 2 in. wide and 3 in. long and pipe apricot jam into the middle and fold over.

You can vary these fillings according to your taste; the important thing is to butter a baking dish and put the pastries on it; mix a little yolk of egg with a little milk and sugar and wash over each pastry. Let them rest for an hour and repeat the washing once more before baking in a medium oven till cooked and nice and golden-brown.

EASTER BUNS (*Kalacs*)

4 lb. (16 cups) flour
1 lb. (1 cup) butter
as much milk as the dough takes
1 lb. (2 cups) sugar
a pinch of salt
10 eggs
2 oz. (3 cakes) yeast

Mix the yeast with a little warm milk and let it rise. Then mix into it the flour, butter and sugar and let it rise again. Mix the beaten eggs with the warm milk and add them bit by bit to the mixture. When it is well blended together leave to rise. Place on a floured pastry board and roll out into strips which can be plaited or left plain. You can make from it small plaited rounds or little buns about 4 in. across. When the dough has sufficiently risen, wash over with a yolk of egg with a little sugar. Let it rise again. Before putting in the oven wash over again with the yolk of egg. You should have ready some hard-boiled eggs painted red with vegetable colouring. When the buns are cooked these eggs are placed in the middle of the buns. One in the middle of small buns and several in the middle of big buns.

RUM BABA

This yeast pastry recipe has an old and romantic origin. It developed from *Guglhupf*. A King of Poland, Stanislaus Leczinski, invented it in 1609. He sprinkled rum and syrup on a *Guglhupf*. My husband invented several variations of this recipe; sponge cakes, rice *soufflets* and pancakes. Whatever he found to be very dry was not just sprinkled with liquid but he would pour on it wine or rum, liqueur or raspberry juice.

King Stanislaus gave to his favourite pastry – at least history claims – the name of the hero of his favourite story in *The Thousand and One Nights* – Ali Baba. Later on, at the beginning of the nineteenth century, it was a great success in Paris. It was then called simply Rum Baba.

1 lb. 14 oz. (7½ cups) sifted flour
1 heaped tablespoonful (1¼ tablespoonfuls) sugar
⅔ oz. (1 cake) yeast
7 eggs
2⅓ fl. oz. (⅓ cup) warm milk
2 oz. (⅓ cup) currants
4 tablespoonfuls (5 tablespoonfuls) sultanas
salt
1 cup rum
3 cups syrup (2 cups sugar, 1½ cups water)

Put the sieved flour into a large wooden bowl, make a well in the middle, put salt and yeast into this well, having diluted the yeast first with warm milk. Add eggs and work the dough with the hands to mix well. Detach those portions of it which stick to the walls of the bowl and add to the mixture; distribute softened butter in small quantities over it. Cover and keep in a warm place till it has doubled its original volume. Then add sugar and salt and knead the paste so that it may absorb the butter. Add the sultanas or currants if used, and mix well. Butter the moulds and fill them up to one-third of their heights. Bake in a hot oven till golden-brown, take it out and allow to cool before turning out of the mould.

Pour syrup over the cake, then sprinkle with any liqueur – rum, kirsch or anything you like. The syrup is prepared by boiling rum, sugar and water at 220°F. (120°C.) till it thickens. The baked and cooled Baba has to be soaked in this syrup for 5 or 6 minutes. Then take out and let it drain on a wire mesh, and brush it over with apricot or some other jam and decorate it with fresh whipped cream or fruit (e.g. pineapple) or both.

I can recommend this pastry: it is very useful. It can be made in several shapes, large or small, individual ones for six, eight or ten people, baked in 'baba rings'.

CHOUX PASTRY

Choux paste is perhaps the best known of all paste or pastries. I cannot tell you for how long choux paste or pastry has been made; it is very easy to make, very light. It is suitable for the most delicate stomach. You can make many kinds of pastries from it including éclairs and chocolate buns. It can be filled with fresh cream, *crème patissière*, vanilla cream or chocolate cream. It is also very good filled with an enormous variety of savoury fillings.

I personally like choux pastry just as it is without any cream and I like it when it is hard and crispy. To make choux pastry is easy, but you have to be precise as in nearly everything else. My experience is that short-cuts do not help, but rather hinder because they often lead to double work in the end.

CHOUX PASTE (1)
4 fl. oz. (½ cup) water
3 oz. (6 tablespoonfuls) butter
pinch of salt
3¾ oz. (scant cup) flour
3 eggs

Bring the water, butter and salt to the boil. When it starts boiling place the pan at the side of the stove and add your flour, little by little. Beat the mixture till smooth. When the paste leaves the sides of the pan the flour is cooked. Now beat the 3 eggs together, and when the paste is cold slowly add the eggs, beating all the time. If your eggs are exceptionally large do not add them all as you must not make the mixture too liquid. Continue beating till the paste is smooth and shiny.

Place the mixture into a forcing bag with a plain tube and pipe in any of the following three ways. (1) Finger shape for éclairs, about 3 in. long. (2) Round for bun shapes, about 2 in. diameter, and (3) very small rounds about the size of a penny for profiterolles.

Take care not to open the oven door for at least the first 8 minutes of cooking. If you want very large buns you can put a deep baking tin over the top of them. Choux paste should be baked at a temperature of 475°F. (247°C.).

To make choux paste is very easy, but it needs experience, so please be patient. If you beat it too much it will be spoiled, so be careful and beat it just right. Again if it is overworked the paste will not rise. Bake till it is hard and crisp; it is lovely when it is fresh. When your paste is smooth and the right consistency, pour it into a forcing bag with a plain tube. Butter and flour a baking sheet and press out from your forcing bag all kinds of shapes. You can also shape tiny balls, which when filled will be profiterolles: they can be very decorative when built up as a tower with a little burnt sugar to hold them together; but of course, before you build up your tower each ball must be filled with fresh cream, chocolate cream, vanilla cream, etc. You can shape your choux paste into long fingers which is the éclair shape; or into rounds, the bun shape. It can also be shaped into a ring about 7–8 in. diameter which makes a very nice St Honoré gâteau (*see* p. 131). This is also a very decorative sweet for your table. The profiterolle tower makes a lovely centre-piece on a buffet and you can decorate it with caramel sugar or serve with raspberry ice cream, or you can pour chocolate sauce on it. This gâteau is also traditionally used as a wedding cake in France.

You can fill both éclairs and buns with a savoury filling; a very tasty one is sardines mixed with anchovy. They can also be filled with chopped ham or mushrooms; indeed any meat or vegetable is suitable so long as it is well seasoned. The top of savoury choux paste may be brushed with Bovril. Now I give you three more choux paste recipes; perhaps they are even easier than the previous one. In any case, you may take your choice.

CHOUX PASTE (2)

4 oz. (1 cup) flour
pinch of salt
3 oz. (6 tablespoonfuls) butter
6 fl. oz. (¾ cup) water
3 eggs

Sieve the flour with a pinch of salt. Leave it on one side. Place the butter and water in a heavy saucepan and put on a low heat. When the butter is melted, bring up to the boil. Then draw the pan to the side of the stove, cool and slowly add the flour. Beat vigorously till smooth. You will know when the flour is cooked as the mixture will no longer stick to the sides of the pan. Beating all the time, slowly add the eggs. The finished paste should be smooth and shiny and should retain its shape.

BAKERY, CAKES AND SIMPLE CONFECTIONERY

CHOUX PASTE (3)

6 oz. ($\frac{3}{4}$ cup) butter
$\frac{1}{2}$ pint ($1\frac{1}{4}$ cups) water
a little sugar
a little salt
6 oz. ($1\frac{1}{2}$ cups) flour
5 eggs

Boil the butter in the water with the sugar and salt. When boiling vigorously, add the flour and cook while mixing with a wooden spoon. It is essential that this paste is well cooked. Allow to cool for a short while and then add the eggs. The eggs must be added singly and well beaten in before the next one is added. The paste can now be used for either éclairs or buns, and these, when piped onto the trays, must be baked in a warm oven.

CHOUX PASTE FILLINGS

You can fill the éclairs or buns with fresh cream, fresh cream flavoured with coffee or, alternatively, you can put chocolate in the fresh cream and fill the éclairs with this. Profiterolles are mostly filled with *crème patissière*. Here are two recipes:

CRÈME PATISSIÈRE (1)

$\frac{1}{4}$ oz. (1 teaspoonful)
cornflour
$\frac{1}{2}$ pint ($1\frac{1}{4}$ cups) cream
$\frac{1}{2}$ pint ($1\frac{1}{4}$ cups) milk
4 yolks of eggs
$1\frac{3}{4}$ oz. (scant $\frac{1}{4}$ cup)
sugar
$\frac{1}{2}$ vanilla pod scraped out

Mix the cornflour with the milk and sugar and boil till it starts to thicken. Remove from the heat and add the egg yolks, one at a time, stirring all the time for about 4 or 5 minutes. Mix in the vanilla pod and put it on the heat again, stirring all the time. Continue cooking till the mixture is thick. Add the cream when the mixture is cold.

CRÈME PATISSIÈRE (2)

2 yolks of eggs
2 oz. (scant $\frac{1}{2}$ cup)
icing sugar
$\frac{1}{2}$ oz. (2 teaspoonfuls)
cornflour
$\frac{1}{2}$ pint ($1\frac{1}{4}$ cups) milk
1 white of egg
a little vanilla pod

Cream the yolks with the sugar; this must be done thoroughly. Add the flour slowly with a little of the milk and heat the mixture. Heat the remainder of the milk, pour it very carefully on the yolks of eggs and then put the whole pot on the heat and stir all the time and bring it slowly to the boil, remove it from the heat and whip the white of egg very stiffly and add a quarter of the cream in a basin and mix in the white of egg, little by little. Return the whole mixture to the pan and cook very slowly for a few minutes stirring very quickly. After removing it from the heat, let it cool.

SHORT PASTRY OR
SHORTCRUST PASTRY

Short pastry is one of the most useful pastries you can make. It keeps uncooked in the refrigerator for a few days, or, cooked, it may be kept for a fortnight. You can make pastries, petits fours, pies, tartlets and a variety of savouries from this pastry. Short pastry if it is carefully made, can be very good and very pleasant. I prefer to make it with butter, but you can make very successful pastry with margarine or with one of the new vegetable shortening. If the weather is cold, rub the butter or margarine well into the flour with your finger-tips. You have to be careful not to work it into a greasy cake or into lumps. If in warm weather the fat used is too soft, it is better to place it in the basin with other ingredients such as eggs and sugar, and mix well before adding the flour. The moistening to use depends on the kind of pastry you want to make. For some purposes, water alone is used; for a richer pastry use eggs instead. In making the dough it is not necessary to rub it too hard and too much, as you will then produce a very greasy pastry. This is a common fault. The ingredients are made smooth and clear by pinching. There is no need to rub the fat into the flour, no need to rub it hard. It is very easy to make short pastry too wet and this is also a common fault. Here are three shortcrust or short pastry recipes for you to try:

SHORT PASTRY (1)

1 lb. (4 cups) flour
4 oz. (½ cup) butter
1 egg
4 oz. (½ cup) lard
2 oz. (¼ cup) caster sugar
¼ pint (⅓ pint) cold water

The method is as above. An alternative way is to cut the butter or lard in small pieces and mix with a fork. The whole operation should be done as quickly and lightly and with everything as cool as possible.

SHORT PASTRY (2)

1 lb. (4 cups) flour
3 yolks of eggs
8 oz. (1 cup) butter
¼ pint (⅓ pint) cold water

Rub the butter into the sifted flour. Make a hole in the mixture and add the yolks of eggs and water and mix together. Store the pastry in a cool place for an hour or two. This pastry is very suitable for rich pies.

SHORT PASTRY (3)

1 lb. (4 cups) flour
10 oz. (1¼ cups) butter
1½ oz. (3 tablespoonfuls)
  caster sugar
1 egg
4 fl. oz. (⅓ pint) water

Rub the butter lightly into the flour, sugar and water with the finger-tips. Beat the egg slightly with the water which should be very cold. Quickly mix into a paste which should be as dry as possible but still workable. Roll out on a floured board; use as required. The oven should be about 400–420°F. (205–216°C.) depending on the recipe.

FRENCH PÂTE

10 oz. (2½ cups) flour
4 oz. (½ cup) unsalted
  butter
1 egg
milk

Sieve the flour into a bowl. Make a well in the centre and add the milk, salt, butter and egg, and gently stir in the flour. Knead this till it is silky and then put it into a refrigerator for 1½–2 hours before using. This is good for anything savoury, pie, or savoury tarts.

FRENCH FLAN PASTRY

4 oz. (1 cup) flour
2 oz. (¼ cup) caster
  sugar
2 oz. (¼ cup) butter
2 yolks of eggs
vanilla

Mix the flour with a pinch of salt on the pastry board. Make a small well in the centre and place the other ingredients in it. Work in the butter, sugar, eggs and vanilla together and quickly make a paste. Roll out thinly and use as required.

CHEESE PASTRY

8 oz. (2 cups) flour
4 oz. (½ cup) butter
4 oz. (1 cup) grated
  Gruyère and
  Parmesan cheese
1 yolk of egg
salt
a little black pepper
a little red pepper
a little milk

Work together carefully the flour, salt and pepper and butter. Rub the butter with your finger-tips. The mixture should look like breadcrumbs. Don't over-work it, especially in the warm weather, as it easily becomes heavy. Add the cheese and stir gently with a fork. Mix the yolk of egg with a little milk. Add the other ingredients and mix carefully to a firm dough. Place on a floured board and knead lightly till it is smooth. Put the dough into a refrigerator for 30–35 minutes before rolling out. Bake in a moderate oven, 370°F. (189°C.). Use for savoury biscuits and tarts, cheese straws, canapés.

HAZELNUT PASTRY

9 oz. (2¼ cups) flour
6 oz. (¾ cup) butter
3½ oz. (scant ½ cup) sugar
3½ oz. (½ cup) ground
   hazelnuts
a little vanilla
red currant jam
icing sugar

Mix together the flour, butter, sugar, ground hazelnuts and vanilla. Roll out thinly and cut out small rounds. Bake till nice and golden brown at about 350°F. (177°C.). Then stick 2 rounds together with red currant jam and dust over with icing sugar, flavoured with vanilla.

APPLE TART

I have never in my life made so many apple tarts, flans, turnovers and pies as here in England. Except for the famous *Apfel Strudel* and apple slices, we never baked anything else with apples in Hungary. Just lately one of our new Scottish pastrycooks made a very successful apple tart. Here is the recipe.

8 oz. (2 cups) flour
2 oz. (¼ cup) butter
1 lb. cooking apples
3½ oz. (scant ½ cup)
   sugar
½ pint (1¼ cups) cream

Cover a 7 in. tin with a pastry which is made of 6 oz. (¾ cup) flour and 2½ oz. butter. Peel the apples and cut them into thin rings. Arrange them around the tin so that they overlap. Try to make it nice and neat. Cover all the pastry, putting the apple slices round and round. Put the tin in the oven at about 400°F. and bake it for 10–12 minutes. Meanwhile mix the remaining flour with the sugar in a bowl and add to it the cream, mix it and pour it over the apple and lower the oven temperature to about 330°F. (160°C.) and bake for another 10 or 15 minutes.

BAKEWELL TART

½ lb. shortcrust pastry
raspberry jam
2 oz. (⅓ cup) ground
   almonds
2 oz. (¼ cup) butter
2 oz. (¼ cup) caster
   sugar
1 egg
almond essence

Line a flat dish with the pastry and place a good layer of jam on the bottom. Cream the butter and sugar, add the egg, almonds and a few drops of essence and beat well. Spread this mixture over the jam. Bake in a hot oven for 30 minutes. You can serve this either hot or cold and I promise you it is delicious.

BRAMBLE TARTLETS

4 oz. (1 cup) flour
pinch of salt
scant pinch of baking
  powder
3 oz. (⅓ cup) butter
2 oz. (2 tablespoonfuls)
  sugar
1 yolk of egg
2 fl. oz. (¼ cup) milk
½ lb. (1 cup) sweetened
  steamed brambles
  (blackberries)
¼ pint (⅓ pint) cream

Sieve flour, salt and baking powder into a bowl. Rub the butter into this and add the sugar. Beat the yolk of egg with milk and stir into the flour, to make a smooth dough. Thinly line tartlet tins with the dough, prick well all over and bake in a hot oven 450°F. (233°C.) till golden-brown. Cool on a wire rack then fill with brambles and decorate with whipped sweetened cream.

Blueberries can be used to fill the same tartlets.

CONGRESS TARTS

These are very pleasant tarts and simple to make.

shortcrust pastry
8 oz. (1 cup) caster sugar
4 oz. (⅔ cup) ground
  almonds
3 whites of eggs
1 oz. (⅙ cup) ground rice
a little granulated
  sugar
raspberry jam

To prepare the filling mix all the dry ingredients together carefully, adding the whites of eggs. Then beat this up a little with a spoon or spatula.

Line the mould with the short pastry and into the bottom drop a small amount of raspberry jam. Then fill it three-quarters full with the almond mixture. Put 2 strips of thin short pastry across the top of each Congress tart forming a cross and dust it with granulated sugar. Bake in a cool oven. These tarts should have a rich surface when finished.

JAM TARTS

Jam tarts and fruit pies and tarts are very popular. The jam should be a bright colour and should be of good quality. It should be thick, otherwise it boils out in the cooking. If the jam is too thick, you can thin it with a little water. For jam tarts roll out the pastry to ⅙ in. thick. Cut out with an oval cutter or a round one – whichever you prefer. Place each piece in a patty tray and seal down with your fingers, making a pattern round the edge. It should be a quarter of an inch higher than the mould. Prick the bottom of it lightly with a pointed knife and fill with jam and bake in a hot oven.

Another method of making tarts is to cut the pastry with a crinkled cutter and thumb up the edge before adding the jam. For variety, small diamonds or strips can be baked separately on a baking sheet. When cooked these should be placed in the centre of the tarts.

It is, perhaps, ridiculous that somebody can be very sentimental about a pastry and about a jam tart. But I am very, very sentimental about this special pastry because many years ago one of Sir Winston Churchill's secretaries told me how much Sir Winston liked jam tarts. She told me that it was his favourite pastry. It is a very plain pastry but it had to be perfect if it was to be made for him. He was a perfectionist in every way and in everything. The next best would never do for him. Once, another secretary told me that Churchill was dictating to him and suddenly he stopped because he had not got the word he wanted to use and he asked the secretary to go away. At 4 o'clock in the morning the secretary was called in and jubilantly he told him that he had found the right word! He was just as precise about his food as well. His favourite pastry was jam tart and I started to experiment with this simple, very English pastry. I made several shortcrust pastries and looked for the best existing jam which I must admit was not always a home-made one.

JAM TARTS (1)

4 oz. (1 cup) flour
2 oz. (¼ cup) butter
a pinch of salt
½ oz. (1 tablespoonful) sugar
a little milk
jam

Rub in the fat to all the dry ingredients, add the milk and allow to rest for 2½ hours before rolling out. Cut in rounds, press into tart trays, and fill with jam. Bake in a hot oven for about 15 minutes. Serve hot or cold.

JAM TARTS (2)

I tried a new short pastry recipe recently. I remembered suddenly that my mother made a short pastry with hard-boiled egg yolks. Jam tarts with a difference!

8 oz. (2 cups) flour
4 oz. (½ cup) butter
2 oz. (¼ cup) sugar
2 hard-boiled yolks of egg
jam

Mix all these ingredients together. It makes mixing easier if the butter is softened a little before use. Mix thoroughly and pack in greaseproof paper and put in the refrigerator to rest for a few hours – or overnight. Roll out thin and cut into rounds. Press into tartlet moulds and fill well with jam. Bake for 20 minutes in a moderate oven about 370°F. (189°C.).

A selection of tarts: 1. Congress tart; 2. jam tarts; 3. fruit tarts; (*centre*) lemon curd tart

MADEIRA TARTS

Use a short pastry as given before. Fill with any mixture – jam or fruit or almond paste.

filling (almond paste):

8 oz. (1 cup) butter
8 oz. (1 cup) caster sugar
5 eggs
6 oz. ($\frac{3}{4}$ cup) flour
2 oz. ($\frac{1}{3}$ cup) ground almonds
4 oz. (1 cup) finely chopped lemon peel
vanilla sugar

Prepare the short pastry for the bottom as before, pricking with a pointed knife, and fill with the above mixture. When baked add a little flavour with vanilla sugar. The vanilla sugar is prepared by blending the vanilla pod with the sugar and then putting it in a sieve and dusting the tarts. If you can obtain it, you can grind the vanilla in a grinder. Before you use vanilla in this way, you have to test it for flavour.

MINCE PIES

You can make these with either puff pastry or short pastry, they both taste very good.

pastry
mincemeat

Roll out the pastry and cut half into rounds. Then roll out the second half a little thinner and cut into rounds to use for the bottom of the pies. Place the thin rounds on a greased baking sheet or line tartlet tins with them. Then put as much mincemeat as possible in the centre of the round; wet the edges with cold water, place the other thicker round on top and press the edges together. Make a hole in the top of the pie with a skewer to let the steam escape and glaze with some milk or yolk of egg. For puff pastry bake in a hot oven, 475°F. (252°C.) or short pastry, 450°F. (233°C.) for about 20 minutes.

PECAN PIE (U.S.A.)

I first ate pecan pie in an American hotel, which was really a road house; the food was excellent and the restaurant good though very homely. After a very good dinner they served an excellent pecan pie. I give you the recipe for this pie, but remember, it is extremely rich.

pastry:
1 lb. (4 cups) flour
salt
4 oz. ($\frac{1}{2}$ cup) butter
4 oz. ($\frac{1}{2}$ cup) lard or
 vegetable shortening
6 fl. oz. ($\frac{3}{4}$ cup) cold
 water
filling:
3 eggs
4 oz. ($\frac{1}{2}$ cup) sugar
salt
8 fl. oz. ($\frac{3}{4}$ cup) golden
 syrup or corn syrup
$\frac{1}{2}$ vanilla pod
8 oz. (1 cup) broken
 pecan nuts
8 oz. (1 cup) whipped
and sweetened double
cream

Mix the salt with the flour; rub in the butter and lard; mix well. Work till the shortening is evenly mixed and the mixture is smooth. Moisten the dough with a little water and make a ball from this dough. Wrap in wax paper and place in a refrigerator for an hour. This will make one or two pies.

Beat the eggs slightly, mix thoroughly with the other ingredients. Line a pie dish with the pastry, pour in the filling and bake for 45 minutes in a slow oven, 300°F. (149°C.). Cover with a layer of whipped cream and garnish with halves of pecan nuts.

RED CURRANT FLAN

4 oz. (½ cup) butter
6 oz. (1½ cups) flour
2 oz. (¼ cup) sugar
little lemon juice
filling:
red currants
2 whites of eggs
4 oz. (½ cup) caster
sugar

Make a pastry: rub the butter into the flour then add the sugar and lemon juice. Line a buttered and floured rectangular flan tin with it. Prick it well all over and bake in a moderate oven till light brown. When baked and still hot cover thickly with red currants and sprinkle with sugar. Whisk the whites of eggs till stiff then whisk in 2 oz. caster sugar and fold in the other 2 oz. sugar. Pile this mixture over the red currants and bake in a cool oven till the meringue top has set. Cut into slices when cold and serve.

STRAWBERRY TARTS

4 oz. (1 cup) flour
2 oz. (¼ cup) butter
2 oz. (¼ cup) sugar
2 yolks of eggs
a little vanilla
filling:
½ lb. (1 cup) cream
cheese
a little sugar
a little fresh cream
small strawberries
¼ pint (⅓ pint) red
currant jelly

Put the flour on a pastry board and rub the other ingredients into it. Add a very little salt and work well and quickly. When it is ready put it in a teacloth or in greaseproof paper and put in the refrigerator for 1 hour.

Roll out very thin and cut into nice round pieces and line 2 in. tart moulds. Bake in a medium oven, 350°F. (177°C.) till nice and golden-brown. Cool.

Add the sugar to the cream cheese to taste. If the cheese is a little dry, add fresh cream.

When the tarts are cold fill with the cream cheese and then on the top place small strawberries. Beat the red currant jelly well till it is smooth and heat a little, but do not let it boil. Cover the strawberries with it.

VICTORIA TARTS

short pastry
4 oz. (1⅓ cups) cake
crumbs
2 oz. (⅔ cup) bread-
crumbs
2 oz. (⅓ cup) ground
almonds
2 oz. (½ cup) peel
3 yolks of eggs
2 fl. oz. (¼ cup) milk

Mix the dry ingredients together with the yolks and sufficient milk to make into a paste consistency, so it can be passed through a forcing bag. Line some small patty moulds with short pastry. Cut out with a plain cutter. Fill each mould three-parts full with the above mixture. This filling is known as frangipane. Sprinkle with a little shredded coconut on the top. Bake in a moderate oven of about 370°F. (189°C.). Remove from the oven and when they have cooled, dust over with cocoa or chocolate powder and vanilla sugar.

VIENNESE HALF MOON PASTRY

This recipe comes from a friend in Chicago. I tasted it in her house, I like it, therefore, I pass it on to you.

1 cup (1¼ cups) butter
1¾ oz. (scant ¼ cup) sugar
8 oz. (2 cups) flour
6 oz. (1 cup) ground almonds (unblanched)
½ vanilla pod, scraped out

Cream the butter and add to it all the ingredients and go on stirring till it is creamy and silky. Make into half moon shapes, like little crescents; put them onto a buttered baking sheet in nice rows, not very near each other. Bake them for 30–35 minutes in a slow oven about 280–300°F. (137–149°C.). When they are cooked dust over with icing sugar.

MISCELLANEOUS PASTRY RECIPES

CHESTNUT PURÉE RINGS (Hungary)

¾ oz. (1 cake) yeast
2½ oz. (scant ⅓ cup) sugar
9 oz. (2¼ cups) flour
9 oz. (1⅛ cups) butter
1 yolk of egg
cream
milk
chestnut cream:
1 lb. sieved chestnuts
1 oz. (2 tablespoonfuls) butter
2 oz. (¼ cup) sugar
1 tablespoonful (1¼ tablespoonfuls) each rum and cream

Mix the yeast with a little of the sugar and a very little warm milk and flour; let it rise in a warm place. When it has risen add the remaining flour, the butter, sugar, the yolk of egg and as much cream as it takes to make a dough soft enough to manipulate easily. Mix well together till it becomes very smooth. Then put it on a pastry board and let it rest for 30 minutes or so. While you wait for the dough to rise make the cream. Add the butter, sugar, rum and cream to the chestnuts. Mix all these very well. Now roll out the rested pastry as thin as a match. Cut out 3 in. squares and put in the middle of each a good tablespoonful of the chestnut cream, roll them up and make them into rings. Arrange them on a greased and floured baking sheet, wash over with milk or yolk of egg and bake in a medium oven for 16–18 minutes.

CINNAMON BALLS

Just a very simple little pastry which can be very useful when unexpected guests arrive because it keeps well for days and costs very little to make.

3 whites of eggs
8 oz. (1 cup) caster
sugar
6 oz. (1 cup) ground
almonds
ground cinnamon to
taste

Whip the whites of eggs with half the caster sugar till very firm indeed. Fold into the meringue the ground almonds, the rest of the caster sugar and the cinnamon. Roll this into balls – small balls I would say, about the size of golf balls – and place on a greased and floured baking tin and bake for 20 minutes at 350°F. (177°C.). When it is baked roll each one in icing sugar.

COFFEE PISCHKOTA (Hungary)

One of the most interesting of pastries which is neither a true pastry, nor a petit four. It looks delightful and is delicious with tea, coffee, or an ice cream. It is not difficult to make, but you do have to be familiar with the method. With practice, I'm sure you will master it and give your family and friends pleasure when you serve them.

1¼ lb. (2½ cups) sugar
Nescafé (mixed with a
little water)
3 whites of eggs
7 oz. (1¾ cups) flour

Boil the sugar and coffee powder with a little water to a temperature of 280°F. (138°C.). While the sugar and coffee are being brought up to the right temperature, whip the whites of eggs till stiff. Add the boiled sugar and coffee and gently stir in 7 oz. flour till thoroughly mixed. Pipe the mixture onto well greased and floured trays. They can be piped in two shapes; either in the shape of dogs' bones, 3 in. long which are left plain, or in round 'dots', 1 or 1½ in. in diameter in the centre of which half a walnut is placed. Now put the *pischkotas* on the tray in a warm, dry place till they develop a thick, dry crust. Finally bake them – still on the trays – at 300°F. (149°C.) for 15-20 minutes.

CHOCOLATE PISCHKOTA

This can be made in the above manner, except that cocoa powder is sieved with the flour and sugar is added, without the coffee.

CSÖRÖGE FÁNK (Hungary)

A charming lady (if she does not mind, I call her a friend of mine) is a great social worker. She and her husband are busy twenty-four hours a day doing good.

One day, she came to me in great excitement and with a long sheet of paper, full of writing. She had on hand an important religious function and on that religious evening they had to have a certain pastry. 'The recipe is here', she said, 'but it is terribly complicated. . . . I am very sorry to bother you', she added in her very modest way, 'but everyone tells me that you are the only one who perhaps can do it'.

She is tiny, fragile, delightful. I would help her with all my might, if I had any might at all. Anyway, I would do anything for her, if I could. I took the recipe and started to read it: half-American, half-English, it really sounded terrifying. Then, a little bit frightened, I told her, 'I must study it a little more'.

I read it again and found that it was the most simple, very common, modest little pastry that every Hungarian peasant woman – any woman – can do. We used to have it at home quite often. I don't believe that any housewife used a recipe for it, but I give it to you because it is really pleasant to eat, and very easy to make. Perhaps not very cheap.

10 oz. (2½ cups) flour
6 yolks of eggs
1 pinch of salt
1 tablespoonful (1¼
tablespoonfuls) sugar
1 tablespoonful (1¼
tablespoonfuls) thick
cream
1 tablespoonful (1¼
tablespoonfuls) rum
oil for frying
vanilla-flavoured icing
sugar
apricot jam

Mix all the ingredients, except the icing sugar, jam and oil, together and knead into a soft dough. It should not be hard and should not be particularly soft; I'm afraid you have to get the feeling for it. Shape into 2 balls and cover them with a teacloth and let them rest for 20 or 25 minutes. Flour the pastry board and roll the balls out into the thickness of a match. With a saw-edged knife, cut out long strips and squares; make bows out of the long strips and cut the squares in two.

Put oil into a large frying pan (use corn oil which has no flavour and no smell) heat it and when it is warm enough, drop as many cut pieces into it as will swim easily. Let them cook till they are golden-brown, then turn them onto the other side; take them out and place them on a sheet of blotting paper or tissue paper. Have ready vanilla-flavoured icing sugar, dust over the pastries generously with it and serve them hot, with hot apricot jam.

FARSANGI FÁNK (Hungary)

You call this a doughnut here, which really hurts me, because *farsangi fánk* is much more than just a dessert after dinner or lunch. It is one of the foods which you have to make, observing the principle of 'cooking for love'. You should only make it for people whom you love and only those people should eat it who love it. In Hungary this dessert was treated with great reverence. I give you the recipe.

½ pint (1¼ cups) milk
1 oz. (1½ cakes) yeast
1 lb. (4 cups) flour
6 yolks of eggs
2 oz. (4 tablespoonfuls) melted butter (lukewarm)
2 oz. (¼ cup) sugar
1 tablespoonful (1¼ tablespoonfuls) rum
1 pinch of salt

Warm the milk and dissolve the yeast and sugar; sieve the flour, add and keep in a warm place for some hours. Add the other main ingredients. Mix till smooth. The dough should not be too hard or too soft. You can adjust it with a little more flour or a little more milk. Put it in a warm place and cover it with a cloth and a small blanket and leave it to rise for 40 minutes. Then put on a floured pastry board, roll out into finger-thickness and cut out with a 3 or 4 in. round cutter. Leave it to rest again for 10 minutes. In the meantime put oil or lard into a very large pot and heat it. When it is hot, put as many round pastries into it as there is room for and cover with a lid. Let them deep fry for 4 or 5 minutes till golden-brown, take off the lid, turn the pastries and let them become golden-brown on the other side, this time without the lid on. Lift them out one by one and place on blotting or tissue paper, dust them over with sugar, and serve them with strawberry, raspberry or apricot jam. If your doughnut is a success, it will be very light and have a white ring round it.

MADELEINES (France)

One of the pleasantest light good little pastries in cake form which is very kind to any delicate stomach and I think, very nourishing as well.

4 oz. (½ cup) butter
4 oz. (½ cup) caster sugar
2 eggs
4 oz. (⅔ cup) ground almonds
2 oz. (½ cup) flour

Cream together the butter and caster sugar till very light and creamy. Add the eggs one at a time, cream the mixture and stir it very well, till very light and fluffy. Now very slowly add the ground almonds and flour. You will need the traditional *madeleine* moulds; they can be very small for petits fours and double size for pastries. Pour the mixture into these moulds which should be very well buttered and floured. Bake for 20–25 minutes at 300°F. (149°C.) depending on the size.

JAPANESE PASTRY

Japanese pastry is very well known in this country and very much liked. I like it too. I don't remember whether I have known it in my old country, but I confess, I am pleased to know this good and modest pastry and I am even more pleased to hand over to you the recipe.

You can make Japanese pastry with any ground nuts, but according to our recipe the most successful mixture combines ground almonds and hazelnuts. I would suggest three-quarters of hazelnuts to one-quarter of almonds as the best proportions.

1 pint (1¼ pints) whites of eggs
1 lb. 14 oz. (3¾ cups) sugar
a small pinch of cream of tartar
1¼ lb. (3 cups) mixed ground almonds and ground hazelnuts
4 oz. (½ cup) cornflour
6 oz. (¾ cup) sugar

Whisk the whites of eggs with the cream of tartar until very firm and stiff. Then slowly add 1½ lb. sugar; stir this till you have a stiff meringue. Then add the nuts, the cornflour and the remaining sugar. Mix these all together. Grease and lightly flour a baking tin and pipe small heaps on it with a plain tube. If you are not experienced mark the floured tray first with a cutter and then pipe on top of these. Then bake at 320–350°F. (160–177°C.) till crisp. Use for the piping a plain ½ in. tube. Be careful not to over-bake as it ruins the flavour of the nuts. Remove from the oven and cool on a wire tray before finishing the biscuits. You can use a wide variety of flavours. I like coffee butter cream best. Put a generous layer of the cream on one biscuit and top it with another one. Spread more butter cream on the top and round the sides and then roll the whole biscuit in roasted or flaked nuts. On top of each one put a nob of chocolate or a whole roasted hazelnut.

MERINGUES

Meringue has been used in pastry making for a very long time; it can be flavoured with anything and can be very decorative and cheap.

4 whites of eggs
9 oz. (scant 2 cups) icing sugar
lemon juice or grated lemon rind
a little vanilla pod

Put the whites of eggs and sugar with the vanilla pod, the lemon juice or grated lemon skin in a copper bowl and whip over a gentle heat till it is thick. Bake at a very low temperature on oiled trays. You can use this mixture for meringues, marron baskets or any shape you like, filling them with whipped fresh cream or fruit.

Meringues and pastries: 1. meringues; 2. vol-au-vent cases; 3 and 4 chocolate éclairs

BANANA MERINGUE TART (Brazil)

1 lb. shortcrust pastry
6 bananas
2 oz. ($\frac{1}{4}$ cup) butter
6 oz. ($\frac{3}{4}$ cup) caster
  sugar
1 level teaspoonful
  ($1\frac{1}{4}$ teaspoonfuls)
  cinnamon
3 eggs

Peel the bananas and cut into long strips. Warm the butter in a frying-pan and gently fry the banana strips till they are golden brown. Line a flan tin with short-crust pastry and cover the pastry with the bananas arranged carefully in rows. Sprinkle with the cinnamon mixed with a spoonful of the sugar. Melt 2 oz. of the sugar in a double saucepan, or over a saucepan half filled with water, add the yolks of eggs slightly beaten, and cook, stirring all the time till the mixture thickens. Pour over the bananas. Whisk the whites of eggs till stiff, fold in the remaining sugar and cover the egg mixture with this meringue. Cook in a slow oven for 30–35 minutes. Leave till cool and sprinkle with sugar.

LEMON MERINGUE PIE

short pastry:

5 oz. (1¼ cups) flour

a little sugar

2 oz. (¼ cup) butter

1 yolk of egg

filling:

1 oz. (1 tablespoonful) cornflour

a little cream

½ pint (1¼ cups) milk

2 yolks of eggs

grated rind and juice of 1 lemon

sugar to taste

2 whites of eggs

Make in the ordinary way and allow to rest for at least 30 minutes. Line a flan ring and bake till nearly cooked. Remove and allow to cool. Then fill with the following mixture.

Blend the cornflour with a little cream. Heat the milk and pour it into the creamed cornflour: add the yolks of eggs beaten a little, the lemon rind and juice. Return to the heat, cook till thick and pour onto the baked flan.

Whip the whites very stiffly and then add to them a tablespoonful of sugar. Put the whites of eggs on top of the flan covering the filling. Dust over generously with icing sugar. Put in a cool oven for 10–12 minutes.

MIRLITON (France)

Very many years ago. I had a French pastrycook who stayed with me a long time. He made the most wonderfully light French pastries. One of these pastries is *mirliton*. Here is the recipe:

shortcrust pastry

filling:

7 oz. (scant cup) sugar

2 eggs

some orange peel

the juice of half a lemon

4 oz. (⅔ cup) ground almonds

Line small tart moulds with the pastry used for jam tarts (*see* p. 159). Cut out rounds with a fancy cutter. Press well down and prick with a pin. Fill with the following mixture.

Beat the sugar and the eggs together till creamy and then add the orange peel and lemon juice. Add the ground almonds and then fill the tartlets with the mixture. Dust over with icing sugar and bake in a medium-hot oven till nice and golden-brown.

OTHELLO or INDIANA

One of the best of pastries. I will give here the recipe but it is only for the very ambitious cook; it is quite a task to make these lovely-looking and delicious pastries. Even for my very able mother it was too big an effort, so she left it to the experts and bought hers from a patisserie. She ordered them specially for great occasions and she only liked the small ones. We agreed they looked very elegant but my brothers and I cared little about elegance – we liked the big ones filled with a lot of beautiful whipped cream, then so many years ago so much better than it is now. Can it be that I have a quite different appetite now? Never mind, it is still a lovely pastry and you just have it and I am sure you will enjoy it. When you make Indiana take a medium-strength flour. Here is the recipe:

6 eggs
3 oz. (full $\frac{1}{3}$ cup) sugar
3 oz. ($\frac{3}{4}$ cup) flour
1 oz. (1 tablespoonful)
  cornflour
a pinch of cream of
  tartar

Separate the eggs. Whisk the whites and the sugar to a very firm meringue. Beat the yolks separately very thoroughly; then slowly and carefully fold in the flour. Then add the cornflour with the cream of tartar. Finally add the meringue mixture. You have to be careful not to allow the meringue to stand or it will collapse. Put on the baking tin a sheet of greaseproof paper; put the mixture into a piping bag with a plain $\frac{1}{2}$ in. tube and pipe blobs of the Indiana mixture. The oven should be heated to 400–420°F. (204–216°C.). Put in the baking sheet, but leave the oven door a little open otherwise the Indiana will collapse. After 5 or 6 minutes touch to see whether it is firm enough – it is very difficult to tell the exact time. When the Indianas are firm quickly and carefully remove the paper and divide the pastries; trim the bottom so that they will stand firmly and scoop a little of the centre out, leave to become cold and fill with whipped cream; be generous with the fresh cream.

You can make three kinds of Indianas; for the first you put sweetened whipped cream; this one is the one which you put the top on and mask with a little boiling apricot jam; the second one you add a little cochineal to the whipped cream and flavour it with rum. The third one has whipped cream flavoured with strong coffee or Nescafé. The white cream one should be covered with chocolate fondant; the rum and pink cream should be covered with coffee-flavoured fondant.

Very fussy people cover the whole Indiana with fondant and then make a little hole in the bottom of the cake and force the whipped cream into the middle with a piping bag.

RICHMOND MAIDS OF HONOUR

4 oz. ($\frac{1}{2}$ cup) butter
4 oz. ($\frac{1}{2}$ cup) caster sugar
4 oz. ($\frac{1}{4}$ cup) cottage cheese
juice and grated rind of 1 lemon
1 oz. (3 tablespoonfuls) ground almonds
2 teaspoonfuls ($2\frac{1}{2}$ teaspoonfuls) flour
1 beaten egg
a very little nutmeg
$\frac{1}{2}$ lb. puff pastry

Cream the butter and sugar together and gradually blend in the cheese, which has first been sieved, lemon rind and juice, the ground almonds, the flour, the beaten egg and the nutmeg if desired. Roll out the puff pastry very thinly and line 18 tartlet tins with it. Divide the mixture between the pastry-lined tins. Bake in a hot oven, 400°F. (205°C.) for 15–20 minutes, till nice and golden-brown.

STRUDEL (Austria)

In Hungary, you would not find a house, small or large, rich or poor, without *Strudel*, called *retes* in Hungary. It is a favourite with men and women because it is really not fattening. It is a little bit tricky to make but once you know the trick, it will become very easy and quick. It is no wonder that it is so well liked, as it is very light and very tasty, and there are so many kinds to choose from. The ingredients are very cheap and you can keep it for days and days. If you put it in a warm oven for a few minutes, it gives you a fresh sweet dish.

I once had a Greek chef who made a *Strudel* paste which he said he could stretch from London to Athens if he really wanted to, and he showed me his secret. He put an extra pinch of salt in the paste and it does not affect the flavour because when it is crisply baked you cannot taste the salt any more. I promise you he made wonderful *Strudel*.

1 lb. (4 cups) flour
1 egg
$\frac{1}{2}$ oz. (1 tablespoonful) lard, oil, butter or margarine
1 teaspoonful ($1\frac{1}{4}$ teaspoonfuls) vinegar
good pinch of salt

Work the ingredients well together, adding enough lukewarm water to make a soft dough. It is important to test how soft or hard it is. We have to learn this by experience. Knead the dough till absolutely smooth; this is very important. When the pastry is smooth and silky, divide into 2 balls and brush the tops with a little melted oil or butter. Leave it on the table and cover with a deep dish. The best is a china pudding dish. Leave it to rest for about 20 minutes.

Cover a large table, at least 6–7 ft long, with a well-floured cloth. Put one of the pastry balls in the middle of the tablecloth. Brush it over with melted butter, oil or margarine and then flatten the pastry with a rolling pin till it is about ¼ in. thick. And now for the tricky part of the operation! Flour your hands and with the palms *underneath* the pastry, pull it towards the edge of the table all round. You will find that the pastry comes easily, shall I say happily, to your hand, and you can pull it and pull it, till it is as thin as paper and reaches the edge of the table and is overlapping it. The test is where the pastry is thin enough for you to be able to read a newspaper laid underneath. The edges will remain somewhat thick. These parts should not be used for the *Strudel* pastry. Now leave the pastry for 12–15 minutes to dry. This is important because if the pastry is not dry enough you will not be able to bake it properly and it will not become crisp. When it is dry enough first sprinkle it with melted butter and after that sprinkle on the filling. If it is apple, slice it thinly; sprinkle chopped almonds, walnuts, a very few breadcrumbs and as much sugar as you like on top. If the apples are sour add more sugar. If your filling is morello cherries, much more sugar is needed, but sprinkle it also with warm butter, almonds or walnuts. You can make *Strudel* filling with cottage or cream cheese mixed with 1 or 2 yolks of eggs and well washed sultanas; and spread this also on the dry *Strudel*. The rolling up is another art. You do it by lifting the tablecloth and rolling it away from yourself to the other end of the table. Cut it according to the size of your baking sheet, which should be well greased before you put the *Strudel* on it. Bake it in a moderately warm oven for 15–20 minutes. It is just as good hot or cold.

TALKELLI (Hungary)

A very simple everyday little pastry, but when we were children, it was one of our favourites.

$\frac{3}{4}$ oz. (1 cake) yeast
2 tablespoonfuls (2$\frac{1}{2}$
    tablespoonfuls) sugar
10 oz. (2$\frac{1}{2}$ cups) flour
4 eggs
pinch of salt

Cream the yeast and sugar. Rest, then mix in the flour. Separate the eggs. Mix everything together, except the whites of eggs, into a somewhat soft dough. Whip the whites of eggs very stiffly, mix them with the dough and let it rest for 25 minutes. Put bun mould tins on top of a moderate oven; pour into each mould a very little oil or fat and then put a tablespoonful of dough in each and let it bake till golden-brown in colour, turn over the dough inside the mould with a fork. When they are golden on both sides, put them into icing sugar and serve them hot with any jam you like.

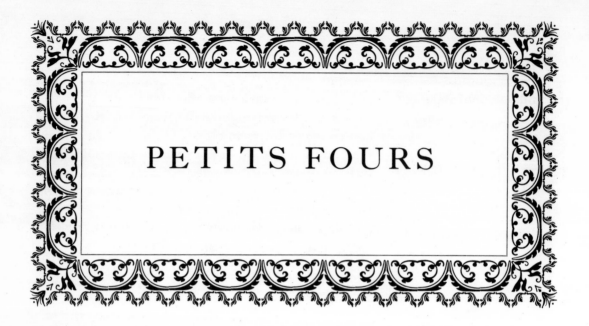

PETITS FOURS

Petits fours are known throughout the whole world, at least in those parts of the world where I have travelled; that is Europe, America and Africa. Everywhere petits fours play a big part in the entertaining world. They belong in the luxury food class.

On the Continent petits fours were called tea biscuits or tea pastries, because no tea party was considered complete without them.

There are two kinds of tea pastries, sweet and savoury. I came across a lot of petits fours in the Arab world. They were mostly made with almonds and were killingly sweet. They were served with a green, over-sweetened tea. Of course, we Europeans would not eat more than one or two and that only to be polite.

On the other hand, the best petits fours of all in our part of the world – that is to say Hungary, Austria, France and Germany – are made in Belgium; all very light, some very crispy, some deliciously fluffy. I am sure there are eighty or a hundred varieties, or rather there used to be when we had more leisure and when households and businesses could afford the time to make them. We still make a very good variety at my place. Our greatest enemy now is lack of time.

I personally serve petits fours after dinner parties, usually with the coffee, and they are always very well received.

The best restaurants in America and here serve *friandises* after dinner with the ice cream or just on their own. These are made of fresh fruit, such as grapes, tangerines or mandarines, or *marrons glacés*; or sugared cherries whose stone has been replaced by an almond, small marzipan balls or squares which have been previously baked – all of them dipped in boiled sugar.

You have to be very careful to dip all these fruits or marzipans in a very thin syrup, otherwise they become very hard and break your teeth. If the sugar is too thin, then you run the risk that the sugar film will melt very quickly and the *friandise* pieces will be runny. But all this is only a question of practice.

We make *friandises* on request; in season we dip strawberries in sugar or in fondant. I am, however, always nervous of serving them, especially in this country, because the humidity spoils them very easily. So I recommend petits fours at the end of dinner on most occasions.

The savoury petits fours – which are all made of puff pastry – are made in different shapes and can have a great variety of fillings – little 'horseshoes' filled with smoked salmon; small crescents stuffed with chopped ham mixed with a little cream; very small 'baskets' filled with cheese (Gruyère cheese is best) or egg; little squares filled with chopped mushrooms; tiny fingers rolled round anchovies; puff pastry rolled out very thin, and filled with chopped cabbage roasted in butter, salt and black pepper.

Roasted hazelnuts to my mind have the best flavour of all in making pastries and petits fours. Of course, it is important here as in everything else that the best raw material should be used. Hazelnuts can be so different, depending on where they come from; the same applies to almonds and walnuts. The best walnuts are French or Rumanian; the best almonds come from Avola in Italy and the best hazelnuts come from Piedmont.

ALMOND or AVOLA STICKS

7 oz. (1¾ cups) flour
7 oz. (full cup) ground almonds
3 eggs
8 oz. (1 cup) sugar
6 oz. (¾ cup) butter

Mix all the ingredients well together till smooth. Allow to stand for about 1 hour in a cool place. Then roll out on a floured board and cut into long sticks. Place the sticks on a buttered baking sheet in neat rows and bake in a slow oven, 240–310°F. (116–154°C.) for for 14–15 minutes. This petit four can be kept for some time.

ALMOND AND DATE PETITS FOURS

10 oz. (1¼ cups) sugar
4 whites of eggs
chopped dates
roughly-chopped almonds

The whites of eggs and the sugar should be whisked ·till they will stand up. It is best to do this by placing your mixing bowl into a saucepan of hot water which is on a very slow gas. When it is stiff enough add the dates and the almonds. Line a baking sheet with grease-

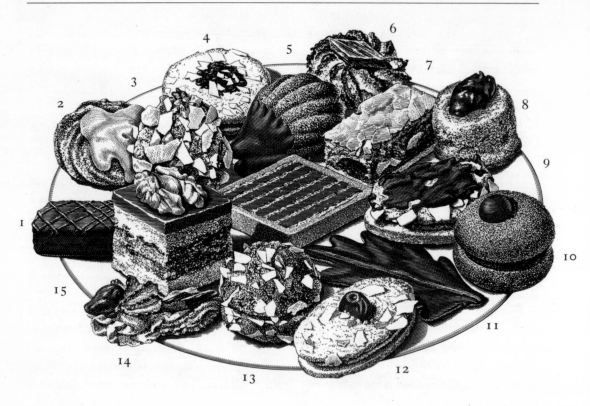

A selection of petits fours: 1. chocolate bar; 2. vanilla crescent (*see* recipe page 205); 3. Florentine (*see* recipe page 179); 4. cherry sandwich; 5. chocolate *beignet* (*see* recipe page 177); 6. chocolate petit four; 7. *restelt* (*see* recipe page 185); 8. almond cherry; 9. duchesse; 10. chocolate Nero; 11. chocolate leaf; 12. cherry *galette*; 13. hazelnut ball (*see* recipe page 180); 14. almond sticks (*see* recipe page 175); 15. walnut square

proof paper and with a spoon make small round petits fours and place on the paper. These are not so much baked as dried in a very slow oven. Do not over dry them.

ALMOND CRESCENTS

1 lb. marzipan
flaked almonds
gum arabic

Divide the marzipan into 32 equal pieces. Mould each piece into a strip 2 in. long, flatten with the fingers and press into each some flaked almonds. Shape like a horse-shoe and place on a greased and floured tray. Place in a very warm oven for 5 minutes at 500–550°F. (261–289°C.), and immediately on taking from the oven, brush lightly with a solution of gum arabic.

ANISEED PETITS FOURS
If you like liquorice you will like these.

½ lb. (2 cups) flour
7 oz. (scant cup) granu-
    lated sugar
4 oz. (1 cup) grated
    lemon peel
2 eggs
1 white of egg
½ oz. (1 tablespoonful)
    caster sugar
aniseed

Mix well all the ingredients together, with the exception of the whites of eggs and the caster sugar. Beat till smooth and silky. The amount of aniseed is entirely a matter for personal taste. Its flavour is strong and not to everybody's liking. Allow to rest for 1 or 2 hours. Then roll out on a floured board and cut out long narrow fingers. Then roll with your palms on the board into ropes. Cut equal lengths and twist into pretzel shapes. Brush the tops with a little beaten white of egg. The white of egg should be only lightly beaten. Sprinkle with caster sugar. Bake in a slow oven for 12–15 minutes.

BEAR'S PAWS

4 oz. (1 pkt) marzipan
1 oz. (2 tablespoonfuls)
    sugar
1 white of egg
3 whites of eggs, stiffly
    beaten
1 oz. (2 tablespoonfuls)
    sugar
nibbed almonds
chocolate butter cream
icing sugar

Mix the marzipan with the sugar and 1 white of egg, till it is light and smooth. Add to this the beaten whites of eggs which should be stiff and firm and have 1 oz. sugar added. Fold till all is absorbed into the mixture. Using a piping bag with a small star tube, pipe out the mixture in the shape of a shell and lightly cover with nibbed almonds. After that dust with icing sugar and bake in the oven at 380°F. (194°C.) for 10–15 minutes. When cooked, stick 2 shells together with chocolate butter cream.

BEIGNETS
Beignet is one of the best of petits fours. Sweets and petit fours are mostly eaten after a meal. Petits fours as we have known them were always made by hand, but I am afraid that they will disappear very soon. Only very ambitious and clever housewives will preserve the old recipes for the coming generation; commercially it will be impossible. I give you the *beignet* recipe because it is one of my favourite petits fours and I want you to pass it on to your children or grandchildren.

1 lb. (2⅔ cups) ground
   almonds
1 lb. (2 cups) sugar
5 whites of eggs
2 eggs
half a vanilla pod
grated peel of 1 lemon
16 whites of eggs,
   stiffly beaten

Mix the ground almonds, sugar and the 5 whites of eggs. Soften this paste with 2 whole eggs. Add to it half a vanilla pod and the grated peel of a lemon; mix all well and add to it 16 very stiffly beaten whites of eggs. Butter and flour a lot of petits fours moulds, if you like put in each *beignet* a small piece of candied lemon peel, sprinkle with icing sugar and bake in a slow oven till firm. For chocolate *beignets* dip one end in melted chocolate.

CATS' TONGUES (*Langues de Chat*)

½ lb. (1 cup) sugar
½ lb. (1 cup) butter
2 large whites of eggs
½ pod of vanilla
8 oz. (2 cups) flour

Beat the sugar and butter till light and fluffy; then beat in the whites of eggs one at a time. Scrape out the centre of the vanilla pod and add it to the mixture. Finally add the flour and stir till all is absorbed. Using a piping bag and plain tube force out the mixture on a greased and floured baking tray, shaped like a dog's bone and about 1 in. long. Bake in the oven at a temperature of 400°F. (205°C.) for about 15–20 minutes.

(When piping the mixture onto the tray ensure that it is piped very thinly and removed from the tray immediately it is taken out of the oven.)

These *langues de chat* can either be eaten plain, with ice cream or fruit salad, or two can be stuck together with praline butter cream. The latter make very good petits fours.

CHOCOLATE ROCKS

7 oz. (full cup) chopped
   almonds
4 oz. (⅞ cup) raisins
1 lb. melted plain
   chocolate

Mix the almonds, raisins and melted chocolate. Using a teaspoon place small amounts onto greaseproof paper and allow to harden. Some of the almond can be replaced by cornflakes if so desired. These are very tasty and so easy to make.

CHOCOLATE MACAROONS

This is a very good macaroon which is useful after dinner, or with tea or coffee; again, good to have in reserve.

5 oz. ($\frac{7}{8}$ cup) hazelnuts,
   roasted just for 3 or 4
   minutes
4 oz. ($\frac{1}{2}$ cup) caster sugar
2 whites of eggs
2$\frac{1}{2}$ oz. (2$\frac{1}{2}$ squares) melted
   plain chocolate
split almonds

Work the ingredients well together. Roll into small balls and put them on a greased and floured baking sheet. Flatten them out with a knife and put in the middle of each a split almond. Bake them in a low oven for 22–26 minutes.

FLORENTINES

1 lb. (2 cups) sugar
$\frac{1}{2}$ lb. nibbed (1$\frac{1}{3}$ cups)
   almonds
$\frac{1}{2}$ lb. (2$\frac{3}{4}$ cups) flaked
   almonds
$\frac{3}{4}$ lb. (3 cups) orange
   peel
$\frac{1}{4}$ lb. (1 cup) chopped
   glacé cherries
2 oz. ($\frac{1}{2}$ cup) chopped
   angelica
$\frac{1}{4}$ oz. (1 tablespoonful)
   ground almonds
a little flour
$\frac{3}{4}$ pint (2 cups) cream

Place all the ingredients (except the melted chocolate or lemon water icing) into a bowl and mix with the cream. When thoroughly mixed use a teaspoon and place equal amounts on a greased and floured tray. Bake in an oven of 420°F. (216°C.) for 15 minutes. Remove the florentines from the tray with a palette knife before they get cold.

   When the florentines are cold the underside can be lightly coated with melted chocolate or lemon water icing, which is made by mixing $\frac{3}{4}$ lb. icing sugar with 2 whites of eggs and the juice of a lemon.

HAZELNUT MACAROONS

7 oz. (full cup) ground
   hazelnuts
3 oz. ($\frac{3}{4}$ cup) finely
   chopped cherries
a little flour
grated rind of $\frac{1}{2}$ lemon
8 oz. (10–11 medium)
   whites of eggs
14 oz. (1$\frac{3}{4}$ cups) caster
   sugar
apricot jam

Carefully mix together the ground hazelnuts, the chopped cherries, the flour and the lemon rind. Whip the whites of eggs and sugar together and blend with the other mixture. Pipe out onto a greased and floured tray using a large plain tube, but making the macaroons as small as possible. Bake at a temperature of 350°F. (177°C.) for 20 minutes and when cool stick 2 pieces together with apricot jam.

DATE PETITS FOURS

1¼ lb. (2½ cups) sugar
1¼ lb. dates
7 oz. (2⅔ cups) split
   almonds
2 whites of eggs

The dates should be cut into long strips. Beat the whites of eggs till very stiff. Mix all the ingredients together. With a spoon make small round petits fours and place on a well-greased and floured baking tin or on rice paper. Bake in a very slow oven till they are more dried than cooked. This will require 1 hour.

FRENCH WALNUT PETITS FOURS

12 oz. (3 cups) flour
5 oz. (⅞ cup) ground
   walnuts
4 oz. (½ cup) sugar
7 oz. (⅞ cup) butter
juice and grated rind
   of 1 lemon
1 tablespoonful (1½
   tablespoonfuls) each
   rum and cream
1 egg
chopped walnuts

Mix all the ingredients together till nice and smooth. Allow to rest for 1 hour in a cold place and then roll out on a pastry board about ¼–¾ in. thick. Then with a pastry cutter cut out small pieces, round, square or oblong. Wash over with a little milk or yolk of egg and sprinkle the top with coarse sugar and a little walnut mixed together. Bake in a moderate oven for 16–18 minutes.

HAZELNUT BALLS

4 oz. (1⅓ cups) cake
   crumbs
4 oz. (½ cup) unsalted
   butter
4 oz. (¾ cup) ground
   hazelnuts
2 oz. (⅓ cup) chopped
   hazelnuts
rice paper
eggs
2 oz. (¼ cup) sugar

Mix well together the cake crumbs, ground hazelnuts, yolks of eggs and the sugar; then add to this the stiffly whipped whites of eggs. Mix carefully, trying not to break the whites of eggs. Put the mixture into a forcing bag.

Place the rice paper on a baking tin and pipe the mixture in little round 'bundle' shapes onto this paper. Sprinkle on the top the 2 oz. chopped hazelnuts and bake in a slow oven for 12–14 minutes.

This petit four keeps quite a long time and is a very useful standby.

KISS FROM A HUSSAR (Hungary)

In Hungary, every young girl (and whether she was a very modest little maid or the heiress of a castle their dreams were the same) wanted to have a Hussar, a soldier or

French Wedding cake (*profiteroles*)

an officer, if not as a partner for lifetime at least for the coming dance season. Perhaps a little pastrycook girl, in her dream, produced a petit four which she called 'Kiss from a Hussar'. I give you the recipe:

6 oz. (1½ cups) flour
5 oz. (full ½ cup) butter
2 oz. (¼ cup) sugar
2 yolks of eggs
1 white of egg
1½ oz. (⅓ cup) coarsely chopped almonds
some candied morello cherries

Mix the flour and sugar and add the softened butter bit by bit. Beat in the yolks of eggs one by one, and mix them very thoroughly. Shape the mixture into balls the size of a walnut and put them on a buttered baking sheet. Press your finger into each ball, making a little dimple in it. Brush each 'dimpled ball' with white of egg, then scatter the coarsely chopped almonds and bake in a medium oven, 350°F. (177°C.) for 12-15 minutes. When they are baked, put the chopped morello cherries into the dimple on each ball.

MARZIPAN DATES

1 date for each petit four
marzipan
1 yolk of egg
a few drops of caramel

Cover the dates very thinly with marzipan and shape them so that they look like a torpedo. Take the yolk of egg add it to the few drops of burnt sugar and wash over the marzipan dates. This should be the same colour and shape as the dates really are. Bake the marzipan dates for 10 minutes at 400°F. (205°C.).

MERINGUE ROCKS

4 whites of eggs
1 lb. (2 cups) sugar
3 oz. (½ cup) walnuts
3 oz. (¾ cup) orange peel
icing sugar

Whip the whites of eggs and the sugar till firm. Then fold in the walnuts, chopped and orange peel. Finally, using a teaspoon, place small amounts on greaseproof paper, lightly dust with icing sugar and bake in an oven at 200–250°F. (93–121°C.) for 1½ hours till nice and firm.

ORANGE PETITS FOURS

2 whites of eggs
2 oz. (¼ cup) sugar
2 oz. (¼ cup) butter
2 oz. (½ cup) flour
very finely-shredded orange peel

Whip the whites of eggs very stiffly, then add the sugar and mix well together. Warm the butter slightly and add it slowly to the mixture and then add the flour. Finally add the orange peel.

Butter a large baking tin and using a teaspoon place little 'bundles' onto the tin in regular rows. When the

Making Strudel pastry

tin is full bang it once or twice to spread the mixture slightly. Bake for approximately 6 or 7 minutes at a temperature of 400°F. (205°C.). When cooked remove the petits fours very quickly from the tin and roll each one round a thin rod such as a pencil or the handle of a wooden spoon or a steel rod made specially for the purpose. You must work very quickly.

This petit four is a very good standby and can be kept in an airtight tin.

ORANGE GALBET

½ lb. (2 pkts.) marzipan
6 oz. (1½ cups) cut orange peel
6 oz. (1 cup) ground almonds
23 whites of eggs
½ lb. (1 cup) sugar
icing sugar
5 oz. (⅞ cup) ground walnuts
5 oz. (scant ⅔ cup) sugar
2 fl. oz. (¼ cup) rum

Mix to a soft paste the marzipan, cut candied peel, ground almonds and 8 whites of eggs. When thoroughly mixed blend with the remaining 15 whites of eggs which have been whipped till firm with ½ lb. sugar. Pipe this onto greaseproof paper (2 in. round flat rings) and lightly place flaked almonds on top. Finally dust with icing sugar and bake in an oven of 400°F. (205°C.) for 20 minutes. When cool stick 2 pieces together with the paste, made by mixing the ground walnuts, sugar and rum together.

RED CURRANT PETITS FOURS

This is a petit four with red currant jam. Red currant jam or jelly is one of my favourite flavourings for petits fours and cakes; before you use it for sauce or for layering cakes you should add enough lemon juice to it to make it sharp and refreshing. This petit four is a very simple little biscuit, the flavour of the central layer giving it piquancy.

4 eggs
4 oz. (½ cup) sugar
3 oz. (¾ cup) flour
2 oz. (¼ cup) melted butter
white icing or white fondant

Mix the yolks of eggs and sugar to a smooth cream. Add the flour to the very stiffly beaten whites of eggs. This must be done very carefully – the flour folded in little by little, lastly add the melted butter. Mix all this together, roll out and cut out little round biscuits. Take a buttered baking tin, place the biscuits on it and bake in a very slow oven for 25–30 minutes till they are crisp. Let them cool and then sandwich two together with red currant jam. When finished, cover them with white icing or white fondant.

PÂTE CRESCENTS

7 oz. (scant cup) sugar
10 oz. (1¼ cups) butter
half a vanilla pod
4 eggs
14 oz. (3½ cups) flour

Beat the sugar and butter till very light. Scrape out the centre of the vanilla pod and mix it into the mixture. Then beat in the eggs one at a time. Finally fold in the flour and continue to stir till the flour is absorbed. Take a piping bag fitted with a small star tube and pipe small crescents on greaseproof paper placed on a baking tray. Bake in the oven at 400°F. (205°C.) for approximately 15 minutes. When cool brush with lemon icing.

PIEDMONTESE PETITS FOURS

8 oz. (2 cups) flour
7 oz. (⅞ cup) butter
2½ oz. (2½ squares) grated chocolate
6 oz. (1 cup) ground hazelnuts
1 oz. (2 tablespoonfuls) vanilla sugar
1 yolk of egg
bitter chocolate

Rub the butter into the flour. Add the grated chocolate, the hazelnuts, the sugar and the yolk of egg. Mix well. Put in the refrigerator for an hour. Then roll out the paste on a floured pastry board and cut out in any shapes you like. Then put these on a buttered baking sheet and bake in a medium oven for about 15 minutes.

When they are cooked put a little melted liquid chocolate in a greaseproof paper forcing bag or cornet and decorate the little pastries with stripes and stars, if you are in an American mood!

RESTELT (Hungary)

4 oz. (¾ cup) crushed walnuts
6 oz. (¾ cup) sugar
1 rind and juice of lemon
3 whites of eggs
cinnamon
shortcrust pastry
apricot jam

Cook walnuts, sugar, lemon juice and rind, whites of egg and cinnamon in a bowl over the heat till the sugar is dissolved. When cooked pour this mixture onto a sheet of shortcrust pastry which has been half-baked and bake for another 15 minutes. The oven temperature should be 350°F. (177°C.). When cooked brush with boiled apricot jam and when cool cut into rectangles.

SAVOURY CREAM CHEESE PETITS FOURS

1 lb. (4 cups) flour
6 oz. ($\frac{3}{4}$ cup) butter
7 oz. ($\frac{7}{8}$ cup) cream
  cheese
salt
3 tablespoonfuls ($\frac{1}{4}$ cup)
  thick cream
1 yolk of egg

Mix these ingredients all well together and add the yolk of egg. Roll out thin and cut into 3 in. finger shapes, using a fancy cutter. Make one or two incisions in the middle of each with a sharp knife and brush over with yolk of egg and bake in a medium oven for 10–12 minutes.

WALNUT STICKS

10 oz. ($1\frac{1}{4}$ cups) sugar
10 oz. ($1\frac{1}{4}$ cups) butter
10 oz. ($2\frac{1}{2}$ cups) flour
10 oz. ($1\frac{3}{4}$ cups) grated
  walnuts
6 yolks of eggs
lemon rind

Mix these ingredients all together and leave to rest for 15 minutes. Roll out thinly and make little round sticks out of it. Put them in rows on your baking tray which should be well greased and floured. Brush over with yolk of egg and bake them till golden-brown.

WALNUT CUSHIONS

7 oz. ($\frac{7}{8}$ cup) butter
7 oz. ($1\frac{3}{4}$ cups) flour
6 yolks of eggs
filling:
6 whites of eggs
7 oz. (full cup) grated
  walnut
7 oz. (scant cup) sugar
a little vanilla

Rub the butter into the flour. Beat in the yolks and then make from the mixture as many little round balls as you can; leave them for an hour or two in a cold place and make the following filling.

Beat the whites of eggs till very stiff. Mix all the ingredients well together. Roll out your little balls and put into the centre of each some of the walnut filling. Shape them to look like little cushions. Put them on a well-buttered baking tray and bake at 330°F. (168°C.) till golden-brown.

BISCUITS

Like wedding cakes, crumpets and muffins are very English, part of the English way of life. They were so foreign to me at first that I could not believe that I would ever make them myself. Making biscuits in England was even more alien to me. I think that nowhere in the world do people eat so many biscuits as in this country and I think that they are made better here than anywhere else.

Therefore I was very surprised, when I got orders from Fortnum and Mason for several kinds of biscuits. It was immediately after the war, or perhaps even during it, that we started to make and pack in Fortnum and Mason tins thousands and thousands of biscuits. Several of the biscuit recipes we got from Fortnum and Mason. We could never make enough. We would send one consignment and it would stay only a few hours in the shop before being sold.

ALMOND BISCUITS (1)

½ lb. (2 cups) flour
½ lb. (1⅓ cups) ground almonds
½ lb. (1 cup) caster sugar
4 oz. (½ cup) butter
4 eggs
half a liqueur glass of rum

Sieve the flour onto a table. Make a well in the centre and put into it the almonds, sugar and butter which should be quite soft. Break the eggs into this mixture, add rum and mix into a paste. If the consistency is too stiff add an extra yolk of egg.

Roll the paste into sausages, cut in pieces and roll into balls. Put them on a buttered baking tin, brush with two coats of egg, slit each ball slightly with a knife. Bake for 20 minutes in a slow oven.

ALMOND BISCUITS (2)

8 oz. almond praline
12 oz. (3 cups) flour
1 oz. (2 tablespoonfuls)
butter
2 yolks of eggs
a pinch bicarbonate of
soda
5 oz. (5 squares)
chocolate
5 oz. (scant $\frac{2}{3}$ cup) sugar

Mix the almond praline with the flour and butter, add to it one by one the yolks of eggs; add the bicarbonate and work all together till the paste becomes smooth and silky. Roll it out very thin and cut again with any shape of cutter you like. Bake the biscuits in a very moderate oven, 400°F. (205°C.) for 14–16 minutes. After taking out of the oven, let the biscuits cool on a wire tray. In the meantime melt the chocolate, add the sugar to it and pour this liquid chocolate over the biscuits.

ABERNETHY BISCUITS

$\frac{1}{2}$ lb. (2 cups) flour
a pinch of baking
powder
3 oz. ($\frac{1}{3}$ cup) butter
3 oz. (scant $\frac{1}{2}$ cup) caster
sugar
caraway seeds to taste
1 beaten egg
1 tablespoonful ($1\frac{1}{4}$
tablespoonfuls) milk

Sift the flour and baking powder together into the basin and rub in the butter. Add to this the sugar, caraway seeds, egg and milk and stir to make a stiff dough. Roll out thinly and cut into rounds 3 in. in diameter. Prick the centres. Bake in a moderate oven 375°F. (191°C.) for 10 minutes. Cool on a wire rack.

AMERICAN COOKIES

6 oz. ($\frac{3}{4}$ cup) butter
7 oz. (scant cup) sugar
1 egg
vanilla
8 oz. (2 cups) flour
1 teaspoonful ($1\frac{1}{4}$ tea-
spoonfuls) baking
powder
salt
5 oz. ($\frac{7}{8}$ cup) chopped
walnuts

Cream the butter and beat in the sugar when the butter is soft and pale, then add the egg and vanilla and beat firmly till the mixture is light and fluffy. Stir in half the flour and the baking powder, then fold in the other half of the flour and the nuts. Now roll the paste into a thick sausage shape about 2 in. thick. Cool in the refrigerator overnight. Then cut your biscuit loaf in thin slices about $\frac{1}{4}$ in. thick and bake in a moderate oven until they are a delicate honey colour. This is a very sensible and useful biscuit for you may keep it for some days in the refrigerator and when you want some fresh biscuits you have only to cut off the slices and bake them with very little trouble to yourself.

ALMOND RINGS

4 oz. (1 cup) flour
2 oz. (¼ cup) butter
1 oz. (2 tablespoonfuls)
  caster sugar
1 pinch baking
  powder
1 yolk of egg
filling:
2 oz. (⅓ cup) ground
  almonds
1 oz. (2 tablespoonfuls)
  caster sugar
a little ground rice
1 white of egg
almond essence
chopped almonds
redcurrant jelly
chopped pistachio nuts

Cream the butter and sugar, beat in yolk of egg and a little flour. Add the rest of the flour which has been sieved with the baking powder. Work until the mixture is smooth then roll out. Cut into rounds and place on a greased baking tin.

To make the filling. Mix the sugar, ground almond, ground rice, almond essence and enough white of egg to make a stiff mixture, all together, and beat very well. Put the mixture into a forcing bag and pipe in a ring onto the biscuit. Sprinkle with chopped almonds. Bake for 25 minutes 320°F. (159–160°C.). Allow the biscuits to cool then fill the centres with jelly and sprinkle with chopped pistachio nuts.

BRANDY RINGS

1 yolk of egg
2½ oz. (scant ⅓ cup)
  sugar
5 oz. (1¼ cups) flour
5 oz. (⅔ cup) butter
5 oz. (⅞ cup) ground
  almonds or walnuts
rind of 1 lemon
brandy
pinch of cinnamon
icing sugar

Sieve together into a bowl the flour and sugar and add the ground almonds. Crumble in the butter, add yolk of egg, brandy, cinnamon and lemon rind. Knead all these ingredients to a smooth dough and then put in the refrigerator to cool for about quarter of an hour. Roll out thinly, a thickness of about ¼ in., cut into rings and put on a buttered and floured baking tin. Brush the rings with brandy and dust with icing sugar, then add a little more brandy so that they are now covered with a thick layer of sugar moistened with brandy. Bake in an oven 370°F. (189°C.) until they are a lovely golden brown colour.

CHEESE STRAWS

In my business we make cheese straws daily, hundreds and hundreds of pounds of them. As it is so good, so useful and so popular I feel I must give you the recipe for cheese straws.

You can always heat them up before serving. You can serve them with drinks, soups or as a savoury.

4 oz. (1 cup) flour
a little salt
Hungarian paprika
(optional)
2 oz. ($\frac{1}{4}$ cup) grated
Parmesan cheese
2 oz. ($\frac{1}{4}$ cup) butter
1 yolk of egg
a little cream to bind

Mix the butter, salt and cheese (the cheese can be Gruyère if you like). Rub into the flour, add the yolk of egg and a little cream; use as much cream as makes a workable but firm dough; knead lightly till firm. Put on a floured pastry board, roll out and cut into strips about 4 in. long and 1 in. wide; then twist the strips holding one end and rolling with the other hand. Put the straws on a buttered baking tin and bake in a medium oven about 375–400°F. (191–205°C.). Bake till golden and cool before serving from the trays. Serve either cold or warm. Alternatively cut rings and straws and if you serve the cheese straws with soup, put four or five of the straws through one of the rings and serve on a bread plate. As a savoury, serve piping hot with freshly mixed English mustard.

CHOCOLATE BISCUITS

2 oz. ($\frac{1}{4}$ cup) margarine
1$\frac{1}{2}$ tablespoonfuls (2
tablespoonfuls) syrup
cocoa to taste
4 oz. (1 cup) flour
pinch of bicarbonate of
soda
2 oz. ($\frac{1}{4}$ cup) sugar

Melt the margarine a little and mix with the syrup and then mix in all the other ingredients. Beat very well. Roll out thinly and cut into rounds. Bake on a greased baking sheet for 15 minutes in a hot oven.

CHOCOLATE WHIRLS

$\frac{1}{2}$ lb. (1 cup) sugar
$\frac{1}{2}$ lb. (2 cups) cashew
nuts
2 oz. ($\frac{1}{4}$ cup) flour
5 fl. oz. (6-7 medium)
whites of eggs

Mix all the ingredients together and pipe on greased trays in small whirls using a $\frac{1}{2}$ in. plain tube. Then flatten out making them as round as possible with a fork. Sprinkle with flaked almonds and bake till golden-brown at 420°F (216°C.). Bend them into an arch shape when still warm. When cold finish by putting chocolate on the smooth side of the bridges.

BRANDY SNAPS
A very interesting sweet biscuit which I met first in this country.

**2 tablespoonfuls
(2½ tablespoonfuls)
golden syrup
2 oz. (¼ cup) butter
2 oz. (¼ cup) sugar
2 oz. (½ cup) flour
ground ginger
a few drops of brandy
lemon juice
whipped cream to fill**

Put all the ingredients – except the whipped cream – in a china bowl, mix them very well. Then butter a baking tin. Drop a spoonful of the mixture on the tin, flatten with a fork making a round 1½ in. in diameter. Fill the tray with these rounds and put into a warm oven, between 350–400°F. (177–205°C.) for five or six minutes. Then take it out and very quickly roll each brandy snap around a wooden or steel tube of about ½ in. in diameter. Slip them off the tube and let them cool and fill with whipped cream just before serving.

CINNAMON CIGARETTES
**6 oz. (¾ cup) butter
6 oz. (¾ cup) sugar
3 whites of eggs
1 teaspoonful (1¼ tea-
spoonfuls) powdered
cinnamon (the best is
to buy the rolled cin-
namon and powder it
yourself)
2 oz. (½ cup) flour**

Cream the butter and sugar together till light and white. Then beat the whites of eggs and add slowly to the mixture. Beat till smooth and light. Add the ground cinnamon, home-made or bought, and finally add the flour. Mix well and let it rest for half an hour. Pipe oblong shapes, 3 or 4 in. long, like a cigarette, on a baking tin. Space well apart because the mixture spreads. Bake in a medium oven 380–400°F. (194–205°C.) for 8–10 minutes. Take out of the oven; working very quickly roll each piece round a pencil shaped handle or tube. The biscuits may be cigarette shape, or you can make them any shape, a cornet or horns. You can replace the cinnamon with ginger powder if you like it better.

COCONUT ROCK BUNS
**7 oz. (1¾ cups) flour
4 oz. (½ cup) butter
3 oz. (1 cup) desiccated
coconut
½ an egg
pinch of bicarbonate of
soda**

Cream the butter and sugar then add the egg which has been beaten. Sieve the flour, soda, cream of tartar and coconut together and add to the butter. Mix until it is stiff. If the mixture will not bind add another half of egg.

COCONUT MERINGUES

2 whites of eggs
5 oz. (scant ⅔ cup) caster sugar
5 oz. (1⅔ cups) dried coconut

Whip the whites stiffly, fold in the sugar and coconut. Pile in very small heaps on rice paper spread on a baking tray. Bake at 200 °F. (93 °C.) for about half an hour. Leave on the tray to cool before removing.

FLAP JACKS

6 oz. (¾ cup) butter
6 oz. (¾ cup) demerara sugar
8 oz. (3 cups) porridge oats

This is one of the quickest and easiest of biscuits to make. It is not very elegant, but homely, and a great favourite with hungry boys when they come home from school.

Warm and beat the butter in a pan. Mix the sugar, oats and salt together and then stir them into the butter. Turn the mixture on a greased baking sheet and press it smooth and firm. Bake in a moderate oven at 330 °F. (168 °C.). When the biscuit is cooked, leave to cool for a few moments to firm, then cut across into slices or squares and leave in the tin till quite cold.

FRENCH BISCUITS

Another very plain, dry biscuit, always very useful to keep for an emergency. The recipe is:

½ lb. (1⅓ cups) ground almonds (add a few bitter almonds which will give a very pleasant flavour)
a few drops of kirsch
5 eggs
½ lb. (1 cup) caster sugar
a pinch of salt
4 whites of eggs
3½ oz. (about ½ cup) potato flour

Separate the eggs, keeping 1 white apart. Moisten the ground almonds with 1 white of egg and the kirsch or any other liqueur you may fancy. Mix to a smooth paste. Add the yolks of eggs, one by one, mix in the caster sugar and a pinch of salt. Add the remaining whites of eggs and sprinkle in the potato flour. Butter and flour a baking tin and pipe out round biscuits from a forcing bag. Bake in a moderate oven.

GINGER BISCUITS

8 oz. (2 cups) flour
ground ginger to taste
½ lb. (1 cup) demerara
sugar
¼ lb. (½ cup) butter
1 egg
1 teaspoonful
bicarbonate of soda
a little milk
split almonds

Mix the flour, ginger and sugar. Rub in the butter. Dissolve the soda in the milk, add the egg and whisk the mixture together. Add this to the flour mixture. Mix well, and roll the mixture into balls. You must flour your hands to stop the mixture sticking to them. Place far apart on a greased baking sheet. Press each ball on top. Place a split almond on top and bake for 30 minutes at 330°F. (168°C.). Leave on the sheet to cool before removing.

GIPSY SLICES

2 eggs
2 oz. (¼ cup) sugar
2 oz. (½ cup) flour
1 oz. (1 square)
chocolate
½ oz. (1 tablespoonful)
butter
filling:
¼ pint (⅓ pint) cream
2 oz. (2 squares) grated
chocolate

Melt the chocolate with the butter. Place the eggs and the sugar in a bowl and whisk over hot water until nice and thick, then take from the heat and whisk until cool. Fold in the flour very lightly and finally the butter and chocolate. Spread to ½ in. depth on a baking tin bake at 410°F. (210°C.) until cooked. Remove the paper while still hot, cut in slices, and fill with the following mixture. Put grated chocolate in a thick saucepan, add cream and bring to the boil very slowly stirring all the time. Let the mixture rise up once, take from the heat and stir until cool. Chill well in the refrigerator, whisk again until it is holding its shape and chill again before using.

HAM BISCUITS

11 oz. (2¾ cups) flour
pinch of salt
7 oz. (⅞ cup) butter
2 yolks of eggs
2 fl. oz. (¼ cup) milk
chopped ham
caraway seeds

Sieve the flour and salt into a bowl. Crumble in the butter. Hard boil the eggs and crumble them in too. Add enough milk to give a stiff paste. Knead very well, make into a round and place in the refrigerator for 1 hour to chill. Roll out to the thickness of ⅛ in. brush with egg and sprinkle with chopped ham. Fold the sides to the middle and roll out again; brush with egg and sprinkle with ham, fold and roll another time. Leave to rest for 20 minutes, roll again brush with egg and sprinkle this time with coarse salt and caraway seeds then leave for a couple of hours. Cut in strips and bake at 410°F. (210°C.) until a beautiful golden brown colour.

HAZEL MACS

½ lb. (1⅓ cups) ground hazelnuts

14 oz. (1¾ cups) sugar

2 oz. (½ cup) glacé cherries

5 oz. (6-7 medium) whites of eggs

a little glycerine

Chop the cherries very finely. Then mix all the ingredients together in a bowl. Then using a ½ in. round tube pipe onto greaseproof paper. Sprinkle with flaked hazelnuts and bake on double trays for 20 minutes at 380°F. (194°C.). Finish by sticking the biscuits together two by two with raspberry jam.

HEDGEHOGS

small sponge cakes

liqueur or brandy

2 oz. (¼ cup) butter

a little sugar

1 yolk of egg

2 tablespoonfuls (2½ tablespoonfuls) strong black coffee

cream

almonds

Prepare the sponge to make it 2 in. in diameter and ½ in. high. Sprinkle them with liqueur or brandy and chill for 15 minutes in the refrigerator. Cream butter and sugar and add yolk of egg then add very slowly the black coffee. Pile some cream on top of each sponge round, spike with the almonds which have been blanched and toasted so that it looks like a little hedgehog. Cut into strips if you like, they are smaller and easier to manage.

LEMON BISCUITS (1)

4 oz. (1 cup) lemon peel

10 oz. (2½ cups) flour

2 oz. (¼ cup) butter

2 whole eggs

8 oz. (1 cup) sugar

pinch of bicarbonate of soda

pinch of salt

Boil the lemon peel in very thick syrup and then dry it and chop very fine, mix with the flour; add the butter, the eggs one by one and the sugar, the pinch of salt and bicarbonate. Mix all this well till it becomes smooth. Make a nice ball out of it; put it on a floured pastry board; roll it out thinly and cut out square or round biscuits. Put them on a buttered and floured baking tin; dot the biscuits and wash them over with egg and bake them in a very moderate oven, 400°F. (205°C.) for 16–18 minutes.

HONEY BISCUITS

3 eggs
honey to taste
9 oz. (full cup) sugar
½ glass rum
pinch of bicarbonate of
    soda
cinnamon
grated cloves
brown flour

Separate the eggs and beat the yolks in a bowl; add the honey, the rum and bicarbonate, the cinnamon and the cloves. When it is all mixed together add the sugar; mix well together. Add as much brown flour as makes the mixture firm but not hard. Put this mixture in the refrigerator. Cut out when firm, and bake in a moderate oven.

HONEY DISKS

12 oz. (3 cups) flour
8 oz. (1 cup) sugar
2 oz. (¼ cup) butter
½ lb. (2 cups) warm honey
1 teaspoonful (1¼ tea-
    spoonfuls) bicarbonate
    of soda
2 eggs

Work these ingredients to a stiff dough; then put it on a floured pastry board and roll out thinly. Cut out with a very large biscuit cutter – it should be as big as a small plate and just as thin. Put on a floured baking tin and bake it in a very slow oven for 18–20 minutes.

LEMON BISCUITS (2)

1½ lb. (6 cups) flour
12 oz. (1½ cups) cube
    sugar
6 oz. (¾ cup) butter
4 eggs
1 oz. (¼ cup) lemon peel
juice of 1 lemon

Rub the butter into the flour. Add sugar which has been pounded and lemon peel finely minced, mix well. Add beaten eggs and lemon juice, beat well. Then drop spoonfuls of the mixture about 2 in. apart on a buttered baking tray. Bake in the oven for 15–20 minutes until the biscuits are a pale brown.

LEMON BISCUITS (3)

6 oz. (1½ cups) flour
3 oz. (full ⅓ cup) caster
    sugar
grated rind of 1 lemo
4 oz. (½ cup) butter
1 egg

Warm the mixing bowl a little and then cream the butter and sugar. Add the flour, then mix in the egg, beaten till creamy, and then the lemon rind. If you prefer orange rind this is just as nice. Leave the paste to rest for 1 hour. Roll out thinly. Bake in a moderate oven at about 350°F. (177°C.) till golden brown. Dust with sugar and serve when the biscuits are cool.

LOBSTER FINGERS

2½ lb. (10 cups) flour
3½ lb. (7 cups) butter
1½ oz. (3 tablespoonfuls) baking powder
¾ pint (2 cups) lobster meal
1 pinch black pepper
enough milk to mix a soft dough

Mix all the ingredients very well till smooth. Let the paste rest for half an hour. Then put it on a floured pastry board, roll out to finger thickness. Cut into finger biscuits. Put them on a buttered baking tin, wash over with yolk of egg and bake them in a moderate oven 375°F. (191°C.) for 15–20 minutes. For lobster meal, use dried lobster soup packets.

MACAROONS

4 oz. (½ cup) caster sugar
2 oz. (⅓ cup) ground almonds
1 teaspoonful (1¼ teaspoonfuls) ground rice
1 white of egg
almond flavouring
split almonds
rice paper
water

Mix the sugar, ground almonds and ground rice, and stir in the white of egg which should not be beaten, and the flavouring. If the mixture is too thick add a little water. Mix well and place spoonfuls on the rice paper spread on a baking sheet. Lightly brush with water to glaze the biscuits. Place a split almond on top of each biscuit and bake for 25 minutes at about 330°F. (168°C.).

ORANGE GINGER CAKES

¾ lb. (3 cups) flour
6 oz. (¾ cup) caster sugar
3 oz. (6 tablespoonfuls) butter
pinch of bicarbonate of soda
pinch of cream of tartar
½ oz. (1¼ teaspoonfuls) ground ginger
grated rind of 2 oranges
2 eggs

Sieve flour and sugar into a bowl; rub in butter and stir in soda, cream of tartar, ground ginger and orange rind. Beat the eggs and add to mixture to make a stiff dough; add a little milk if it is too stiff. Place piles of the mixture on a greased baking tin. Bake for 30 minutes in a moderate oven 350°F. (177°C.). Sprinkle with orange icing sugar.

MELTING MOMENTS

6 oz. ($\frac{3}{4}$ cup) butter
4-6 oz. ($\frac{1}{2}$-$\frac{3}{4}$ cup) sugar
2 eggs
8 oz. (2 cups) cornflour
2 teaspoonfuls (2$\frac{1}{2}$ tea-
spoonfuls) baking
powder
grated rind $\frac{1}{2}$ lemon

Cream the butter till light, add sugar and beat again till fluffy. Add eggs and sieved cornflour and baking powder and mix well together to make quite a soft mixture; add some milk to it if too stiff. Stir in lemon rind. Fill patty pans half full and bake in a moderate oven 425°F. (219°C.) for 15-20 minutes.

OAT BISCUITS

I like everything made with oatmeal. I wouldn't mind eating porridge every day; I like it for breakfast, I wouldn't mind it for lunch. I would be pleased to have it for my supper, but I never do! But I don't want to talk about myself I want to give you a good biscuit recipe.

3 oz. ($\frac{3}{4}$ cup) flour
4 oz. (1$\frac{1}{2}$ cups) porridge
oats or oatmeal
a pinch of baking
powder
salt
3 oz. (6 tablespoonfuls)
unsalted butter
sugar to taste
a little milk to blend

Mix the flour with the porridge oats or oatmeal, the baking powder, and the salt. Rub in the butter till the dough is smooth, add the sugar, then mix all together till crumbly. Then use as much milk as makes a firm dough. Let it rest for half an hour or so, then roll out $\frac{1}{4}$ in. thick and cut out into 2 in. squares. Butter a baking tin and bake in a moderate oven at 380-400°F. (194-205°C.) for 18-20 minutes.

PARMESAN BISCUITS

You never can tell when people are coming in for a drink, or your husband or sons will bring some friends for a drink. It is always good to be prepared. I was once terribly embarrassed, when I took a friend to a family, where I had been invited and asked to bring this friend. At first we had difficulty in being admitted. The puzzled servants did not know what to do; at last our host came and showed us in. With a few embarrassed words he ushered us into a beautiful sitting room. A few minutes later the lady of the house appeared and tried to entertain us.

'I'm so sorry I have not a drink in the house', she said apologetically. 'I have nothing to offer you'.

We answered, though surprised: 'We only wanted to see you. We have only a minute. We are invited to dinner.' We made our stay as short as possible and left. I decided then never to be without something, however modest, to offer to unexpected guests. So I give you a very simple and inexpensive recipe for such occasions.

10 oz. (2½ cups) flour
1½ oz. (3 tablespoonfuls) butter
1 oz. (2 tablespoonfuls) grated Parmesan cheese
salt according to taste
milk
1 yolk of egg

Rub the butter into the flour, add the salt and cheese. Add just 1 or 2 teaspoonfuls of milk to make a fairly soft dough. It has to be kneaded very well. It should be a smooth and silky dough. Put it on a floured pastry board and roll out to matchstick thickness. Cut out pieces from it with a biscuit-cutter – any size or shape you like – put them in a buttered baking tin and brush them over with the yolk of egg which can be diluted with a little water. Then bake the biscuits at 350–400 °F. (177–205 °C.) for 5–8 minutes.

These biscuits are very nice served hot and you can warm the left-overs before serving a second time.

PARKIN

¼ lb. (1⅓ cups) oatmeal
4 oz. (1 cup) flour
4 oz. (½ cup) sugar
½ egg
a pinch of mixed spice
a pinch of ground ginger
a pinch of cinnamon
1 teaspoonful (1¼ teaspoonfuls) bicarbonate of soda
2 oz. (¼ cup) lard
3 oz. (½ cup) golden syrup
split almonds

Mix all the dry ingredients and then mix in the lard with your fingers. Now add the egg, which should have been beaten first and then the syrup. Mix to a quite stiff paste. Grease a baking sheet and spoon small heaps of the mixture on this. These must be far apart from each other as the biscuits will spread till they are as much as 3 in. across. Put a split almond on top of each little pile and bake 20–25 minutes at about 375 °F. (191 °C.). The parkins should be a rich brown colour when they are ready and you must leave them on the tray to cool, before removing them. They will keep very well and are a useful standby.

PLAIN BISCUITS

Just something very easy to have at home in reserve when somebody drops in for tea. They can be kept in the larder in a tin. It's nothing but a little shortbread.

Gâteaux; Dobos Torte and friandises; Baumkuchen; Nougatine gâteau; coffee hazelnut gâteau; fruit flan; mignons; fruit gâteau

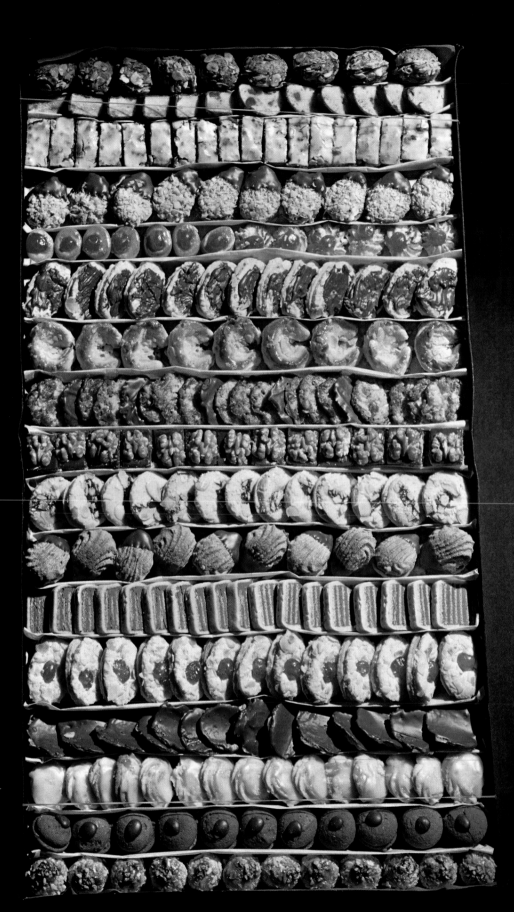

½ lb. (2 cups) flour
a little salt
6 oz. (¾ cup) unsalted
    butter
4 oz. (½ cup) sugar
1 egg
glacé cherries for the
    middle of the biscuits

Mix all the ingredients together with the finger-tips, knead or beat until smooth. Leave to rest for half an hour or so, then put on a pastry board and roll out very thin. Then cut out with a biscuit cutter into rounds, crescents or any shapes you like. Prick with a fork, mix a yolk of egg with a drop of heated milk and wash the biscuits before putting them in an oven. Put a cherry on each biscuit and bake for 12–14 minutes in a low oven at 200°F. (93°C.).

RATAFIA BISCUITS

Once this biscuit was made by the industrious housewife; now it is usually made commercially, mainly in Holland. I include it because from time to time, some nice old lady asks for them and seems disappointed to learn that we don't make them, as she had hoped to get them from us. Thus I give you a recipe for this modest and very old-fashioned biscuit:

½ lb. (1⅓ cups) ground
    almonds
3–4 bitter almonds,
    grated or ratafia
    essence
¾ lb. (2¾ cups) icing
    sugar
2 whites of eggs

The bitter almonds are optional. Mix the almonds with 1 white of egg and slowly stir in the sugar and add the remaining whites of eggs. Beat till very creamy and frothy. The mixture should be white. Put the whole mixture into a piping bag and using a small plain tube, pipe onto a large baking tin covered with rice paper. The biscuits should be very small, smaller than a shilling. Bake in a warm oven for 10–12 minutes at 360–380°F. (182–194°C.). It should be firm and crisp; put in a tin when cold and they will keep for weeks and weeks.

RED SAVOURY BISCUITS

1 lb. butter
1¼ lb. (2¼ cups) grated
    Gruyère cheese
½ lb. tomato purée
1 pinch of cayenne
    pepper
5 lb. (20 cups) flour
½ lb. (1 cup) lobster meal

Mix all these ingredients together till they become very smooth. Make a ball out of the paste and let it rest for a full half an hour. Then put on a floured pastry board, roll out, cut into long finger shapes and twist into screw shapes. Put the biscuits on a floured and buttered baking tin and bake them in a very slow oven, 400°F. (205°C.) for 18–20 minutes. They ought to be very crisp. Use dried lobster soup packets as meal.

A selection of petits fours

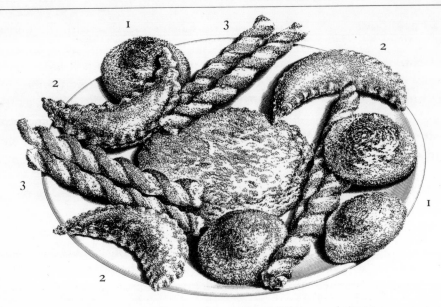

A selection of biscuits: 1. almond biscuits; 2. cheese crescents; 3. cheese straws; (*centre*) lemon biscuit

RICE BISCUITS

¼ **lb. (1 cup) flour**
salt
pinch of baking powder
¼ **lb. (⅔ cup) ground rice**
3 oz. (full ⅓ cup) caster
    sugar
¼ **lb. (½ cup) butter**
lemon or vanilla
    essence
beaten egg

Sieve flour, salt and baking powder into a bowl, add ground rice and sugar. Rub in the butter. Add lemon or vanilla essence to the egg and stir into dry ingredients; knead. Roll out on a floured board and cut in rounds, put on a greased baking tin. Bake in a moderately hot oven for 10–12 minutes at 400°F. (205°C.).

If you like, sandwich together with apricot or raspberry jam.

SHORTBREAD

1 lb. (4 cups) flour
12 oz. (1½ cups) butter
4 oz. (½ cup) sugar
2 eggs

Mix the flour and sugar together. Rub in the butter with the finger-tips, add the eggs, slightly beaten, stir well together till the paste is firm, malleable and smooth. Turn out onto a floured board, and roll or press to your required thickness. Shortbread may be rolled out to average biscuit thickness and cut out in rounds, fingers or crescents; alternatively it may be pressed into a round sandwich tin about $\frac{1}{2}$ in. to $\frac{3}{4}$ in. deep, the edges pinched and the centre pricked with a fork, and the round marked into segments. Alternatively cut into fingers up to 1 in. thick.

Bake in a moderate oven till golden-brown: leave to cool completely in the tin before removing. Dust with sugar.

Cut peel may be incorporated in the paste and the shortbread is then known as Pitkaithly bannock. Some people prefer the biscuits flavoured with vanilla; in which case omit the eggs and increase the proportion of sugar.

SHORTCAKE BISCUITS

1 oz. ($\frac{1}{4}$ cup) **icing sugar**
4 oz. (1 cup) **flour**
4 oz. ($\frac{1}{2}$ cup) **unsalted butter**
vanilla pod

Leave the vanilla pod in a jar with the sugar overnight. Cream the butter in a warm bowl and gradually beat in the sifted icing sugar and the flour. Beat till very creamy and soft. Pipe the mixture with a fluted nozzle to the bag straight onto a greased baking tray. Press half a glacé cherry on top of each biscuit. They may be any size you like. Tiny ones are elegant for coffee or parties, or bigger ones for tea. Bake at about 330°F. (168°C.) for 25 minutes.

SPICE BISCUITS

2 oz. ($\frac{1}{4}$ cup) **butter**
2 oz. ($\frac{1}{4}$ cup) **caster sugar**
1 teaspoonful ($1\frac{1}{4}$ teaspoonfuls) **treacle**
a pinch of baking powder
mixed spice
1 **egg**
4 oz. (1 cup) **flour**

Beat the butter and caster sugar to a cream. Mix in the treacle. Mix the flour, baking powder and spice and add to the butter and sugar. Add the beaten egg bit by bit, alternately with the flour. Roll out on a floured board, cut into rounds $\frac{1}{4}$ in. thick. Bake for 25 minutes at 330°F. (168°C.).

TEA BISCUITS

A very useful biscuit to have as a handy standby. Just a nice bite.

1¼ lb. (5 cups) flour
6 oz. (¾ cup) butter
10 oz. (1¼ cups) sugar
3 eggs
¼ pint (⅓ pint) cream
1 pinch of bicarbonate
   of soda

Cream the butter, then add the eggs, the sugar and cream, the bicarbonate of soda and then add, slowly, folding in the flour. Knead thoroughly till smooth and silky. Mould it into a big lump, then roll it out on a floured pastry board and cut out with biscuit cutter several different biscuit shapes. Put them on a greased and floured baking tin and bake it in a medium oven for 15–20 minutes. Be careful not to brown too much. When cooked, dust with icing sugar flavoured with the inside of a vanilla pod. This quantity will make about 3 lb. biscuits.

WAFFLES

When I was in America, I much enjoyed the famous waffles. Already in the boat crossing the Atlantic I had them for my breakfast. Waffles with maple syrup was a breakfast indeed!

4½ oz. (1⅛ cup) flour
2 teaspoonfuls (2½ tea-
   spoonfuls) baking
   powder
1 pinch of salt
1 tablespoonful (1¼
   tablespoonfuls) sugar
1 egg
2½ spoonfuls of melted
   butter
a little less than ½ pint
   (1¼ cups) milk

Put the flour in a china bowl; put the yolk of egg in the middle; add a little of the milk and slowly the melted butter. Mix very well, add the baking powder, salt, sugar, and enough milk to make a smooth batter. Then beat the white of egg very stiff and mix all together. Now grease your waffle-iron, with an absolutely tasteless and smell-less oil. Maize or corn oil is the best. Then heat the waffle-iron in your oven. Your iron is really hot when you see a little steam coming out of it. When it is hot enough, pour in the batter. Do not over-fill the waffle-iron, because it comes out. The baking time is 2½–3½ minutes. It depends how hot your oven is and how thick your iron is. But don't worry, experience will teach you, as with everything else. But it is worth the trouble. Of course, you can make savoury-waffles as well. You make the same batter, just leave out the sugar. You may add grated cheese, Parmesan or Gruyère, about 2 oz., or you may add chopped ham. But the tastiest addition is cabbage.

Chop a small cabbage, salt it a little and let it rest for 15 minutes or so. In the meantime put the frying pan in your oven with a good spoonful butter or corn oil, press out the cabbage and put it in the frying pan. Then roast it until it is golden-brown; add black pepper and salt according to your taste and mix the cabbage (about $2\frac{1}{2}$ oz. when roasted) with the batter and cook waffles as before.

WALNUT BISCUITS

10 oz. ($2\frac{1}{2}$ cups) flour
1 oz. (2 tablespoonfuls) butter
3 oz. ($\frac{1}{2}$ cup) grated walnuts
$\frac{1}{2}$ oz. (1 tablespoonful) lemon peel
6 oz. ($\frac{3}{4}$ cup) sugar
1 egg

Mix all the ingredients very well, roll out very thin and cut out with a round cutter. Bake the biscuits in a very moderate oven. Before putting them in the oven wash them over with a little sugared milk.

WINE BISCUITS

$\frac{1}{2}$ lb. (1 cup) unsalted butter
4 oz. ($\frac{1}{2}$ cup) sugar
$\frac{3}{4}$ lb. (3 cups) flour

Cream the butter and sugar, add the flour. Mix all the ingredients well together until smooth. Allow the paste to rest for half an hour and then roll it out thinly and cut out with a fancy cutter; you can cut out long strips and make finger biscuits. Then place the biscuits in a buttered and floured baking tin and bake at 380°F. (194°C.) till crisp and golden coloured.

VANILLA CRESCENTS (Austria)

2 oz. ($\frac{1}{3}$ cup) ground almonds
4 oz. (1 cup) icing sugar
6 oz. ($\frac{3}{4}$ cup) butter
8 oz. (2 cups) flour
vanilla sugar

Sift the flour and sugar together. Mix in the ground almonds. Unblanched ones are best, but if you discover these impossible to find, do not worry blanched ones will do, but the biscuits will be a little paler in colour. Now rub in the butter, knead into a firm paste and roll into crescent shapes. Bake on a buttered and floured baking tray at about 375°F. (191°C.) and remove when the crescents are a golden brown. Roll in vanilla sugar and leave to cool. These biscuits keep beautifully.

CONFECTIONERY

Many years ago, the craft of the confectioner was distinct from that of the bread maker. It is still so today. There is evidence that the art of confectionery can be traced back to Egypt some 3,500 years ago and while this art was by no means primitive at that time, it was not until Greek and Roman influence became paramount that the confectioner took his place in the select band of skilled craftsmen.

At this time the basic raw material for the confectioner was honey. This was due to the fact that the process of sugar refining was not known. This process was first used in India and was basically the evaporation of the juice from sugar cane. This skill passed from India to China and thence to Persia where the first sugar refinery was started in the seventh century A.D.

The first mention of sugar in England was in 1319, when 100,000 pounds was imported by way of Venice from India. The price of sugar at that time was 1/9½d. per pound, in those days a very considerable sum. Sugar in fact was not sold at a reasonable price until the use of beet sugar became more common during the Napoleonic wars at the beginning of the nineteenth century. Beet sugar had been discovered by Margraff of Berlin in 1747 but was not developed until 1801 when a factory was established by Archard in France. This did not prosper, however, until the British Continental blockade made it impossible to obtain supplies of cane sugar from outside Europe, and so beet sugar manufacture was quickly developed on the European continent.

This had the effect of putting much more sugar on the market and as a result sugar prices quickly dropped Far more sugar and confectionery became generally available.

Confectioners in the past were much concerned with sugar and sugar-boiling. The modern confectioner has still to know a great deal about this subject.

Today sugar is cheap and very thoroughly refined, in fact it may be said that there are few purer foods available. Quite a large proportion of the sugar used in this country today is made from beet and the finished article is undectectable from that obtained from sugar cane.

As a food sugar is invaluable as a fuel, and so is a source of energy.

There is now hardly any demand for the elaborate and costly confections made from pulled and spun sugar, so typical of late Victorian and Edwardian cookery. The place of this type of sugar work is taken over by fondant. We colour the fondant, we flavour it, we use it a great deal for icings, fillings as well and the French use it even more than we do here; they like fondant more than chocolate and so do I. For sweet-making in France they use fresh fruit juices: we, in our sweet or cold chocolate kitchen, use only fresh fruit covered with a thin layer of chocolate. It is very convenient to have in your food cupboard a jar of both white and chocolate fondant. You can make chocolate fondant to add to the already prepared fondant. To make this, melt the fondant with the help of a little syrup, then add to it a little unsweetened and sweetened chocolate mixed. Of course all this is quite a lot of trouble – so if I may corrupt you try to be friendly with your local pâtisserie and ask them to sell you a pound or a half pound of fondant. It is no trouble to them; it has to be made anyway! It is a shame that you cannot buy ready-made fondant anywhere in the shops because it is such an effort and a lot of work for the housewife to make it. I have a few friends who became friends through being my customers and I let them have ready made fondant when they want to make their own Christmas cakes or any other cakes at home.

FONDANT

1 lb. (4 cups) cube sugar
1½ pints (2 pints) water
a pinch of cream of tartar
1 teaspoonful (1¼ teaspoonfuls) glucose

Put the sugar and water into a heavy, thick-bottomed saucepan. Allow to heat up slowly until the sugar is dissolved. Then add the cream of tartar dissolved in a spoonful of water. Mix these well together. Lower the heat under the syrup and allow to come to the boil. Add the glucose. Remove the lid and then place in your sugar thermometer (sacrometer). Let the sugar boil rapidly until it reaches about 240°F. (116°C.). Wash the sides of the pan with a soft wet brush from time to time. Stop the sugar boiling immediately when it reaches 240°F. (116°C.). The best way to do this is to stand the saucepan in cold water. When the syrup has cooled slightly pour it on a watered marble slab. Sprinkle the surface of the syrup slightly with cold water and allow to cool for a few minutes; then work it with a sugar scraper or a wooden spoon; do this without stopping until the fondant turns snow white. Then taking a little fondant at a time begin to knead it into a ball. Cover it with a damp cloth and let it mellow for an hour or two before using it.

It is possible by making even the slightest variations of recipes and cooking processes to produce a different creation. The most important thing to remember is to note the ingredients and the precise method of cooking adopted, so that should something different and pleasing materialize, it will be possible to reproduce it.

A good example of variation in ingredients and method giving different textures and tastes is apparent in the making of fudge.

A basic recipe is shown from which, with a little practice, a good, smooth and creamy fudge will be produced. If, however, the dextrose content is reduced by half, the finished texture will be much rougher and quite crumbly. If the dextrose content is doubled, the finished article will be very soft and could be used as a filling or a topping for a cake. By cooking the batch very slowly the sugars will have far more time to caramelize and a much more pronounced flavour will be noticed. With the addition of some plain chocolate or some coffee, different fudges will be produced. Similarly, chopped walnuts, ginger or seedless raisins will all give striking variations.

The important thing is to be willing to experiment and make careful notes and in this way you may well produce a sweetmeat that will be truly yours and one that cannot be readily copied.

ACID DROPS

1½ lb. (3 cups) granu-
  lated sugar
½ pint (1¼ cups) water
pinch of cream of tartar
the grated rind of ½
  lemon
½ tablespoonful tartaric
  acid

Boil in a copper pan the sugar, water and the cream of tartar to 320°F. (159°C.) – or until it turns slightly yellow. Add the lemon rind and pour the mixture on an oiled slab.

Sprinkle over this one dessertspoonful of tartaric acid and mix thoroughly. When cool enough to handle, form it into thin rolls. Cut each one with scissors and roll into small round drops. Sift sugar over them and leave to dry. Keep the drops in an airtight container.

ALMOND HALVA (India)

**8 fl. oz. (1 cup) granu-
   lated sugar water**
8 oz. (2 cups) flour
2 oz. ($\frac{1}{4}$ cup) butter
pinch of saffron
grated almonds
pistachio nuts

Boil the sugar with water to make a thin syrup and add the flour. Cook until thick and then slowly add the butter and saffron. Remove from the fire and pour on a tray to set. Sprinkle with grated almonds and pistachio nuts and cut out into squares.

ALMOND TOFFEE

**$\frac{1}{2}$ lb. (1$\frac{1}{3}$ cups) blanched
   almonds**
**1$\frac{1}{2}$ lb. (3 cups) granu-
   lated sugar**
$\frac{3}{4}$ pint (2 cups) water
a little marzipan
pinch of cream of tartar

Halve the almonds and dry them in a cool oven. Put the sugar, water and cream of tartar in a copper pan and boil until it becomes deep amber in colour. Remove from heat and add almonds. Bring up to boiling point again, and pour into a buttered tin. Let it cool.

BARLEY SUGAR

1$\frac{1}{2}$ lb. (3 cups) sugar
$\frac{1}{2}$ pint (1$\frac{1}{4}$ cups) water
$\frac{1}{2}$ white of egg
**1 teaspoonful (1$\frac{1}{4}$ tea-
   spoonfuls) lemon
   juice**

Mix in a saucepan and bring up to boiling point the sugar, water and the white of egg. Skim and then strain through muslin. Then put the mixture back in the pan and bring up to 310°F. (154°C.). Remove from the heat, add the lemon juice and stir. Pour into a greased dish. Cut into strips before it sets, and twist each strip. Cut into pieces with scissors.

BLACK BOBS

**1 pint (1$\frac{1}{4}$ pints) black-
   currant purée**
$\frac{1}{4}$ lb. ($\frac{1}{2}$ cup) sugar

Make the blackcurrant purée by heating the black-currants in a wet preserving pan and mashing them all the time. Then rub them through a fine sieve, place in a clean pan with sugar and stir over a low heat until the sugar has dissolved, then bring it to the boil and boil for 45 minutes, stir almost all of the time if you can. Pour mixture into saucers, put before the fire to dry out for 4 days, turning the cakes every day. Then place the cakes between folds of paper and hang up to dry again. Cut into lozenges and keep in jars with tightly fitting lids. These are excellent to eat when you are feeling low with a cold and your throat is sore. They will help you feel better much more quickly.

BLACK TREACLE AND ALMOND TOFFEE

1 lb. (2⅔ cups) treacle
¼ lb. (½ cup) unsalted butter
½ lb. (1 cup) caster sugar
2 oz. (⅓ cup) chopped blanched almonds

Put the treacle, butter and sugar into a saucepan. Bring to the boil slowly stirring all the time. Let it boil for 20 minutes stirring all the time. Remove from the heat, add almonds; pour into a buttered tin. When set break into pieces with the handle of a heavy knife or a hammer.

BULLS' EYES

2 lb. (8 cups) cube sugar
8 fl. oz. (1 cup) water
a pinch of cream of tartar
yellow colouring
a pinch of lemon essence

Stir the sugar, water and cream of tartar in a saucepan over a low heat until the sugar is dissolved, then continue stirring and allow the mixture to boil; continue boiling and do not stir until brittle *i.e.* when a small drop is tested in a cup of cold water. Pour a small portion onto a buttered or oiled slab. Wearing gloves pull it out until it is creamy white. Now stir a little yellow colouring and tartaric acid and lemon essence in the remaining portion. When blended, lay strips of the pulled portion an inch apart onto the pulled coloured portion. Fold the whole in two, stripes outwards and draw the two ends together. With oiled scissors cut into strips and then into bull's eyes.

BUTTERSCOTCH

8 oz. (1 cup) granulated sugar
4 oz. (½ cup) brown sugar
4 fl. oz. (½ cup) water
4 oz. (1 cup) dextrose
6 oz. (¾ cup) butter

Place the sugars, water and dextrose in a pan; bring to the boil and cook until the temperature reaches 290°F. (146°C.). Add the melted butter slowly and continue cooking to first crack. Pour on a lightly greased metal tray while still very hot; mark with a knife to sizes required while the butterscotch is still soft. ('First crack' means that when a little toffee is dropped in a cup of cold water it will spread out thinly and when flicked with fingers it will shatter. *See* p. 225.

CARAMEL

8 oz. (1 cup) granulated sugar
4 oz. (½ cup) brown sugar
4 fl. oz. (½ cup) water
6 oz. (1½ cups) dextrose
6 oz. (¾ cup) unsalted butter
6 oz. (¾ cup) condensed milk

Place the sugars, water and dextrose in a pan, bring to the boil and cook until the temperature reaches 280°F. (138°C.). Remove from the heat and slowly add the butter and milk previously mixed and warmed. Stir thoroughly and continue cooking slowly till hard crack is reached. Pour onto a metal tray, lightly greased with butter. Allow to cool and harden, cut with a knife using light and very brisk strokes. ('Hard crack' means that on a trial the toffee will snap when a little is cooled in a cup of cold water. *See* p. 225.)

COCONUT ICE

1 lb. (4 cups) cube sugar
¼ pint (⅓ pint) milk
6 oz. (1 cup) desiccated coconut
little cochineal

Put the sugar and milk in a saucepan, bring to boil slowly stirring all the time, until it reaches a temperature of 240°–245°F. (116°C.) – firm ball stage. Take the pan from the heat and stir in coconut then quickly pour half the mixture into small oiled, oblong tin. Colour the other half a light pink and pour over the first half. When almost set cut into pieces 4 × 1½ in. and leave again until cold.

FRIANDISES

Friandises are made from all kinds of fruit and from marzipan. They are very decorative. They look well on the table. If cleverly arranged in a silver platter, they can look like a little flower garden.

To make, have ready dates, stuffed with marzipan or with a blanched almond; dried prunes, from which you remove the stones and replace with any kind of nut you like. Also green almonds, marrons glacés, green and black grapes, stem ginger, glacé ginger and in season; cherries on the stem. I think that nothing is more decorative than red and black currants, Cape gooseberries and, if in season, our own big, sweet gooseberries or stick three or four hazelnuts together with a little bit of caramel sugar and so on. When these are all prepared, then prepare a very thick syrup by boiling about 1 lb. lump sugar in ½ pint (1¼ cups) water. You have to test the syrup for thickness. I don't suggest for a minute that you must have a sugar thermometer, but you can test the syrup in the nice old way. To do this put ice cold water in a big bowl near your syrup, be brave and put your two fingers and thumb in the water and then – in a very quick and neat movement – dip them into the boiling syrup and pull them out at once. Separate the two fingers from the thumb. If the syrup then forms a string between the two fingers and the thumb, then the thickness is the right one. It should not be *too* thick, because the result will not be nice if the sugar is too thick and too hard.

Tip all your fruit into the syrup quickly on a fork and then put them on a oiled tray.

Here I remember, when I was a very young girl, my mother took me out to the kitchen so that I should learn to cook from her and from our delightful, fat cook. Both explained to me what to do and when I wanted to do it, my mother always told me: 'Oh, wait! Let me do it for you.' That's what I want to tell you too.

CREAM CANDIES

**2 lb. (4 cups) granu-
    lated sugar**
8 oz. (2 cups) glucose
½ pint (1¼ cups) water

Place all the ingredients in a copper pan and mix. Bring to the boil and continue cooking till 250°F. (121°C.) is reached. Remove from the heat and add colour. Rub the syrup against the side of the pan with a wooden spatula. The mixture will cloud and thicken. Add the flavour (see below)* and stir. Mix until the whole batch has become grainy and thick. Pour into a warm, oiled tray and allow to cool. When set, mark into squares with a knife and break up when cold.

*Colours and flavours suggested: Red – Strawberry; Green – Lime; Orange – Orange; Yellow – Lemon; No colour – Coconut.

GINGER CANDY

**¾ lb. (1½ cups) granu-
    lated sugar**
¼ pint (⅓ cup) water
**4 oz. (½ cup) preserved
    ginger**
ginger syrup to taste
1 pat of butter
2 oz. (½ cup) glucose

Put the sugar into the water to dissolve. Then add the glucose and the butter and boil up to 240°F. (116°C.). Add the preserved ginger and the ginger syrup. Stir gently and boil up again to 250°F. (121°C.). Pour the mixture into a basin rinsed in cold water and leave for 5 minutes. Stir with a wooden spoon until thick and creamy. Cover with wax paper and a thick towel and allow to stand for 20 minutes. Knead the mixture and pat it out on wax paper. When set, cut into cubes.

GINGER FUDGE

The recipe is the same as for vanilla fudge, but just as the batch thickens in the sauce-pan, add a cup of chopped and drained ginger.

GOOSEBERRY CHIPS

1 lb. gooseberries
½ lb. (2 cups) cube
    sugar

Put the gooseberries which should be unripe, green but fully grown, into a pan and boil until quite soft. Then slowly and gently add the sugar. Pour into saucers, and dry in the sun or in England, where there is little sun, in front of the fire or in a low oven. When sufficiently dry cut into strips and twist into fanciful shapes. They keep well in tins packed between layers of paper.

GULAB JAMAN (India)

2 tablespoonfuls (2½
    tablespoonfuls) flour
4 oz. (½ cup) dried milk
4 oz. (½ cup) granu-
    lated sugar
4 fl. oz. (½ cup) water

Mix the flour with the dried milk, and knead together. Shape into balls and fry till a rich brown. Prepare a syrup from equal quantities of sugar and water and soak balls in this.

HONEY TOFFEE

1 lb. (2 cups) granu-
    lated sugar
¼ pint (⅓ pint) water
a little glucose
¼ lb. (½ cup) honey
¼ lb. (½ cup) butter
3 tablespoonfuls (3¾
    tablespoonfuls) cream

Dissolve the sugar by heating gently, then add the water and boil. As it boils add glucose, honey, butter and cream. Boil up to 290°F. (144°C.) stirring continuously. Then pour the mixture on a buttered marble slab and mark into squares when cool. Break them up, and wrap each piece separately in wax paper.

KARANJI (India)

8 oz. (2 cups) flour
2 oz. (⅓ cup) semolina
1 tablespoonful (1¼
    tablespoonfuls) butter
half a grated coconut
2 oz. (¼ cup) sugar
2 oz. (¼ cup) raisins
2 oz. (⅔ cup) sliced
    almonds
crushed cardamoms

Prepare a soft dough from the flour, semolina and butter. Roll it out as far as possible without breaking it and cut into 1 in. pieces. Flatten each piece into a thin round. Prepare the filling by mixing all the other ingredients together.

Place a spoonful of filling on each dough round and deep fry to a golden-brown. Clarified butter is the ideal frying medium.

HELENSBURGH TOFFEE

4 oz. ($\frac{1}{2}$ cup) unsalted
  butter
2 lb. (4 cups) caster sugar
8 fl. oz. (1 cup) water
1 tin sweetened
  condensed milk
vanilla essence

Melt the butter then add sugar, water and milk; stir until boiling, then simmer for 25 minutes stirring all the time. Add vanilla essence. Pour into greased tins. Mark into squares before it is completely set.

JALEBI (India)

1 lb. (4 cups) flour
water
1 teaspoonful ($1\frac{1}{4}$ teaspoonfuls) sour milk
butter
8 oz. (1 cup) granu-
  lated sugar
a pinch of saffron
8 fl. oz. (1 cup) water

Make a thin paste with the flour and water and allow to ferment. Add the sour milk and mix thoroughly. Melt the butter in a pan and when hot slowly drop in the paste, shaping it into rings by passing it through a small funnel. Fry till golden brown.

Prepare the syrup by boiling the sugar, saffron and water and soak the Jalebi rings in this.

MAPLE CARAMELS (U.S.A.)

1 lb. (2 cups) brown
  sugar
16 oz. ($1\frac{1}{2}$ cups) maple
  syrup
4 fl. oz. ($\frac{1}{2}$ cup) cream
1 tablespoonful butter

Put the sugar, syrup and cream in a heavy pan and stir over a strong heat until the sugar is dissolved, continue cooking until it reaches firm ball stage 242°F. (117°C.) then add the butter. Pour the mixture into a buttered tin. When the mixture has almost set cut into squares.

Nuts can be added with the butter or they may be sprinkled on the buttered tin before pouring in the caramel.

MARRONS GLACÉS

2 lb. chestnuts
1 oz. ($\frac{1}{4}$ cup) flour
syrup:
1 lb. (4 cups) cube sugar
$\frac{1}{2}$ pint ($1\frac{1}{2}$ cups) water
1 in. vanilla pod

Carefully peel the chestnuts, then put them in a pan with enough cold water to cover them and the flour (this cleans them). Boil for about $\frac{1}{2}$ hour until tender. Take them out one at a time and remove all the husks being careful not to break them. Pack closely together in an earthenware vessel.

To make the syrup, boil sugar and water with vanilla

pod to 218°F. (108°C.). Remove the vanilla pod and pour syrup when almost cold over the chestnuts. Bring the chestnuts to simmering point and then allow to get cold. Let them stand in the syrup for 2–3 days adding more syrup if necessary (this should be added hot, or, if added cold heat the chestnuts as before). Put back in the pan, pour on some fresh syrup boiled to 220°F. (110°C.). Bring carefully to the boil, then grain the syrup a little by rubbing the spoon against the side of the pan to give a cloudy appearance. Lift out the chestnuts, drain well. When dry put in paper cases.

MARSHMALLOWS

½ lb. (2 cups) icing sugar
¼ lb. (1⅓ cups) gum arabic
2 whites of eggs
½ pint (1¼ cups) water
little caramel essence

Soak the gum arabic in water until soft then heat gently until dissolved and strain through a fine muslin. Return to pan add sugar and when this is dissolved add whites of eggs and whisk until mixture is stiff. Flavour to taste then pour into a tin and leave it for 10 hours. When set cut into small squares and sprinkle thickly with icing sugar.

MARZIPAN SWEETS

1 lb. (3 cups) blanched almonds
13½ oz. (1⅔ cups) sugar
2 oz. (¼ cup) vanilla-flavoured sugar
4 whites of eggs

Pound together very finely, preferably in a mortar, the almonds and sugars. Add gradually the whites of eggs. Leave the mixture to stand for a little while. Roll out ⅛ in. thick. Cut the sweets out using different-shaped pastry cutters. Ice with royal icing (*see* p. 140) flavoured with orange-blossom water. Then place in a slow oven to dry.

MEXICAN TABLET

1½ lb. (2⅔ cups) demerara sugar
6 fl. oz. (¾ cup) milk
1 lb. (3 cups) chopped walnuts
2 oz. (¼ cup) butter
vanilla essence

Boil the milk and sugar together and then add the butter. Continue boiling until the mixture hardens; test this by dropping a piece in cold water. Beat well for three minutes. Add the walnuts and the vanilla essence and beat again. Then turn the mixture into a buttered tin and mark it into squares before it cools. Break up when cold or keep in a single tablet.

NOUGAT

4 oz. ($\frac{3}{4}$ cup) icing sugar
4 oz. ($\frac{1}{2}$ cup) honey
8 oz. ($1\frac{1}{2}$ cups) blanched
   almonds
2 whites of eggs
1 oz. (3 tablespoonfuls)
   pistachio nuts
1 oz. ($\frac{1}{4}$ cup) glacé
   cherries

Blanch and dry the nuts thoroughly. Line the box of suitable size first with white paper and then with rice paper. Put the sugar, honey and whites of eggs into a copper pan and stir over a gentle heat until thick and white. Test by dropping a little of the mixture into cold water, if it hardens immediately it is ready. Take from the fire and stir in nuts and quartered glacé cherries. Dredge a slab with icing sugar, place the nougat on it and make into a ball. Press this into the prepared box and cover with paper then put some heavy object like a book, on top of this and leave it until cold. Then cut into squares.

PEPPERMINT CREAMS

8 oz. ($1\frac{3}{4}$ cups) icing
   sugar
small pinch tartaric
   acid
1 white of egg
peppermint essence
1 tablespoonful ($1\frac{1}{4}$
   tablespoonfuls) cream

Sieve the sugar and tartaric acid then mix to a stiff paste with the cream, and about half of a lightly beaten white of egg. Mix well and knead lightly, make into ovals and let them dry on greaseproof paper for several hours. Flavour to taste with the essence.

Orange creams can be made by adding orange juice instead of the cream and colouring with a little yellow colour.

POPCORN CANDY (U.S.A.)

1 pint popcorn
1 lb. (2 cups) sugar
2 fl. oz. ($\frac{1}{4}$ cup) water
2 fl. oz. ($\frac{1}{4}$ cup)
   molasses
1 oz. (2 tablespoonfuls)
   butter
tiny pinch cream of
   tartar

To pop the corn you should first buy the best popping corn, then put a thin layer of this into a wire frying basket then shake over a very slow fire till all the corn has popped and looks white and floury. It will taste nicer if you sprinkle it with icing sugar.

Now boil the sugar, cream of tartar, water and molasses to 240°F. (116°C.). Let the bubbling die down and cease then add the butter. When dissolved add popcorn. Stir until the corn is coated all over and pour onto an oiled slab. When it is cool enough so that you can handle it, roll into balls. When quite set wrap in greaseproof paper.

RUSSIAN TOFFEE
1 lb. (4 cups) cube sugar
½ lb. (1 cup) butter
1 lb. red currant jelly
½ pint (1¼ cups) cream
few drops vanilla
essence

Place all the ingredients in a saucepan, stir over low heat until the sugar has dissolved. Continue cooking and stirring until the toffee leaves the sides of the pan clean. Pour into oiled tin and mark into squares when almost set. Wrap in wax paper when cold. I must warn you not to let the mixture boil as it will spoil your toffee.

STUFFED DATES
dates
walnuts if required
marzipan:
8 oz. (1⅓ cups) ground
almonds
4 oz. (½ cup) caster sugar
4 oz. (¾ cup) icing sugar
2 whites of eggs
1 tablespoonful (1¼
tablespoonfuls) brandy
vanilla essence
almond essence

Make the marzipan by mixing the almonds and the caster and icing sugars. Make a well in the centre and drop in the whites of eggs, mix, then add the brandy, vanilla and almond essence. Mix very well.

Now slit the dates and remove the stones; stuff with the marzipan mixture, or if you prefer wrap it round a walnut. Close up the dates as tightly as possible and roll in some caster sugar. Serve in paper cases.

VANILLA FUDGE
8 oz. (1 cup) granulated
sugar
4 oz. (½ cup) brown
sugar
4 oz. (½ cup) water
3 oz. (¾ cup) dextrose
3 oz. (6 tablespoonfuls)
butter
4 oz. (½ cup)
condensed milk
6 oz. fondant

Place the sugars, water and dextrose in a saucepan, bring to the boil and cook until the temperature reaches 260°F. (126°C.). Remove from the heat and add the butter and milk, previously mixed and warmed. The butter and milk should be added slowly. Continue cooking, stirring continuously to avoid burning, until the mixture forms a firm ball. Remove from the heat and transfer to a clean saucepan; cool for about 10 minutes, or until the mixture becomes bearable to handle.

Break the fondant into pieces and stir in. Continue stirring for about five minutes or until the mixture thickens. Pour into greaseproof paper lined trays and allow to set for 24 hours.

SCOTTISH TABLET

2 lb. (4 cups) sugar
1¼ pints (3 cups) cream
oil of cinnamon or clove
4-6 oz. minced dried
**   figs**
vanilla or lemon
**   essence**
12 oz. (2 cups) chopped
**   walnuts**
2 tablespoonfuls (2½
**   tablespoonfuls) golden**
**   syrup**

Dissolve the sugar in the cream over a slow heat; stir until boiling, and boil for about 10 minutes to soft ball consistency and remove from the stove. Stir in one of the flavourings (if making walnut tablet boil the golden syrup with the cream and sugar). Place the pan in a bowl of cold water and stir rapidly until the mixture starts to thicken and become slightly granular – this can be done in an electric mixer if you have one. Pour into a butter tin and cut into squares when cold.

TRUFFLES

½ lb. (1 cup) condensed
**   milk**
1 oz. (2 tablespoonfuls)
**   sugar**
1 lb. plain melted
**   chocolate**

Place the milk and sugar in a saucepan, warm in a *bain-marie* until the mixture reaches 140°F. (60°C.) and then remove from the heat.

Stir in the melted chocolate and mix thoroughly with a hand whisk. Pour into a greaseproof paper-lined tray and allow to cool. When set, tip in a slab and remove the paper; dust with chocolate powder and roll out until the mixture is about ½ in. thick. Cut into ½ in. squares with a knife and dust each piece with chocolate powder.

TURKISH DELIGHT

2 lb. (4 cups) sugar
¾ lb. (3 cups) glucose
3½ pints (6¼ cups)
**   water**
pinch of cream of
**   tartar**
6 oz. (¾ cup)
**   cornflour**

Put the sugar, glucose, 1½ pints (2 pints) of water and the cream of tartar in a copper saucepan and bring to the boil. Mix the cornflour and remainder of the water together and pour into the boiling mixture.

Cook slowly for 1 hour, stirring the mixture continuously, by this time the mixture should be thick and when a knife is put into, and drawn out of it, it should form a springy thread. Add a little pink colour and flavour with rose essence to taste. Pour into a tray lined with paper and dusted with icing sugar. Allow to set for 2 days. Turn out and cut with a knife into chunks and roll each piece in icing sugar.

WALNUT FUDGE
Same as for ginger fudge, but using 6 oz. (1 cup) chopped walnuts.

WALNUT KISSES
1 lb. (2 cups) brown sugar
1 tablespoonful (1¼ tablespoonfuls) glucose
¼ pint (⅓ pint) water
½ vanilla pod
6 oz. (1 cup) chopped walnuts

Boil all the ingredients in a saucepan till the mixture reaches 240°F. (116°C.). Pour this syrup into a wetted bowl. Allow to cool for three minutes and knead or stir until it becomes creamy; then add the chopped walnuts. Stir until a paste is formed. Cover the bowl and leave for 10 minutes. Turn the mixture on a marble slab and knead it. Shape into small logs and roll those in chopped walnuts. Cut in small pieces.

CONCLUSION

I feel that I cannot close this book without an account of the beginning of my little business. The story of my early struggles, my doubts, worries and fears would fill another book and be a long story. After weeks and months of talks, correspondence, negotiations, hopes and disappointments the day came at last when my bakery was to open. It was January 4, 1939.

I left home very early indeed and walked to the nearest Underground station, where I bought a workman's ticket. I emerged from the station at Leicester Square and started to walk in the direction of Soho. It was quite dark and bitterly cold.

I felt frozen and my heart was an icy lump in my chest. I walked in the darkness. It seemed an endless journey, looking for the right turning. The streets were empty and I was lost. Suddenly I noticed a silhouette. I was pleased, stopped in the dark and asked the way. I could not see the face but a pleasant young voice said, 'I am sorry but I don't know the way. It is so dark and cold, wouldn't you like to come and have a cup of tea with me?' Suddenly I felt better, happy and cheerful. I answered the kind young man that I was in a hurry and couldn't stop but thanked him all the same. Then I went briskly on my way. It was a very long time since a strange man had invited me to tea. Suddenly the darkness lifted; in no time I found the right street and found myself in my own bakery. In a strong, cheerful voice I called for the lift. The lift came, I pressed the button, I entered and went up to the workroom. There I found my six bakers had already started work. That was the beginning of my first day. I was confident, I was self-assured, I knew that I would succeed.

I would like to leave you with a story from my youth. It is appropriate to a book on bread and bakery because it shows what a big part this plays in our lives. It happened to me in my courting days. One evening the man who wished to be my husband walked me home. We went on talking in the doorway of my house. He was standing with his back to the door, blocking my way. I wanted to go in, but he pleaded for yet one more minute and then one more again. His eyes were shining and my heart was beating, but in the end I was firm and said a quick goodnight and went indoors. It was pretty late and I went straight to my own room. I went to bed but could not sleep. I had a bad conscience about keeping him so long in suspense, I hated myself; I decided that I would tell him next day that I would marry him. I waited impatiently for the morning, for our next meeting. When he came at last, charming, pleasant, interesting, good humoured as always, my first question was, 'tell me how did you go home last night?' He answered with a big smile, 'I didn't walk, I ran all the way, I was suddenly so desperately hungry. I rushed to the kitchen, cut three or four slices of bread, toasted them quickly, spread them with butter and sat down and ate them there and then'. Was there ever such an anti-climax? My beloved bread had spoilt my romance, even bread can let you down! But it all came right in the end for me as I hope you too will have found in trying some of these recipes. It has been a great pleasure for me to seek and find them for you. Your success will be my reward.

GENERAL INSTRUCTIONS
CAKES

A few simple rules, a few common errors to avoid, will make all the difference to successful cakemaking. Once these are grasped, however, commonsense and experience are the best guides. Differences in utensils, materials, the temperament of the oven and of cooking conditions all play a part.

Utensils

There are many different types of cake tins, baking sheets and so on. Some are designed for a particular purpose, others are suitable for a variety of uses. Examples of specialized cake tins are *guglhupf*, a deep fluted tin; angel cake, a deep tin with a funnel; and *savarin* mould, a ring mould. Cake hoops or rings are useful for gâteaux, especially for those with a nut and egg base. Removable bottoms are helpful when cakes are inclined to stick to their tins. For small cakes use paper cases, patty tins, *madeleine* moulds or bun trays.

The cake tins most in use can be either round, square, or rectangular. The most common sizes are 6, 7, or 8 in. in diameter; they range from those 1 in. deep for sponges, tortes and flans, to ones 3 in. or more for large cakes. It is false economy to buy any except the best available. Tins made from poor materials are difficult to keep clean, and may warp. Also if the material is thin, the edges and bottoms of the cake may burn before the centre is cooked through. Cake tins should be quite clean and dry before use. It is often a good idea to warm the tin before greasing. It is advisable to line large tins meant for fruit cakes with greaseproof paper or tinfoil. The paper lining the bottom of the tin should be cut to fit the tin and the lining paper should be a little higher than the sides.

The quantity of the cake mixture in relation to the size of the tin may be important. Rich mixtures should fill the tin to about two-thirds of its depth. Sponge cakes and those cakes which will rise and increase their volume greatly should about half fill the tin. As a rough guide, a cake with 3–4 eggs will require a tin 7 in. in diameter; a 2 egg mixture, a tin 5 or 6 in. in diameter; while a mixture with 6 and more eggs will

need a 7, 8, or 9 in. tin. This criterion obviously will depend also upon the remainder
of the ingredients. In making light sponge cakes, a 2-egg mixture will require a 7 in.
sandwich tin. A cake baked in a large shallow tin will cook more quickly than the same
quantity in a smaller deeper tin.

Fruit cakes and rich cake tins should be greased. Some authorities say that it is
advisable to use a salt-free fat, such as one of the vegetable fats now on the market, or
fresh butter, to prevent sticking. Sponge cakes and gâteaux tins are usually floured
after greasing. Generally speaking large cakes and fruit cakes and pastries should be
left to cool in the tin, but light cakes and sponges should be turned out immediately.

Materials

It is advisable to collect all the ingredients before starting. Flour should be sifted,
eggs and butter brought to room temperature; bowls, tins and trays cleaned and
dried. When using dried fruits, toss them in a little flour before adding to the mixture.
This will help to prevent them sinking to the bottom of the cake. The consistency
of the mixture may vary according to the size of the eggs, quality of the flour and so on.
The amount of liquid may be adjusted accordingly.

Methods

There are different techniques for the principal ingredients involved in cakemaking,
that is, flour, eggs, sugar and butter. Let us consider them in turn. The difference
in flour qualities, the raising agents, together with the method of adding them to
the mixture will all influence the texture of the cake. If a close texture is desired, add
the eggs and flour alternately: if an open spongy texture, lightly fold in the flour last
of all. In some recipes, cake crumbs or ground nuts take the place of the flour, but
the same principles apply. Eggs should be fresh, but not less than three days old,
as new laid eggs do not beat or whisk so well. When the recipe calls for very stiffly
beaten whites of eggs, whisk until the mixture will not start to slide out of the bowl
or jug when it is inverted. When whisking yolks and sugar together, warm the bowl
first or beat over a pan of hot water. A copper bowl is considered by some the ideal
for whisking whites of eggs.

Creaming butter and sugar is again facilitated both by warming the bowl and
making sure that the butter is at room temperature. Do not, however, heat the butter
till it melts; this is fatal, except where the recipe calls specifically for melted butter,
as in Genoese cakes. Cream the butter alone just a little before adding the sugar. The
blessing of an electric mixer for beating and whisking in cakemaking cannot be over-
estimated. But remember always to cream or beat butter at a slow speed, reserving
the high speed for incorporating eggs to a mixture, or for whisking yolks or whites.

The actual baking should present few difficulties providing you have an oven thermometer or thermostatic heat control. It is difficult to overcook rich cakes. The richer the cake, the lower the temperature is a useful rule. The higher the proportion of eggs, butter, etc. to the flour, the richer the cake will be. Cakes with a high proportion of fruit must cook at a low temperature for long periods. If the top browns before the cake is cooked through, cover with paper or foil. To test, pierce with a knife or skewer. When the cake is cooked, this will be clean on removal.

For light cakes, sponges, etc., there is one absolute rule. Do not open the oven door to look at your cake before the prescribed time is up. A sponge is cooked when a finger mark leaves no lasting impression on the surface of the cake. Meringue mixtures should be cooked very slowly and never touched until they are quite cold.

PASTRY

There are fewer rules to be observed for pastry making, and such as they are are no more than commonsense. It is very easy to make pastry successfully and this requires the minimum of utensils. All that is needed is a bowl, baking board, rolling pin, spoon, fork and jug. The essence of successful pastry making is speed of work, lightness of touch and a cool, even temperature in both cook and kitchen.

Materials

The materials used are flour, fat, and liquid. The fat may be butter, lard, vegetable fat or a combination of these. The minimum of liquid necessary to form a workable paste is the ideal for shortcrust pastry. The methods for puff pastry and choux pastry have been described in the chapter on pastries.

Lightness and sureness of the fingertips when rubbing the fat into the flour and the speed at which this is done are essential to success. It is however possible to achieve this with a fork when using vegetable fat or lard. The liquid – ice-cold water, egg yolk or lemon juice – must be added after the fat, again with the exception of puff pastry. Rolling is an art that only experience can perfect. It needs quick, firm, but not heavy, movements away from the body to ensure even pressure on the pastry which should be turned between rollings. Reflour both the rolling pin and your hands as necessary to prevent sticking. Many experts state that resting the pastry in a cool place before final shaping and baking will improve the result and prevent shrinking during cooking.

Pastry is more often spoiled by baking at a too low temperature than the reverse. Eggs will add richness but will make it more liable to crumble and break while it is being handled. Be careful with sugar. Granulated sugar is apt to spot the pastry in cooking. It is safer to use icing sugar. Nut pastry is delicious, but requires care in handling.

SCONES

The art of making scones is a very simple one. Scones are cheap, quick and appetizing. They are extravagant only in that they should be eaten absolutely fresh, and are only eatable the day after baking, if they are toasted. The secret of making good scones is that the dough or paste should be as wet as is consistent with handling. The mixing should be done as quickly as possible and there should be the minimum of handling. The raising agents may be buttermilk, sour milk or cream, eggs, cream of tartar, bicarbonate of soda or baking powder. Oven scones should be baked very quickly in a very hot oven and should be wrapped at once in a soft cloth. Griddle scones, oatcakes, drop scones or pancakes should be cooked on a flat greased hot plate, heavy pan or griddle (girdle in Scotland) and should be turned over once during cooking.

CONFECTIONERY

Sweetmaking has become a highly technical and professional craft. However, there are many sweets which may be made at home. These are roughly divided into two classes, the cooked and the uncooked sweets. The uncooked are obviously easier and call for little instruction. Proper wrapping will help to give a professional air and will also improve storing. Cooked sweets require some specialized equipment for the most satisfactory results. A little knowledge of the nature and behaviour of sugar when heated will be helpful in achieving success.

Sugar melts at 320°F. (159–160°C.); if it is heated further it becomes honey coloured, then brown, dark caramel and lastly black. It is easily soluble in water. Cold water will dissolve double its weight of sugar. If sugar is boiled its characteristics will alter at different degrees and each of these degrees has its own name. Sugar is best boiled as a syrup, that is in a water solution. A practical guide is to allow $\frac{1}{2}$ pint ($1\frac{1}{4}$ cups) to 2 lb. sugar. Boiling the sugar will evaporate the water, and when the surface is covered with little bubbles, cooking has started and from then on it must be very carefully watched. The different degrees relevant to making simple confectionery are:

Large thread, 219°F. (104°C.), when threads form if a little sugar is pulled between finger and thumb.

Small ball, 220°F. (104–5°C.) a little sugar dropped into cold water will form a soft gluey ball. Also known as *soft ball*.

Large ball, 230°F. (106°C.) when sugar is dropped into water the ball will be harder and more resistant to the fingers.

Small crack, 264°F. (129°C.) when dipped in water and touched with a finger the sugar will break but will cling to the teeth. Also known as *first crack*.

Hard crack, 289°F. (143°C.) now the sugar will break like glass when dipped in water and will have become a rich brown. Any overcooking will caramelize the sugar which will taste burnt and be extremely hard.

These remarks and tests apply to toffee mixtures of all kinds as well as pure sugars. The addition of glucose will help prevent graining during boiling and will also give a glossy appearance to the sweets.

Utensils

To make confectionery at home, therefore, successfully, a proper sugar thermometer is essential, although with these guides to sugar degrees it makes it possible to make some confectionery with a reasonable chance of success. But wastage is avoided and results are much more certain with a thermometer. These are not very expensive and cover a very wide range of temperatures. A marble slab for cooling and pulling the confectionery and a large heavy pan are also very useful.

Comparative Cookery Terms and Measures

BRITISH MEASURES	AMERICAN MEASURES	AMERICAN CUP EQUIVALENTS
Liquid Measures		
1 teaspoon	1¼ teaspoons	
1 tablespoon	1¼ tablespoons	
1 fluid ounce	1 fluid ounce or 2 tablespoons	
2 fluid ounces	2 fluid ounces or 4 tablespoons	¼ cup
2⅔ fluid ounces	5⅓ tablespoons	⅓ cup
4 fluid ounces	8 tablespoons	½ cup
5⅓ fluid ounces	10⅔ tablespoons	⅔ cup
8 fluid ounces	8 fluid ounces or ½ U.S. pint	1 cup
10 fluid ounces or ½ Imperial pint	10 fluid ounces	1¼ cups
16 fluid ounces	1 U.S. pint	2 cups
20 fluid ounces or 1 Imperial pint	1¼ U.S. pints	2½ cups
1⅗ Imperial pints	2 U.S. pints or 1 U.S. quart	4 cups
2 Imperial pints or 1 Imperial quart	2½ U.S. pints	5 cups
6⅖ Imperial pints	8 U.S. pints or 1 U.S. gallon	16 cups
8 Imperial pints or 1 Imperial gallon	10 U.S. pints	20 cups

British and American Equivalent Ingredients

BRITISH	AMERICAN
Icing sugar	Confectioners sugar
Cornflour	Cornstarch
Sultanas	Raisins
Rusk	Zwiebach
Single cream	Light cream
Double cream	Heavy cream
Bicarbonate of soda	Baking soda
Scone	Biscuit
Soft brown sugar	Brown sugar
100 per cent wholemeal flour	Graham flour
Digestive biscuits	Graham crackers
Trex or Spry	Soft shortening
Butter or margarine	Shortening
1 oz. cooking chocolate	1 square chocolate
$\frac{2}{3}$ oz. bakers yeast, or	
3 level teaspoonfuls dried yeast	1 cake yeast
Okra	Gumbo
$\frac{1}{3}$ oz. powdered gelatine, or 1 level tablespoonful	1 envelope gelatine
Caster sugar	Granulated sugar
Biscuit	Cookie or Cracker
Minced meat	Ground meat
2 oz. egg (standard)	2 oz. egg (large)

Equivalent Gas and Electric Oven Temperatures

GAS	$\frac{1}{4}$	$\frac{1}{2}$	1	2	3	4	5	6	7	8	9
ELECTRICITY	240°	265°	290°	310°	335°	355°	380°	400°	425°	445°	470°

1 British fluid ounce is equal to 1 U.S. fluid ounce
British Standard Measuring Cup is equivalent to 10 fluid ounces
American Standard Measuring Cup is equivalent to 8 fluid ounces

In general British and American solid weights are equivalent

Throughout this book British measurements are given first: the American equivalents for both solids and liquids follow in brackets

Vintage Chart

YEAR	CLARET	BURGUNDY	WHITE BURGUNDY	SAUTERNES	RHONE	RHINE	MOSELLE	CHAMPAGNE	PORT	LOIRE
1945	7	6	–	6	7	–	–	5	7	–
1946	1	1	–	2	5	–	–	–	–	–
1947	5	6	–	6	6	–	–	6	7	–
1948	5	5	–	5	4	–	–	–	7	–
1949	6	5	–	5	7	–	–	6	–	–
1950	5	3	–	6	6	–	–	–	6	–
1951	0	1	–	2	4	–	–	–	–	–
1952	6	5	5	6	6	5	4	7	4	–
1953	6	5	4	5	6	7	6	6	–	–
1954	4	3	1	2	7	2	2	–	6	–
1955	6	5	4	6	6	5	4	6	7	–
1956	0	1	1	2	5	1	1	–	–	–
1957	5	5	5	4	7	4	4	–	5	–
1958	4	3	4	4	5	5	5	–	6	–
1959	6	7	6	6	6	7	7	7	–	6
1960	4	1	1	3	6	2	2	–	7	2
1961	7	7	7	5	7	5	4	7	–	5
1962	6	5	6	6	6	3	3	6	5	4
1963	1	4	3	2	5	3	2	–	7	1
1964	6	7	7	5	6	6	7	7	–	7
1965	0	1	2	2	5	1	1	–	4	1
1966	6	7	7	6	6	6	6	–	7	5
1967	5	5	7	5	6	5	4	–	6	6
1968	1	1	1	0	5	1	1	–	–	3

0 = No Good   7 = The Best

Fresh Food in its Best Season

	JANUARY	FEBRUARY	MARCH	APRIL	MAY	JUNE	JULY	AUGUST	SEPTEMBER	OCTOBER	NOVEMBER	DECEMBER
MEAT												
Beef	x	x	x	x	x	x	x	x	x	x	x	x
Veal		x	x	x	x	x						
Spring lamb					x	x	x	x	x			
Fed lamb	x	x	x	x						x	x	x
Pork	x	x	x	x	x	x				x	x	x
POULTRY												
Chicken	x	x	x	x	x	x	x	x	x	x	x	x
Duck	x	x	x	x	x	x	x	x	x	x	x	x
Turkey	x	x	x	x	x	x	x	x	x	x	x	x
FISH												
Bass	x	x	x	x	x	x	x	x	x	x	x	x
Carp	x	x	x	x	x	x	x	x	x	x	x	x
Cod	x	x	x	x	x	x	x	x	x	x	x	x
Dab	x	x	x	x	x	x	x	x	x	x	x	x
Eel	x	x	x	x	x	x	x	x	x	x	x	x
Flounder	x	x	x	x	x	x	x	x	x	x	x	x
(Grey) mullet	x	x	x	x	x	x	x	x	x	x	x	x
Haddock	x	x	x	x	x	x	x	x	x	x	x	x
Hake	x	x	x	x	x	x	x	x	x	x	x	x
Halibut	x	x	x	x	x	x	x	x	x	x	x	x
Herring	x	x	x	x	x	x	x	x	x	x	x	x
Lemon-sole	x	x	x	x	x	x	x	x	x	x	x	x
Mackerel		x	x	x	x	x	x	x	x	x	x	x
Pilchard	x	x	x	x	x	x	x	x	x	x	x	x
Salmon	x	x	x	x	x	x	x	x	x	x	x	x
Sardine					x	x	x	x	x	x	x	x
Sole	x	x	x	x	x	x	x	x	x	x	x	x
Trout	x	x	x	x	x	x	x	x	x	x	x	x
Whiting				x	x	x	x	x	x	x	x	

	JANUARY	FEBRUARY	MARCH	APRIL	MAY	JUNE	JULY	AUGUST	SEPTEMBER	OCTOBER	NOVEMBER	DECEMBER
CRUSTACEANS												
Crab	x	x	x	x	x	x	x	x	x	x	x	x
Lobster	x	x	x	x	x	x	x	x	x	x	x	x
Prawns – Shrimp	x	x	x	x	x	x	x	x	x	x	x	x
MOLLUSCS												
Mussel	x	x	x	x	x	x	x	x	x	x	x	x
Oyster	x	x	x	x					x	x	x	x
Scallop	x	x	x	x	x	x	x	x	x	x	x	x
Clams	x	x	x	x	x	x	x	x	x	x	x	x
FRUIT AND VEGETABLES												
Anise	x									x	x	x
Apples									x	x	x	
Apricots						x	x					
Artichokes	x	x	x	x	x						x	x
Asparagus			x	x	x							
Avocados	x	x	x	x	x	x	x	x	x	x	x	x
Beans, Lima							x	x	x	x		
Beans, green			x	x	x	x	x	x				
Beets					x	x	x	x	x	x		
Blackberries						x						
Dewberries						x						
Loganberries						x						
Blueberries						x	x	x				
Huckleberries						x	x	x				
Broccoli	x	x	x							x	x	x
Brussels sprouts	x									x	x	x
Cabbage	x	x	x	x	x					x	x	x
Cantaloupes						x	x	x	x			
Carrots (home-grown)								x	x	x	x	
Cauliflower (home-grown)									x	x	x	x
Celery	x	x	x	x	x						x	x
Cherries					x	x	x					
Collards	x	x	x								x	x
Corn							x	x	x			
Cranberries										x	x	x
Cucumbers					x	x	x	x				
Currants							x					

FRUIT AND VEGETABLES (continued)	JANUARY	FEBRUARY	MARCH	APRIL	MAY	JUNE	JULY	AUGUST	SEPTEMBER	OCTOBER	NOVEMBER	DECEMBER
Eggplant							x	x	x	x		
Endive and Escarole								x	x	x		
Grapefruit (imported)	x	x	x	x						x	x	x
Grapes (home-grown)								x	x	x		
Kale					x	x			x	x		
Lettuce					x	x	x					
Melon (Cantaloupe)						x	x	x				
Mushrooms	x	x	x	x					x	x	x	x
Mustard Greens	x	x	x									
Okra							x	x	x	x		
Onions, dry	x	x	x						x	x	x	x
Onions, green				x	x	x	x					
Oranges	x	x	x	x	x							
Parsley	x	x	x	x	x	x	x	x	x	x	x	x
Parsnips	x	x	x							x	x	x
Peaches						x	x	x	x			
Pears								x	x	x	x	
Peas, green				x	x	x	x					
Peppers								x	x	x		
Persians								x	x	x		
Plums						x	x	x	x			
Potatoes	x	x	x	x	x	x	x	x	x	x	x	x
Sweet potatoes	x								x	x	x	x
Pumpkins										x		
Radishes			x	x	x	x	x					
Raspberries						x	x	x				
Rhubarb			x	x	x	x						
Shallots	x	x	x	x								x
Spinach			x	x	x	x						
Squash									x	x	x	x
Strawberries				x	x	x	x					
Tangerines	x										x	x
Tomatoes						x	x	x	x	x		
Turnips and Rutabagas	x	x	x							x	x	x
Watermelons						x	x	x				

INDEX